CAMBRIDGE
UNIVERSITY PRESS

40 West 20th Street, New York, NY 10011-4211

For Review

Smith

APR 1995

The Theology of the Gospel of John

Hardback   0-521-35514-1 $ 44.95
Paperback 0-521-35776-4 $ 12.95

We would appreciate three copies of the review. — Publicity Department

D. Moody Smith treats the theology of the Gospel of John in its narrative form and historical context, both ancient Jewish and early Christian. His work draws upon the most recent scholarly investigations of the Gospel's historical purpose and setting. The major theological themes of the Gospel, especially its christology, are treated in relation to the context of the work, since Johannine theology is not simply a by-product of controversies that produced the Gospel, but is rather related to them in significant ways. As Professor Smith shows, John marks an important watershed between Christianity and Judaism. His study will thus serve equally well as an introduction to the question of the origin of John and as an introduction to its theology. It also consistently pays attention to the relationship of the Gospel to other major New Testament witnesses as well as to its important influence upon the development of later Christian doctrine.

NEW TESTAMENT THEOLOGY

General Editor: James D. G. Dunn,
Lightfoot Professor of Divinity, University of Durham

The theology of the Gospel of John

This series provides a programmatic survey of the individual writings of the New Testament. It aims to remedy the deficiency of available published material, which has tended to concentrate on historical, textual, grammatical and literary issues at the expense of the theology, or to lose distinctive emphases of individual writings in systematised studies of 'The Theology of Paul' and the like. New Testament specialists here write at greater length than is usually possible in the introductions to commentaries or as part of other New Testament theologies, and explore the theological themes and issues of their chosen books without being tied to a commentary format, or to a thematic structure drawn from elsewhere. When complete, the series will cover all the New Testament writings, and will thus provide an attractive, and timely, range of texts around which courses can be developed.

THE THEOLOGY OF THE GOSPEL OF JOHN

D. MOODY SMITH

George Washington Ivey Professor of New Testament, Duke University

CAMBRIDGE
UNIVERSITY PRESS

Published by the Press Syndicate of the University of Cambridge
The Pitt Building, Trumpington Street, Cambridge CB2 1RP
40 West 20th Street, New York, NY 10011–4211, USA
10 Stamford Road, Oakleigh, Melbourne 3166, Australia

First published 1995

Printed in Great Britain at the University Press, Cambridge

A catalogue record for this book is available from the British Library

Library of Congress cataloguing in publication data
Smith, D. Moody (Dwight Moody)
The theology of the Gospel of John / D. Moody Smith.
p.   cm. – (New Testament theology)
Includes bibliographical references and index.
ISBN 0 521 35514 1 (hardback) – ISBN 0 521 35776 4 (paperback)
1. Bible. N.T. John – Criticism, interpretation, etc. 1. Title.
II. Series.
BS2615.2.S626 1994
226.5′06–dc20   93–29256   CIP

ISBN 0 521 35514 1 hardback
ISBN 0 521 35776 4 paperback

Contents

J. Louis Martyn
and
Paul W. Meyer

teachers and friends

Editor's preface

Although the New Testament is usually taught within Departments or Schools or Faculties of Theology/Divinity/Religion, theological study of the individual New Testament writings is often minimal or at best patchy. The reasons for this are not hard to discern.

For one thing, the traditional style of studying a New Testament document is by means of straight exegesis, often verse by verse. Theological concerns jostle with interesting historical, textual, grammatical and literary issues, often at the cost of the theological. Such exegesis is usually very time-consuming, so that only one or two key writings can be treated in any depth within a crowded three-year syllabus.

For another, there is a marked lack of suitable textbooks round which courses could be developed. Commentaries are likely to lose theological comment within a mass of other detail in the same way as exegetical lectures. The section on the theology of a document in the Introduction to a commentary is often very brief and may do little more than pick out elements within the writing under a sequence of headings drawn from systematic theology. Excursuses usually deal with only one or two selected topics. Likewise larger works on New Testament Theology usually treat Paul's letters as a whole and, having devoted the great bulk of their space to Jesus, Paul and John, can spare only a few pages for others.

In consequence, there is little incentive on the part of teacher or student to engage with a particular New Testament document, and students have to be content with a general overview, at best complemented by in-depth study of (parts of) two or three New Testament writings. A serious corollary to this is the degree to which students are thereby incapacitated in the task of integrating their New Testament study with the rest of their Theology or Religion courses, since often they are capable only of drawing on the general overview or on a sequence of particular verses treated atomistically. The growing importance of a literary-critical approach to individual documents simply highlights the present deficiencies even more. Having been given little experience in handling individual New Testament writings as such at a theological level, most students are very ill-prepared to develop a properly integrated literary and theological response to particular texts. Ordinands too need more help than they currently receive from textbooks, so that their preaching from particular passages may be better informed theologically.

There is need therefore for a series to bridge the gap between too brief an introduction and too full a commentary where theological discussion is lost among too many other concerns. It is our aim to provide such a series. That is, a series where New Testament specialists are able to write at a greater length on the theology of individual writings than is usually possible in the introductions to commentaries or as part of New Testament Theologies, and to explore the theological themes and issues of these writings without being tied to a commentary format or to a thematic structure provided from elsewhere. The volumes seek both to describe each document's theology, and to engage theologically with it, noting also its canonical context and any specific influence it may have had on the history of Christian faith and life. They are directed at those who already have one or two years of full-time New Testament and theological study behind them.

University of Durham   JAMES D. G. DUNN

Preface

To write the theology of John is a daunting and almost presumptuous undertaking. The evangelist has already written his theology in narrative form. Who are we to rewrite it for him? Moreover, Rudolf Bultmann masterfully set forth the theology of the Gospel and Epistles of John in slightly less than a hundred pages of his *Theology of the New Testament*. Why should we now need more than half that much space again?

The mere fact that John wrote a narrative of Jesus' ministry means that we should ask whether that historic ministry provides the proper, or complete, context or frame for interpreting what he has written. Apart from that ministry his narrative is unthinkable, but, as J. Louis Martyn argued in *History and Theology in the Fourth Gospel*, the narrative operates at two levels, that of Jesus himself and that of the Johannine Christians and community. To elucidate John's theology means not to destroy his narrative, but to show how its theological emphases arose from and relate to the emergence of that Christian community on Martyn's second level.

The length of the book is partly the consequence of its intended audience and pedagogical purpose, but mainly a reflection of our increased knowledge. As John Ashton (*Understanding the Fourth Gospel*) has pointed out, Bultmann did not deal adequately with the question of the historical setting of the Fourth Gospel, particularly as it impinges upon its theology. Yet my own indebtedness to Bultmann, as well as to Martyn, Raymond Brown, and others, should be clear enough. Like Ashton, from whose comprehensive treatment I have learned a great deal, I attempt to bring some of the theological insights of

xi

Bultmann into conjunction with the work of Martyn and Brown.

This book also reflects the experience of many years teaching the Gospel of John at the Divinity School of Duke University. In an earlier form it was the basis for lectures in courses on the theology of John at Duke (spring semester, 1992) and at Princeton Theological Seminary (summer session, 1992). I am especially grateful to students in those classes for their insightful questions, as well as the encouragement their interest afforded me. This book is dedicated to, and intended for, such students.

Friends and colleagues in the Johannine Seminar of the Society for New Testament Studies, particularly Alan Culpepper, Robert Fortna, Robert Kysar, John Painter, and Fernando Segovia, have kept me aware and abreast of the range of issues to be considered. I am grateful also to a number of other people who in different ways have been of great help: Sarah Freedman, who put my work in its many drafts on disk; Eric Greaux, my graduate assistant, for his careful reading of the typescript; Professor Marianne Meye Thompson, who read the typescript in penultimate form, offering detailed observations and suggestions; and Professor James D. G. Dunn, who invited me to write this volume for the series and offered much constructive advice. Of course, the author alone must assume responsibility for the contents of a book. A sabbatical leave at the Center of Theological Inquiry in Princeton enabled me to write without interruptions, and I once again have the pleasure of thanking the director, Professor Daniel W. Hardy, and his administrative assistant, Kate Le Van, for providing a wonderful place in which to work among good friends and congenial colleagues.

Where I have quoted the Gospel of John or other parts of the New Testament I have offered my own translations, albeit influenced primarily by the RSV, although I do follow the NRSV's use of inclusive language, where appropriate. For such ancient writers as the Apostolic Fathers, Eusebius, and Philo I have used the appropriate volumes of the Loeb Classical Library, and for Justin Martyr and Irenaeus the venerable *Ante-Nicene Fathers*. As far as possible, however, I have cited quotations of ancient sources from the accessible collection and translation of C. K. Barrett, *The New Testament Background: Selected Documents* (London and San Francisco, 1987 and 1989), which in a representative way covers the *Umwelt* of the Fourth Gospel admirably. The concluding list of further reading is limited to books available in English. These are the works most likely to be accessible to undergraduates or theological students. Moreover, this seems a reasonable and not altogether arbitrary way of reducing the publications cited in a crowded field.

Abbreviations

CBQ	*Catholic Biblical Quarterly*
JBL	*Journal of Biblical Literature*
JSNTSS	Journal for the Study of the New Testament Supplement Series
KJV	King James (Authorized) Version
NRSV	New Revised Standard Version
NTS	*New Testament Studies*
RSV	Revised Standard Version
SBLDS	Society of Biblical Literature Dissertation Series
SBT	Studies in Biblical Theology
SJT	*Scottish Journal of Theology*
SNTSMS	Society for New Testament Studies Monograph Series
TDNT	*Theological Dictionary of the New Testament*, ed. G. Kittel and G. Friedrich, trans. G. W. Bromiley (9 vols., Grand Rapids, 1964–1974).
ZNW	*Zeitschrift für die neutestamentliche Wissenschaft*

CHAPTER I

Introduction

John the evangelist obviously did not write a theological treatise, but a Gospel, a narrative of the ministry of Jesus Christ that stands alongside three broadly similar narratives in the New Testament. Moreover, the Greek words *theologia* and *theologos* (theology and theologian) are nowhere to be found in the New Testament. These terms only gradually came to be applied to discourse about God in the Christian tradition, however, so it is no surprise that John does not use them or that we do not find them in the New Testament. Yet in antiquity John was given the title of theologian, if not already in the second century by Papias, then in the fifth by Philip of Side, who quotes him.[1] Certainly the title has seemed apposite, for John more than any of the other Gospel writers deals with theological matters. That is, in John's Gospel more than in any of the others, Jesus, the Son, talks about his relationship with God, the Father.

Christian theology begins with the fact of Jesus Christ. That fact became first the object of faith and then the object of thought. "It was a complex fact: a man who is Son of God, dead yet living, weak yet Lord. It demanded that God be seen as Father of a Son, the two of them acting through a Holy Spirit who is at once immanent in the 'hearts' of the faithful and transcendent over them."[2] John more than any other New

[1] See C. K. Barrett, *The Gospel According to St. John: An Introduction with Commentary and Notes on the Greek Text*, 2nd ed. (London and Philadelphia, 1978), p. 103. Yves M.-J. Congar, OP, *A History of Theology*, trans. and ed. Hunter Guthrie, SJ (Garden City, NY, 1968), p. 29, ascribes the attribution of *theologos* to John to Eusebius of Caesarea.

[2] Yves Congar, OP, "Christian Theology," in *The Encyclopedia of Religion*, ed. Mircea Eliade (New York, 1987), vol. XIV, p. 456.

Testament writer deals with Jesus Christ as the object of distinctly Christian faith and reflects, as he leads the reader to reflect, upon the meaning and importance of this faith for those upon whom the Holy Spirit has come. Anyone who has read the rest of the New Testament will readily acknowledge that John deals with the same subject matter. The Fourth Gospel presupposes the same fact of Jesus Christ as the object of faith but at the same time introduces new ways of describing him and thinking about the character and implications of this faith.

Therefore, it scarcely seems necessary to defend theology as the discipline or discourse that is appropriate to deal with the subject matter of the Gospel of John. Nevertheless, the problem of how to treat the theology of John, or in what context to understand it, has engaged and divided New Testament study for a good part of this century. One question has been how to organize and present the theology of the Gospel of John. To present John's theology under the doctrinal rubrics of a classical Christian orthodoxy that was centuries developing seems anachronistic. Yet it is quite obvious that there is a strong relationship between the two, as between no other New Testament writing and the theological doctrine of the ancient church.[3] Another question concerns the cultural and religious traditions represented and assumed by this Gospel, so familiar are its themes and yet so distinctively framed. One must also ask what manifestation of early Christian religion or what life-setting in the early Christian church lies behind this unique Gospel. The religious issues and life that surely underlie this Gospel find expression in theological concepts and forms. To ignore the centrality and importance of such theological expression to the fourth evangelist, and the readers for whom he wrote, would be an even greater mistake than to read the Gospel primarily in light of later Christian dogma or creeds. The theological content and narrative form of the Gospel of John are its most obvious characteristics. The life-setting – while also very important – remains implicit, and in the nature of the case hypothetical, although we shall see that the Gospel

---

[3] On the relation of the Gospel of John to the development of christological doctrine, see T. E. Pollard, *Johannine Christology and the Early Church* (Cambridge, 1970).

itself provides evidence that allows one to make significant inferences about the circumstances of its origin. An appreciation of the Gospel's origin lends depth and perspective to our understanding of the text.

Questions about the origin of the Gospel of John, particularly authorship and its relationship to the Synoptic Gospels, were already the subject of discussion in Christian antiquity. Modern introductions to the New Testament have concerned themselves with such questions as the date and place of composition of the individual books, their authorship, intended readers, purpose, sources, and stylistic features. In the case of the Gospel of John, the questions of date, place, and authorship once loomed very large. The discussion of them has reached an impasse, however, if not a solution, and there would be no point in attempting to resolve them in this book, although it will be worthwhile to note what is at stake in these matters. Questions of readers, purpose, sources, and style and literary character have more recently come into the foreground of discussion as more profitable, and we shall deal with them in some detail before attempting to treat the theological themes of the Gospel directly.

The title of this book is *The Theology of the Gospel of John*, and we repeatedly refer to this Gospel by that traditional name. The John in question is, presumably, the prominent member of the twelve, brother of James and son of Zebedee, who is mentioned not infrequently in the Synoptic Gospels and with Peter in the early chapters of the Book of Acts. Christian readers have since the second century assumed that the Beloved Disciple, who first appears in chapter 13 and to whom the Gospel is ascribed (21:24), is this same John. Given John's prominence in the Synoptics and Acts, together with the fact that he is not otherwise mentioned by name in the Gospel of John (but see 21:2), this seems a reasonable conclusion. On the other hand, it requires believing that John as author, although he modestly refrained from naming himself, could nevertheless refer to himself as the Beloved Disciple. Moreover, all the Synoptic episodes in which John figures are missing from the Fourth Gospel. (See, for example, Mark 1:16–20, 29–31;

3:13–19; 5:35–43; 9:2–8, none of which have Johannine parallels.) Nevertheless, when this Gospel was accepted by most Christians as authoritative – something that happened toward the end of the second century – it was taken to be the work of that disciple and Apostle who was an eyewitness of Jesus' ministry.

Irenaeus, the first great theologian of the church after John, writing toward the end of the second century, makes frequent use of the Gospel of John, refutes what he regards as heretical or erroneous interpretations of it, and calls the author John the disciple of the Lord. (Already a decade before Irenaeus, Tatian, in composing the *Diatessaron*, a compilation of the four Gospels, had used the Gospel of John as equally authoritative with the Synoptics.) Earlier, there are hints and indications of the use and influence of the Gospel in Justin Martyr at the middle of the second century and in Ignatius of Antioch as early as the second decade, while between them Polycarp clearly seems to have known the quite closely related First Epistle of John.[4] But the clear attribution of the Fourth Gospel to the Apostle John had to await the latter decades of the second century. As we enter the third century, however, the Gospel of John is frequently cited as such, and there seems to be little or no trace of any doubt about its origin and authorship. Clement of Alexandria called it a spiritual Gospel, in distinction from the others, and that has proven an apt designation.

A generation later Clement's brilliant student Origen wrote a commentary on the Gospel of John, in which he took issue at points with earlier interpretations, particularly those of a certain Heracleon, who was a learned exegete and a disciple of the great gnostic teacher Valentinus. Valentinus apparently wrote his own gospel or treatise known as the *Gospel of Truth*. As the title by which it is known already implies, the *Gospel of Truth*, although not a narrative, has strong affinities in termin-

---

[4] See Irenaeus, *Against Heresies* III.11.1–6, who rejects gnostic interpretations of the prologue of the Gospel of John; Justin Martyr, *First Apology* 61, who quotes John 3:5; Ignatius, *Romans* 7:2–3, who refers to the seemingly Johannine themes of water (4:10; 7:38), bread (6:33), and blood (6:53); and Polycarp, *Philippians* 7:1, who apparently reflects knowledge of 1 John 4:2–3 or 2 John 7.

ology and conceptuality with the Gospel of John. Obviously the Gospel of John was known and cherished by gnostic Christians. Whether for that reason it was suspect among many other Christians cannot be known for sure, but it is a reasonable surmise, and we do know there were otherwise orthodox Christians who opposed the Gospel of John and rejected its authority.[5] Doubtless the Gospel eventually prevailed and became a part of the New Testament, not only because of its intrinsic quality but also because of its attribution to the Apostle.

Our concern is not with the identity of the author *per se*, which cannot be established on the basis of New Testament evidence, but with the meaning and implications of this Gospel's claim that it is the work of an eyewitness or is at least based on the testimony of an eyewitness. What does this claim imply for any assessment or presentation of the theology of John? Certainly that such theology cannot hang in the air, so to speak, unrelated to or unaffected by the *realia* of history. As much as the history of Jesus may be selectively presented (20:30; 21:25) and interpreted (14:25–26; 16:12–15), it is the history of Jesus, in whom the word became flesh, and that fact is of crucial importance for understanding the Fourth Gospel. At least one major aspect of the role of the Beloved Disciple is to underwrite the authority of the Gospel as a first-hand witness to Jesus' ministry (21:24; 19:35). Thus this disciple is presented as an historical personage, whoever he may have been. At the same time, he is also a figure of symbolic significance, a kind of ideal disciple of Jesus. His role, with its claim of eyewitness authority for the Gospel, must be taken into account in any treatment of its theology, and in ways we shall have to examine.

As to date and place of origin, probably neither question affects our apprehension of Johannine theology in a way germane to its presentation. We shall assume the traditional view that the Gospel of John was written late rather than early

---

[5] Barrett, *The Gospel According to St. John*, p. 14, refers to the *alogoi*. See the important unpublished work of Joseph Daniel Smith, Jr., "Gaius and Controversy over the Johannine Literature," Ph.D. diss., Yale University, 1979.

in the first century. The earliest writers to comment on the Fourth Gospel took it to be late, in the time of the Roman Emperor Trajan (AD 98–117), and many stated that it was written with the other canonical Gospels in view. Whether the latter view is correct is a matter we shall have to examine, but the reflective, retrospective character of the Gospel's narrative supports the tradition that it is a relatively late Gospel, not an earlier one, and most critical scholarship has assented. The occasional argument that John is an early Gospel is the child of modern criticism, not ancient tradition.[6]

Tradition has it that the Gospel was written in Ephesus. If one visits the ancient site of Ephesus today, a modern guide will confidently confirm this as she shows the Church of St. John, erected at the site at which the Apostle supposedly composed the Gospel and was later buried. Not surprisingly, modern gospel criticism has become quite skeptical of this tradition. Among other things, in the early second century Ignatius of Antioch wrote a letter to the church at Ephesus, in which he makes a good deal of Paul's residence there, but says nothing of John's having worked or written there also. In fact, he does not mention John at all. But according to the tradition of the late second century, John would have been in Ephesus more recently than Paul, much closer to the time of Ignatius himself. If John had written his Gospel in Ephesus just a quarter of a century before, would Ignatius have ignored that fact while extolling Ephesus' connection with Paul? Moreover, Ignatius himself seems to know the Gospel of John or its constituent traditions. Of course, this whole argument assumes that the Gospel of John was actually written by the Apostle of that name. If this was not the case, but it was rather the work of some other ancient witness, this argument loses a great deal of its force.

In examining the sketch of church life in Ephesus found in Acts 18 and 19, one finds a setting in which Christian believers of Jewish origin like Paul, Priscilla, Aquila, and Apollos are

---

[6] Barrett, *The Gospel According to St. John*, p. 100, cites the statements of Irenaeus (*Against Heresies* II.22.5 and III.3.4) quoted by Eusebius (*Ecclesiastical History* III.23.3f.) that John lived until the time of Trajan (AD 98).

engaged in conversation and controversy with other Jews, who do not believe in Jesus. Moreover, there is a group there whose members seem to be followers of John the Baptist (19:1–7). Paul debates with other Jews in a synagogue, where he is ultimately rejected (19:8–10). Through Paul God works mighty miracles, and the pretensions of Jewish exorcists who illegitimately pronounce the name of Jesus are exposed (19:13–16). In fact, there are some remarkable correspondences between the Acts portrayal of the church at Ephesus and some recent proposals about the setting and purpose of the Gospel of John. Nevertheless, cogent arguments have also been made for John's origin in Syria or Alexandria.

As reckless as it would be simply to dismiss ancient traditions of an Ephesian origin of the Gospel of John, or for that matter other ancient traditions of the Gospel's origin, neither can such traditions be used uncritically in an effort to establish a solid base from which to understand this Gospel. Most early statements about the Gospel of John express an obvious interest in its authenticity and validity. While they should not be regarded as baseless for that reason, neither can they be taken at face value. Fortunately, the kinds of introductory questions most relevant for understanding Johannine theology can best be addressed on the basis of a study of the text of the Fourth Gospel itself and an effort to set it in its historical context. The stylistic character and quality of the Gospel, its purpose in relation to its anticipated readers, and its sources can only be adequately assessed and understood on the basis of such a study.

Therefore, in Chapter 2 of this book the character, sources, and historical setting of the Fourth Gospel will be discussed. There is first of all a brief sketch of the general setting of the Gospel in the religious world of its time (Chapter 2, A). The Gospel draws upon broadly familiar terms and concepts. This is followed by an initial or provisional assessment of the literary character and sources of the Gospel of John. Much can be learned by paying attention to its movement and structure, as well as the ways in which it is parallel to but different from the Synoptic Gospels (Chapter 2, B). We shall examine these matters with a view to asking about the reasons behind, or causes of, its differences.

The obvious facts that the Gospel of John, like most New Testament writings, is full of references and allusions to the Old Testament and that it constantly refers to "the Jews" as a people or group opposed to Jesus raise questions about the relation of this Gospel to Judaism that cannot be avoided in any effort to understand its purpose, message, and the particular emphases of its theology (Chapter 2, c, 1). Jesus was a Jew, as was Paul, and neither is intelligible historically outside a Jewish context. If they can be understood in a Christian context, that is in no small part because Christianity has imbibed a great deal from its parent religion. In the Gospel of John we may be witness to a critical stage in the relationship of Christianity to Judaism. Indeed, we may find here a point at which what we have now come to know as two distinct religions are coming into being, precisely over the question of the role ascribed or denied to Jesus and the implications of various confessions of loyalty to Jesus for the old community and a new one just now taking shape. This sunderance, which lies at or near the root of Christianity *per se*, had an important bearing on Christian theology, which is reflected nowhere more clearly than in the Fourth Gospel.

In this connection it will be instructive to compare and contrast the Fourth Gospel not only with other Gospels, but with the message of early Christianity, particularly as represented by the Apostle Paul and with the very closely related Letters of John (Chapter 2, c, 2). If the latter are not the work of the author of the Fourth Gospel himself, they were certainly written by a disciple, someone so heavily influenced by him that he imbibed the style and vocabulary of the Gospel as well as its literary themes. Obviously, the Gospel of John shares a common subject matter with the rest of the New Testament. If the lines of connection cannot be drawn with certainty from our vantage point, they are nevertheless real. Moreover, Paul's Letters also reflect the centrality of Jewish-Christian issues, as do the Letter to the Hebrews and several other New Testament books (for example, the Gospel of Matthew).

The theological themes of the Fourth Gospel (Chapter 3) then arise directly out of its historical setting in ancient Judaism, early Christianity, and particularly the nexus and polemic between them. While to see these themes or doctrines simply as the product of such polemic fails to do them justice, neither can they be fully or properly understood apart from this historical and polemical context. The order of our treatment of these themes will thus reflect the ancient conflict and context. Our general framework of revelation to the world (Chapter 3, B) and to the community (Chapter 3, C) sets the theological, as well as historical, context of these themes. The revelation of God in Jesus Christ is the projection of God himself as light and life into a world of darkness and sin, creating within that world a new one, the community of those who follow Jesus and live in love and fellowship with him and therefore with God, and one another. This is not only a theological statement, but one that assumes an historical setting and sequence: first Jesus; then the church. It is, of course, the case that the theological themes of John's Gospel have generated a life of their own within the Christian church, and have contributed enormously to the development of its theology. Also, the theme of revelation within the Gospel has contributed importantly to the function of the Gospel itself as a source or medium of revelation in the church. The latter consideration, important as it may be, is not, however, the subject of our treatment.

The final part of the book (Chapter 4) deals with three issues that arise out of the Gospel of John and our treatment of its theology: mythology, anti-Semitism, and the nature or essence of Christianity. Obviously, these matters are too large and important to be dealt with exhaustively or definitively here. Nevertheless, they are indicative of the importance of the Fourth Gospel in several aspects or dimensions: for the understanding of the gospel message in the modern world; for its relation to other religions, particularly its parent faith, from which it has been so long estranged; and for the Christian church's understanding of who she is and what she is about.

CHAPTER 2

The setting and sources of Johannine theology

A THE GENERAL RELIGIOUS SETTING

If the question of authorship was the crucial problem and issue
for late nineteenth-century and early twentieth-century scholarship, the question of the background or setting and sources of
the Gospel came to dominate twentieth-century research and
the determination of the nature and character of Johannine
theology. At issue is the question of the Johannine world. From
what world of Hellenism, Judaism, or early Christianity does
the Fourth Gospel stem? Quite obviously these are not
mutually exclusive possibilities, for it is clear that whatever else
its background, the Gospel of John stems from some early
Christian environment. Moreover, recent scholarship has
shown us that Judaism itself existed within the cultural and
conceptual world of Hellenism, distinctive though it may have
been.[1]

1 Hellenism

Within the broader Mediterranean world, John was once
thought to have originated among Greeks or pagans, that is,
among Christians who had not previously been Jews.[2] Such a

---

[1] This insight is associated with the work of Martin Hengel, *Judaism and Hellenism:
Studies in their Encounter in Palestine During the Early Hellenistic Period* (Philadelphia,
1974).

[2] The title of Benjamin W. Bacon's book, *The Gospel of the Hellenists*, ed. Carl H.
Kraeling (New York, 1933), seems to represent that view, although by "Hellenists"
Bacon actually meant the Greek-speaking Jewish Christians we encounter in Acts 6
and 7.

view arose in recognition of the fact that the Gospel of John, and even the Jesus of that Gospel, speaks a language different from the Synoptic Gospels and the Synoptic Jesus. His vocabulary and style, as well as his phrasing, are more like those of 1 John than those of the Synoptic Jesus. The very beginning of the Fourth Gospel, the prologue (1:1–18), appears philosophical or even metaphysical in its aim or interests. John does not seem to breathe the air of first-century Palestine, but rather that of the fourth-century Christian creeds, and thus of earlier Greek philosophy and metaphysics. This is already apparent in the prologue, which is a fair barometer of the atmosphere of the Gospel generally.

The subject of the prologue is the *logos*, usually translated *word*. The *logos* personified turns out to be Jesus Christ (1:17), but why should Jesus be designated in this way? Of course, Jesus preached the word (Mark 2:2), and the good news about him could be called "the word" (Acts 4:4), but elsewhere Jesus himself is not presented as the word. Old Testament prophets characteristically spoke the word of the Lord, but not simply the word. Nor did they personify the word in the manner of the prologue of the Gospel.

In ancient Greek thought, however, *logos* had a long history, and standard Greek lexicons give more than a dozen possible renderings of the term: "speaking," "assertion," "speech," "subject," "thing," and "account," to mention only a few. Heraclitus, the pre-Socratic philosopher (fifth century BC), apparently spoke often of the word, but the remnants of his writings are so fragmentary as to leave us in doubt about what role it actually played in his thought. More to the point was the use of *logos* by the early Stoics, such as Zeno, who lived well into the third century BC. He equated Zeus, the high god, with *orthos logos*, right reason.[3] The philosophical followers and descendants of Plato took up the word and concept of *logos* to designate the mediation of the divine presence in creation and elsewhere. We find a later outworking of that usage in the quasi-philosophical Hermetic literature, dating from about the

---

[3] Cited by C. K. Barrett, *The New Testament Background: Selected Documents*, rev. ed. (San Francisco, 1987), p. 67.

third century of our era, but with earlier roots. There one can read of a "holy word" active in the moment of creation or of a "luminous word" called "son of God."[4] How much the Hermetic literature is influenced by the Bible, and even by the New Testament, is, however, a real question.

Clearly influenced by the Bible (i.e., the Old Testament), as well as by Platonism, is the Jewish philosopher Philo of Alexandria, who was a contemporary of Jesus and the earliest Christians. Although he was a loyal Jew, Philo's conceptuality and thought owe as much to Plato as to Moses, particularly with respect to his use of *logos*: "to his Word, his chief messenger, highest in age and honor, the Father of all has given the special prerogative, to stand on the border and separate the creature from the Creator."[5] Philo goes on in the same context to describe the *logos* as neither uncreated like God nor created, but in a very real sense a mediator. Not surprisingly, this most Hellenistic of Jews seems, like John, to be a mediator between Greek philosophy and biblical religion.[6]

2   Gnosticism

Naturally, the whole question of the conceptual and cultural background of the Gospel of John does not hinge upon the term *logos*, although it provides a good test case. *Logos* as intermediary belongs to a philosophical and religious vocabulary that was common in Mediterranean antiquity. Such a vocabulary, largely shared with the Fourth Gospel, appears also in Christian and gnostic texts that are later than the first century but may have more ancient roots. A large cache of such texts was found at Nag Hammadi on the Nile River in Egypt in 1945, and they have since been edited and

---

[4] See the tractate *Poimandres*, 5–6; cited by Barrett, *New Testament Background*, pp. 95f.

[5] *Quis Rerum Divinarum Heres?*, 205–206; cited by Barrett, *New Testament Background*, p. 263.

[6] C. H. Dodd, *The Interpretation of the Fourth Gospel* (Cambridge, 1953), pp. 54–73. Dodd concludes: "It seems clear, therefore, that whatever other elements of thought may enter into the background of the Fourth Gospel, it certainly presupposes a range of ideas having a remarkable resemblance to those of Hellenistic Judaism as represented by Philo" (p. 73).

published.[7] The essence of gnosticism was salvation through knowledge, primarily knowledge of one's heavenly origin. This basic insight was often complicated by theories about how the divine essence fell into the material world. The ancient gnostics are described in negative and tendentious terms by Irenaeus in a work entitled *Against Heresies.* Irenaeus' descriptions lead us to think that these Christians were presenting foreign philosophy, speculation, and superstition under the guise of Christianity. In a sense, or in part, Irenaeus was correct, particularly if one takes as the norm of Christianity the books of the New Testament, which were only just being collected as a canon of scripture when Irenaeus wrote. (Irenaeus is, in fact, one of the earliest witnesses to the existence of something very much like our New Testament.) The gnostic texts, however, drew upon a vocabulary with marked affinities to the Gospel of John; not only *logos*, but such dualities as truth and falsehood, light and darkness, and life and death figure prominently in them. The elect belong to God, as in John, and Jesus' function is to gather them to himself (John 12:32). Moreover, God is often described as the Father and Jesus simply as the Son. That kind of language is also found in the Synoptic Gospels, but it is much more common in the Gospel of John. Of course, in John as in Christian gnostic writings, knowing Jesus or God is very important, but in John knowing one's own, heavenly origin does not occupy the same role.

While gnosticism is known mostly in some Christian version, there is a gnostic corpus of literature and community that is clearly not Christian, namely the Mandaean. The Mandaeans, now only a few thousand in number, still inhabit a strip of territory between Iraq and Iran, where they have presumably lived since late antiquity. Yet there are references in their traditions to figures of the Old Testament and to the Jordan River, as if they once lived in Palestine. Indeed, it is now thought that they migrated from there to their present

---

[7] For the Nag Hammadi documents the most accessible and comprehensive collection in English translation is James M. Robinson (ed.), *The Nag Hammadi Library in English*, 3rd rev. ed. (San Francisco, 1988).

location in the early years of our era.[8] Moreover, John the Baptist figures prominently in their religious texts, as he does in the Fourth Gospel, and they themselves practice baptism. Their primary emissary from God, the mythical Manda d-Hiia ("knowledge of life"), descends into this world from the world of light above to gather and deliver such human beings as are really alienated citizens of the world above. The revelation discourses of the Mandaean *Right Ginza* are reminiscent of words of Jesus in the Fourth Gospel.

> I am the messenger of light,
> whom the Great One sent into the world.
> The True Messenger am I,
> In whom there is no falsehood ...
> I am the messenger of light ...
> Whoever receives his word,
> his eyes are filled with light.[9]

Not surprisingly, some commentators on the Fourth Gospel have seen in the Mandaeans its proximate background.[10] The problem with that view is that the Mandaean literature in its present form is centuries later than the New Testament, and it cannot be shown that they or their traditions antedate early Christianity. Nevertheless, since it is also unclear that they were fundamentally influenced by Christianity, the possibility remains that they represent an independent offshoot of Judaism. In that event the points of similarity to the language of Johannine Christianity would be remarkable.

Similarly, the Manichaean religion, to which St. Augustine once belonged, possessed marked similarities to Christianity.

---

[8] Conceivably, their ancestors, like the Johannine community, felt that they had been persecuted and driven out of Judaism. A leading authority on Mandaeism, Kurt Rudolph, has come to this conclusion. Rudolph's views are accessible in summary form in English in his *Gnosis: The Nature and History of Gnosticism* (San Francisco, 1983), pp. 343–366. Simone Pétrement resists this view in her recent general work on gnosticism, *A Separate God: The Christian Origins of Gnosticism* (San Francisco, 1990), pp. 476–481; but her own discussion reveals how ambiguous is the evidence and how cloudy the issues.

[9] Cited by Barrett, *New Testament Background*, p. 115.

[10] Most notably, Rudolf Bultmann, *The Gospel of John: A Commentary* (Oxford and Philadelphia, 1971), takes this position and uses the Mandaean materials to help reconstruct the hypothetical gnosticism over against which he places the Gospel of John.

Indeed, the third-century founder, Mani, apparently knew the principal New Testament books, and at least some of his adherents regarded Manichaeism as the true Christianity. Unlike the Mandaeans, the much more numerous Manichaeans can be dated more exactly in relation to early Christianity, and the lines of influence are clear. Yet, like the Mandaeans, the Manichaeans cannot simply be explained as an offshoot of Christianity, for their roots too go back deep into the myths and traditions of the Near East. Characteristic of the Manichaeans and the Mandaeans, to whom they are perhaps related, is the pervasive dualism, similar to John's, that reflects a profound pessimism about this world. Historians of ancient Near Eastern religion are inclined to trace such dualism and world pessimism, whether in Mandaeism or Manichaeism, to ancient Iranian religion, specifically Zoroastrianism.

Zarathustra (Zoroaster), the founder of Zoroastrianism, lived well before the beginnings of Christianity, perhaps nearly a millennium earlier, in the vicinity of present-day Iran. In the earliest sources he is already an almost mythical figure. His chief emphasis or insight, or at least what flowed from him in Zoroastrianism, was an uncompromising monotheism, accompanied by a stark dualism. This dualism, the division of the world into good and evil, light and darkness, explains the present evil in the world without attributing it to the creator God Ahura Mazda, or Ohrmazd.[11] Although the lines of connection can scarcely be traced, the influence of Zarathustra, or at least the later movement bearing his name, can quite possibly be seen a thousand or more years later in such movements as gnosticism, Mandaeism, and Manichaeism. A strong dualistic influence appears at points in early Christianity, particularly in the Gospel of John, but also in Judaism, especially in what may well be the nearest identifi-

[11] See James H. Charlesworth, "Critical Comparison of the Dualism in 1Q5 3:13–4:26 and the 'Dualism' Contained in the Gospel of John," *NTS*, 15 (1968–69), 389–419 (reprinted in *John and the Dead Sea Scrolls*, ed. Charlesworth [New York, 1990], pp. 76–106), who traces the Qumran dualism to a specific form of Zoroastrianism known as Zurvanism (pp. 88f.).

able relative of Johannine Christianity within the mother religion, the Essene community, which produced the Dead Sea
Scrolls.

3   Judaism: The Dead Sea Scrolls

The Dead Sea Scrolls, discovered by accident near the ruins of
an ancient Jewish monastery of Qumran in 1947, consist of a
large number of biblical manuscripts, mostly in fragmentary
form, as well as other documents. Because the manuscripts
have been shown on the basis of paleography and carbon-14
tests to date from the period of Christian origins (200 BC–AD
70), they are of great interest to New Testament scholarship, as
well as Old Testament research and the history of Judaism. Of
particular relevance to the origins of Christianity are the
distinctive books of the community itself, particularly its so-
called *Community Rule* or *Manual of Discipline*.

Much of the dualistic theological vocabulary of gnosticism
and the Gospel of John turns up also in the Scrolls. Thus in the
Community Rule (cols. 3 and 4) we read:

He has created man to govern the *world*, and has appointed for him
two spirits in which to *walk* until the time of his visitation: the *spirits of
truth* and *falsehood*. Those *born* of *truth* spring from a fountain of *light*,
but those *born* of *falsehood* spring from a source of *darkness*. All the
children of righteousness are ruled by the *Prince of Light* and walk in the
ways of *light*, but all the children of *falsehood* are ruled by the *Angel of
Darkness* and *walk* in the ways of *darkness*.

And again:

And as for the visitation of all who *walk* in this *spirit*, it shall be
healing, great *peace* in a long *life*, and *fruitfulness*, together with
everlasting blessing and *eternal joy* in *life without end*, a crown of glory
and a garment of majesty in *unending light*.[12]

The words and phrases italicized are reminiscent of early
Christian literature, and typical of the Fourth Gospel especially.[13] Particularly striking are the dualism and the

---

[12] The translation is from Geza Vermes, *The Dead Sea Scrolls in English*, 3rd ed.
(London, 1987), pp. 64–65.

[13] See Charlesworth, "Critical Comparison."

emphasis on eternal salvation. This is all the more remarkable in that the *Community Rule* is written in Hebrew, while the Gospel of John is in Greek. If the *Rule* were to be translated into Greek, the natural Greek words chosen would be those we find in the Fourth Gospel: *pneuma* (spirit); *alētheia* (truth); *phōs* (light); *skotia* (darkness); *zōē* (life); *eirēnē* (peace); etc. Thus the similarity that is quickly recognized in English translation is quite real and significant. Of course, the affinities with the Fourth Gospel are unusually strong in these passages of the *Rule*, but this fact does not render them less important. Just at this point in the *Rule* the theological nature of the community and the promise of its salvation are being described. In other words, what we find here is fundamental to the community's theological self-understanding.

Increasingly, the search for the proximate background or milieu of the Gospel of John has centered upon Judaism, in no small part because of the discovery of the Scrolls. But there are other elements in the Gospel that also call attention to its strong Jewish roots, despite the fact that "the Jews" seems to be a technical term and a label of opprobrium in the Gospel. Most obvious are the frequent references to the scriptures that Christians now call the Old Testament. In John Jesus can refer to something being written in "your law" (8:17), by which he obviously means scripture, as if the scriptural law pertained to Jews, and not to himself or his followers. On the other hand, all references to scripture are positive, at least implicitly so, and scripture is said to find its fulfillment in Jesus (5:39,46). Moses and the law or scripture, when rightly understood, testify in favor of Jesus. There is then a significant interplay between Moses and Jesus in the Fourth Gospel.[14]

4 *Judaism: Wisdom motifs*

Furthermore, there are more subtle biblical motifs or allusions, one of the most important of which is wisdom, although neither the Greek word *sophia* (wisdom) nor the adjective *sophos* (wise)

[14] Most recently dealt with by M.-Emile Boismard, OP, *Moses or Jesus: An Essay in Johannine Christianity* (Minneapolis, 1992). See also T. Francis Glasson, *Moses in the*

actually occurs in the Fourth Gospel. Nevertheless, the role
and function of the *logos* in John's prologue (1:1–18) is closely
paralleled by the personification of wisdom in biblical and
later Jewish wisdom texts, notably in Proverbs 8:22–31 (cf.
Genesis 1), where wisdom is personified and said to be present
with God at creation. Moreover, whoever finds wisdom is said
to find life (Proverbs 8:35), even as in John the *logos* is the
source of life (1:3–4). In the deutero-canonical Wisdom of
Solomon, a part of scripture for most ancient Christians as well
as those in the Catholic tradition, wisdom is called "the
fashioner of all things" (7:22) and "a pure emanation of the
glory of the Almighty" (7:25). Interestingly, the word for
wisdom is feminine in both Greek (*sophia*) and Hebrew
(*hochmah*); perhaps for this reason the masculine term *logos* was
selected by John to describe Jesus, who was male, although
logos has other connotations having to do with expression or
communication that may have influenced the evangelist's
choice. Of course, the word of God, or of the Lord, is itself an
important biblical term and concept, especially in the prophetic literature, although the absolute use of "word" (without
"of the Lord") is not. In any event, if one asks where the idea
that God uses a mediator in creation, and ultimately in redemption, originates, an important answer may be found in
the biblically based personification of wisdom. Already wisdom
could be identified with the word, as in the synonymous paral-
lelism of Wisdom 9:1–2: "God ... who made all things by your
word, and in your wisdom fashioned man ..." (Revised
English Bible). While the designation of Jesus as the *logos*
occurs only in the prologue of the Gospel of John, the perspective on Jesus and the role ascribed to him there are by no means
isolated, but pervade and underlie the whole Gospel.

Of course, the Jewish background and character of the
Fourth Gospel are already evident from the opening line of the
prologue. The Gospel's "In the beginning was the Word" (1:1)
closely parallels the opening line of the Hebrew Bible: "In the

Fourth Gospel, SBT 40 (London, 1963); and especially Wayne A. Meeks, *The Prophet-
King: Moses Traditions and the Johannine Christology*, Supplements to Novum Testamentum 14 (Leiden, 1967).

beginning God created heaven and earth" (Genesis 1:1). In John God creates through the word, who is portrayed as a personal being, paralleling the personification of *sophia* in the wisdom literature. In Genesis there is no personification of the word, but God speaks and thereby creates. God says, "Let there be light, and there was light" (Genesis 1:3). In John the word itself is light as well as life (1:4). The allusions to Genesis are clear, as John provides a fresh reading of that ancient text.

Moreover, John betrays particular interest in, and knowledge of, groups or sects within, or at the fringes of, Judaism. John the Baptist plays a large role in the Gospel and the reader learns that he, like Jesus, has disciples (1:35; 3:25; cf. Luke 7:18–30; 11:1; Matthew 11:2–15; also Acts 18:25–19:4). In fact, from the outset the evangelist seems intent on defining John's role precisely so that the reader will not mistake him for the Christ (1:6–8). Yet John himself is portrayed in an entirely positive light and his disciples are open to Jesus (1:35–42), not hostile to him (even in 3:26). By the same token the Samaritans, personified initially by the woman at the well (4:1–42), are attracted to Jesus and many are persuaded by him (verses 39–42). Samaria itself will prove a rich mission field according to Jesus' own word (4:31–38; cf. Acts 8:4–25). John the evangelist knows the gulf of hostility that separates Jew and Samaritan, and that Jesus is a Jew, not a Samaritan (4:9; cf. verses 20–24). Yet Jesus' opponents will accuse him of being a Samaritan (8:48), thus suggesting that he or his followers have relation to, or affinities with, the despised Samaritans.[15]

Although the question of the religious and cultural milieu or antecedents of the Gospel of John has been the subject of intensive research through most of this century, our brief summary will suffice to indicate the range and importance of these matters. The vocabulary and concepts of the Gospel find their place in the world of late Hellenistic and Jewish anti-

---

[15] On the Baptist and Samaritan connections of the Gospel, see Raymond E. Brown, *The Community of the Beloved Disciple* (New York, 1979), pp. 39–40, 69–71 (on the Baptist), and pp. 34–40 (on the Samaritans). The possible relation of Samaritan veneration of Moses to Johannine christology is discussed by Meeks, *The Prophet-King*, pp. 215–257.

quity. They would not have seemed strange to the original or intended readers. Yet an effort to begin from a single presumed background in order to interpret the Gospel against it will be too narrow, or ill focused, or both, at least until we establish what is distinctive about the Fourth Gospel as compared with the other Gospels or what we know about early Christianity generally. For influences ascribed to some other background or source may actually have been mediated by, or through, the early Christian milieu of which this Gospel was a part. Thus we turn now to the Gospel itself in order to make a brief analysis of its structure and an inventory of its content, with a view to uncovering and highlighting its distinctiveness.

B   THE NARRATIVE SETTING AND SOURCES

Like the other Gospels, the Gospel of John is a story, a narrative of Jesus' ministry rather than a theological treatise, although Christian theological themes are far more evident in it than in the others. Its literary style, as well as its genre, is obvious enough. Some of the Johannine narratives attain a subtlety and sophistication scarcely matched in the other Gospels, for example, the healing of the man born blind (chap. 9) and the risen Jesus' appearance to Mary Magdalene in the garden (20:11–18). Yet there are also breaks in the narrative. For example, at the beginning of chapter 6 we find Jesus suddenly in Galilee, although he had just previously been in Jerusalem (chap. 5); or after the Gospel has seemingly ended (20:30–31) there is yet another resurrection scene, now also in Galilee. Yet the Gospel of John has as clear an overall outline or structure as any: after an introductory section (chap. 1), there follows an account of Jesus' public ministry (chaps. 2–12), which is, as we shall see, very different from that of the Synoptics. Jesus' passion and resurrection (chaps. 18–21) are preceded by a scene at the Last Supper much longer than in the other Gospels. This second half of the Gospel (chaps. 13–20) is called by one commentator (Bultmann, *The Gospel of John: A Commentary*) "The Revelation of the Glory to the Congregation," corresponding to the earlier "Revelation of the Glory before the World." The sharpness of this distinction matches, and is perhaps an expression of, the dualism of the Gospel: the congregation of Jesus' disciples withdraws from the fatally hostile world to be alone with him.

The composition and content of the Fourth Gospel set it apart from the Synoptics, which – as their name implies – have a common view of the ministry of Jesus: they see it together. Every student and careful reader from antiquity on has noted John's differences in time frame and geographical setting, but the most striking difference has to do with the portrayal of Jesus, his deeds, and particularly the issues he addresses. They are issues of faith and unbelief, and they seem to be cast in the form of a dispute involving the beliefs of Judaism and the innovations of Christianity. Jesus debates with the Pharisees, not about the interpretation of the law, but about who he is. Although until recent times it has been assumed that John wrote after the other evangelists and with knowledge of them, it is not evident that knowledge of other Gospels *per se* is required to understand John, and therefore not clear that the fourth evangelist presupposed the Synoptics or used them as sources. Obviously, they share certain knowledge and beliefs. In surveying the narrative of the Fourth Gospel we gain a clearer impression of its distinctiveness over against the others. Whatever may have been the relation between John and the Synoptics, John's distinctive emphases do not appear simply to have been derived from them.

They do not in themselves suggest how or why he presented what he received in the way he did. Likewise, the general religious and cultural setting of the Fourth Gospel provides the conceptuality and vocabulary with which the evangelist worked, but does not explain his distinctive emphases. Therefore the student must read the Fourth Gospel with a view to asking why and how they arose. That is, the reader should look for hints or indications of the specific setting and purpose of the Gospel that may be revealed in the narrative. This may not be such a difficult task, because the evangelist often lets us know that he is aware of a significant difference between his own time and setting and that of Jesus. Moreover, there may be anachronisms in the narrative that he has made little effort to hide.

1　The introduction of the Gospel (1:1–51)

The prologue of the Gospel of John (1:1–18) is entirely distinctive among the Gospels, although there are similar christological passages with hymn-like characteristics that extol Jesus Christ's role in creation or redemption elsewhere in the New Testament: Philippians 2:5–11; Colossians 1:15–20; cf. Hebrews 1:1–4. Moreover, each Gospel begins in a distinctive way. A remote parallel with John can be seen in the Matthean and Lucan birth narratives, which seek to establish the role and purpose of God in Jesus' advent. Yet John is typically different, and it is noteworthy that this evangelist seems deliberately to avoid explaining Jesus' ultimate origin by reference to his Davidic lineage and birth (cf. 7:40–44). This seems strange, and many suggest that John, like Paul and Mark, did not know the stories of Jesus' birth. But perhaps John would not have been satisfied with the very earthly stories of Jesus' humble birth as adequate explanations of his heavenly origin. That origin is a paradox to be held in stark contrast to outward, worldly appearances. Jesus is, on the one hand, the son of Joseph from Nazareth (1:45), a town noted for no one and nothing (1:46); but he is, on the other, the *logos* and Son of God. Indeed, he can be called *theos* (God), as he is at the beginning of the narrative (1:1,18) and again at the end (20:28). Yet despite the otherworldliness of Jesus, his human origins are not a matter to be overcome. They remain with him throughout the story. Otherwise, the kind of eyewitness to him that the Gospel underscores (1:14; 2:11; 19:35; 21:24) might be unthinkable. The Johannine Jesus has his own very earthly side (see 1 John 1:1–3). It is also evident, however, that the Gospel of John is not out to prove the humanity of Jesus – that is a given – for its more pressing interests lie elsewhere.[16]

---

[16] Marianne Meye Thompson, *The Humanity of Jesus in the Fourth Gospel* (Philadelphia, 1988), p. 122: "It does not set out to prove that Jesus was truly human or that he

Jesus' encounter with John (never called "the Baptist" in the Fourth Gospel) closely parallels the Synoptic accounts, with some notable differences. Perhaps the most obvious – although it can easily be overlooked – is that the narrative never tells us that Jesus himself was baptized by John in the Jordan River (Mark 1:5,9). John's baptizing activities are said to have taken place across the Jordan (10:40), and once at an otherwise unknown Bethany beyond the Jordan (1:28). John's account complements the Synoptics' so well that we scarcely realize we are not told that Jesus was baptized, or we read the event in, thinking that was the author's intention. It is a typical case of John's relation to the Synoptic narratives. Indeed, in this case the omission is quite understandable as a deletion from the Synoptic account, made because the Fourth Gospel wishes to emphasize Jesus' superiority to John (1:15,30; 3:28–30; 5:33–36). Remarkably, most of the words spoken at Jesus' baptism are preserved in John, despite the absence of the event itself! Moreover, as if to be sure the reader keeps the Baptist in his place, the evangelist has him tell the entire story, so to speak, in retrospect to his disciples (1:30–34). John's account of his encounter with Jesus then leads immediately into a narrative in which, in effect, John sends his disciples to follow Jesus, "the Lamb of God, who takes away the sins of the world" (1:34–37; cf. verse 29). From the beginning (1:6–8) the Fourth Gospel makes unmistakably clear the relationship of John to Jesus: he is his witness, not his rival. Indeed, there is apparently a need to be sure that John is accorded his proper place, but nothing more.

While the evangelist clearly has a theological purpose in describing the events in the way he does, and the narrative is replete with his theology, he nevertheless produces a scene that has a certain verisimilitude or historical plausibility. It is not unlikely that some of Jesus' disciples, like Jesus himself, had been followers of the Baptist. Moreover, John provides a basis for understanding why the disciples would follow Jesus in the

possessed a real body of flesh and blood. Instead, this is exactly what the Gospel assumes."

first place, one that is lacking in the terse Marcan account (1:16–20). There the disciples follow at Jesus' bare command.

Between the Baptist narrative and the account of Jesus' calling or gathering disciples there are, however, a couple of noteworthy omissions in John that are altogether typical of the theology of that Gospel. In the first place, nothing is said of Jesus' being tempted by Satan or the devil. Correspondingly, there is in John no account of Jesus' anguish in the Garden of Gethsemane (but see 12:27). The Johannine Jesus is neither subject to temptation nor beset with anxiety. In the second place, there is no announcement of the imminence of God's kingdom or rule (Mark 1:15; Matthew 4:17; but Luke also lacks such an announcement). As we shall see, John dramatically shifts the focus of eschatology from the future to the present. Both these omissions will prove typical of Johannine theology.

The conclusion of the first chapter of John, and of the Gospel's introduction, has Jesus uttering a rather enigmatic suggestion of what Nathanael, and Jesus' disciples, may expect to witness during his ministry (1:51). What is meant by the heavens opened and the angels of God ascending and descending upon the Son of Man is not obvious. But the saying evokes Genesis 28:12, where in Jacob's dream at Bethel angels ascend and descend upon the ladder into heaven, or as it is possible to construe the Hebrew, upon Jacob (Israel!) himself. Of course, *Bethel* in Hebrew means "house of God," and in the Genesis story Jacob exclaims after his dream: "This is none other than the house of God, and this is the gate of heaven" (Genesis 28:17).

Three inferences or conclusions about how John should be read may be drawn from John 1:51 and its Old Testament background. First, the continuing importance of scripture for understanding the Fourth Gospel is underscored. The revelation in Jesus Christ harks back to and recapitulates the revelation of God to Israel. Second, revelation, that is, God's making himself known, is precisely the theme of this Gospel. Indeed, there is a real sense in which it is the theme of all the Gospels, but it is even more explicitly articulated in the Fourth. Third, the enigmatic and symbolic nature of this statement must not be lost on us. That is, John does not paint a photographic picture of what the disciples, or Jesus' opponents, would have seen or heard. Rather, his language is deliberately, consciously, symbolic or suggestive, evoking both the Genesis scene and the coming ministry of Jesus.[17] This Gospel is interested in the historical, but this is no flat, or even three-dimensional, presentation of history. An overriding theological dimension finds expression here.

2   The beginning of the public ministry (2:1-4:45)

As in the other Gospels, Jesus' public ministry begins in Galilee, but at Cana, a place never mentioned elsewhere (except in John 4:46 and 21:2). As if he has prepared the reader for what to expect (1:51), the evangelist now narrates a tale unparalleled in the Synoptic Gospels. Jesus keeps a wedding feast going by changing water into wine. The episode concludes with the steward of the feast uttering a piece of commonsense, and utterly banal, wisdom (2:10). The reader is led to ask whether the surface meaning is all that is intended. Or does the statement really refer to the revelation of God in history, which like the good wine has been kept until last?[18] It is not coincidental that the water from which the wine appeared has been kept in Jewish purification vessels (2:6). Also not coincidentally, Jesus' mother appears. Although Jesus appears to rebuff her (2:4), she will return at the end of his ministry (19:25-27).

Following this wonderful but strange tale, Jesus goes to Jerusalem at Passover. Immediately he enters the temple and cleanses it (2:13-22), something he does only at the end of his public ministry in the other Gospels. What does the evangelist

---

[17] The symbolic character of John's language is succinctly described by Xavier Léon-Dufour, "Specificité symbolique du langage de Jean," in *La Communauté johannique et son histoire: la trajectoire de l'évangile de Jean aux deux premiers siècles,* ed. Jean-Daniel Kaestli, Jean-Michel Poffet, and Jean Zumstein, Le Monde de la Bible (Geneva, 1990), pp. 121-134. See also R. Alan Culpepper, *Anatomy of the Fourth Gospel: A Study in Literary Design* (Philadelphia, 1983), pp. 180-198.

[18] See Paul W. Meyer, "John 2:10," *JBL,* 86 (1967), 191-197, for a sensitive probing of the theological significance of the good wine's being held until the last.

accomplish by narrating this story here, so early in the Gospel? Once again, the theme of revelation is sounded as Jesus makes his epiphany at the temple, the place of revelation, in Jerusalem. It is *bethel*, the house of God, where God reveals himself and deals with his people, and when Jesus speaks of his own body as "this temple" (verses 19,21), it is immediately clear that this juxtaposing of Jesus and the temple is intended and significant. In a veiled way Jesus speaks of his own resurrection, so that not even the disciples understood immediately, but only when he has been raised from the dead (verse 22). Here we get another important hint about how the Gospel is to be read and understood. It can best be read as a retrospective account of who Jesus is and what he has accomplished, for only in light of his resurrection can the questions raised by his ministry and crucifixion be answered. (At this point we find two sharp departures from the Synoptic narrative of Jesus' itinerary. First, Jesus goes to Jerusalem not at the end of his ministry, but at its beginning, and, second, we have already reached a Passover season.)

While in Jerusalem for this same Passover (2:23–25), Jesus is approached by the Pharisee Nicodemus, described as a ruler of the Jews (3:1), and their conversation is recounted. No such encounter is reported in the Synoptics. During this conversation Jesus tells Nicodemus that he must be born again, from above, by water and Spirit, else he cannot see or enter the kingdom of God. Thus the theme of rebirth is introduced (cf. 1:13) with an allusion to baptism, which was to become the Christian rite of initiation. Nicodemus has approached Jesus in a friendly way, acknowledging him to be a teacher sent from God, and Jesus' responses to him appear to be nothing short of sharp, uncalled-for, rebuffs, as he answers questions Nicodemus has not asked, or does not answer the questions he has asked, and in response to Nicodemus' perplexity over the possibility of rebirth says, "Are you the teacher of Israel and you do not know these things?" (3:10). After a veiled allusion to his own approaching crucifixion (3:14–15), there follows in verse 16 a succinct, characteristically Johannine, statement of the nature and purpose of the gospel message: "For God so loved the world that he gave his only Son, that whoever believes in him should not perish but have eternal life." Whether Jesus or the evangelist here speaks is probably a matter of indifference, for their voices typically become one. That is, the message of the Gospel of John is the message that Jesus himself delivers. The critical nature of the advent of the Son is now described (3:17–21); it is either judgment and condemnation (the Greek word *krisis* is the same for both) or salvation, depending on one's response.

The encounter between Jesus and Nicodemus marks an early turning point in the narrative. Jesus receives a friendly reception from this representative of the establishment, which he curtly rejects. Although Nicodemus disappears from the scene in the course of the narrative, he will return later to defend Jesus' right to a fair trial (7:50–52) and finally to help bury him (19:39). After this scene Jesus' reception by the Jews, also called Pharisees, is by no means so friendly. They reject him and he condemns them. Chapters 5 through 10 are a kind of manual of religious polemic, a handbook of Christian denunciation of Judaism and Jewish response. Only when one has read through this central part of the Gospel can he return to chapter 3 and understand what is really going on between Jesus and Nicodemus. Nicodemus approaches Jesus as an innocent party might. His encounter is with some reason compared with the friendly approaches of the rich young man (Mark 10:17–22 parr.) or the scribe who is not far from the kingdom of God (Mark 12:28–34 parr.). In both cases those approaching Jesus feel that they have with him a common basis for discussion, as does Nicodemus. In the Synoptics Jesus tacitly accepts that common basis. In the Gospel of John, however, Jesus clearly does not accept it, for there can be no further discussion until Nicodemus is born from above by water and Spirit. Thus there is, and can be, no conversation between Jesus and Nicodemus at this stage. Nevertheless, the fact that Nicodemus does not reject Jesus, but returns to defend and to bury him, means that the possibility for a conversation, and for Nicodemus' conversion, remains open.

Jesus' sharp rebuff of Nicodemus should not be understood

in normal relational categories applying to conversational and similar interchange between persons, so that Jesus could be described as arrogant or rude. From the standpoint of *the Gospel* narrative there seems already to be a deep gulf between Jesus and Nicodemus, which Jesus appreciates but Nicodemus does not. He does not realize that the lines are now sharply drawn between Jesus and his opponents, and one must decide to be on one side or the other. In John 3:16–21 the sharpness of the alternative is clearly drawn. It is as if two communities, two groups, whose interests were once common, but have now become divergent, and even opposed, are confronting one another. (In verse 11 there is a significant shift in the verbs from the singular to the plural.) Because they speak different languages, they can no longer converse.[19]

After a brief interlude in which John the Baptist appears once again to bear testimony to Jesus (3:22–36), Jesus goes to Samaria, to Sychar near Jacob's well, and there encounters a Samaritan woman, with whom he carries on a conversation (4:1–42), having first asked her for a drink. Although this woman, from a despised and rejected relative of orthodox Jewry (4:9), at first has as much trouble as Nicodemus understanding Jesus, she ultimately comes to a point where she can bear testimony to him, however inadequately (4:29,42). The implications can scarcely be missed. The one who is despised by upright, Pharisaic Jews – even a woman and a Samaritan – is better able to understand and receive Jesus than the well-intentioned Nicodemus, whose ethnic, religious, and academic pedigree is impeccable. This should tell us something about the distinctive life-setting and purpose of this Gospel, and where its message has found a friendly reception.

3   Confrontation and controversy (4:46–10:42)

After a couple of healing miracles (4:46–54; 5:1–9) not unlike those found in the Synoptic Gospels, Jesus, again in Jerusalem, becomes involved in an acrimonious discussion with "the

---

[19] See Wayne A. Meeks, "The Man from Heaven in Johannine Sectarianism," *JBL*, 91 (1972), 44–72, esp. 66–72 (reprinted in John Ashton [ed.], *The Interpretation of*

Jews." It begins with their accusing a man Jesus has just healed of violating the sabbath by carrying his pallet (5:10), but quickly moves to a confrontation with Jesus over his alleged claim to make himself equal with God (5:18), for which they seek to kill him. The basis for this allegation is Jesus' statement, "My Father is working still, and I am working" (5:17), which need not be taken as a claim to equality with God. Jesus, however, does not deny that is what his statement implies, and only qualifies the claim by asserting that he does nothing on his own, "only what he sees the Father doing" (verse 19). No such claim is made in the Synoptic Gospels, nor do his opponents make such an accusation against Jesus. Again, as in the case of the Nicodemus discourse, a gulf seems to lie between Jesus and his interlocutors, one for which the preceding narrative has scarcely prepared us. But now the Jews, unlike Nicodemus, are fully aware of how the land lies. Is the reader? Surely the evangelist's intended readers would have been; they would have known what was going on between the followers of Jesus (i.e., themselves) and their Jewish opponents. In fact, Jesus' own statements following upon the initial accusation of 5:18 show that these opponents are well informed of the claims about Jesus, and there is no disagreement about where the lines of separation lie. Obviously, Jesus, and by implication his followers, put one interpretation on these claims and the Jewish opponents another, but there is a clear advance over the Nicodemus discourse in that both sides now seem to be aware of what the issues are. For our purposes it is worth observing that the disagreement is thoroughly theological in nature, but not abstractly so, for the theological disagreements obviously involve life-or-death questions.

As chapter 6 begins, it is once again near Passover (6:4), but Jesus is now unaccountably back in Galilee (6:1), and we find some strong parallels to the Synoptic accounts, particularly Mark's. (It is a conundrum of exegesis that we are told nothing of how or why Jesus returned to Galilee, and some commentators suggest that chapter 6 has been misplaced, for it fits better

John, Issues in Religion and Theology 9 [Philadelphia and London, 1986], pp. 141–173).

before chapter 5, while Jesus is still in Galilee.[20]) Jesus feeds a multitude of five thousand people (6:1–15; Mark 6:32–44 and cf. 8:1–10), and later comes to his disciples walking on the sea while they are in a boat (6:16–21; Mark 6:45–52); and there is a crowd scene (6:22–25, which is quite different in detail from Mark 6:53–56). In John Jesus then launches into a long discourse and dialogue arising out of the feeding scene (6:26–59), which has no close parallel in the Synoptics, except that there is a curious and obscure conversation about bread after Mark's second feeding narrative (8:14–21). In Mark (8:11–13) one even finds a question from the crowd about a sign, which is strangely paralleled in John (6:30). After the bread discourse of John, a conversation between Jesus and some of his disciples (6:60–65) leads to Peter's affirmation of his loyalty (6:66–71; cf. Mark 8:27–30) after some have fallen away. This scene concludes with an allusion to Jesus' coming death (6:70f.; cf. Mark 8:31) in the reference to Judas' betrayal. In both Mark and John, then, the disciples' loyalty to Jesus comes under a cloud.

The Johannine Jesus' discourse about bread is clearly a discourse about himself: he is the bread from heaven. Now comes the first of the predicative "I-am" sayings (*egō eimi*) so typical of the Gospel of John: "I am the bread of life" (6:35). As will now happen repeatedly in the Gospel, Jesus applies a symbolic, salvific, predicate to himself. Usually, as here, the predicate (bread, light, shepherd, resurrection, vine) is drawn from scripture, and therefore has rich connotations. The crowd quickly become "the Jews" (verse 41) as they show their hostility to Jesus. Interestingly, *Ioudaioi* (Jews) can mean simply "Judeans," residents of Judea, but here such a meaning is not likely, for the scene is set in Galilee, indeed, in the synagogue of Capernaum (verse 59), a town frequented by Jesus, according to the Synoptic narratives. Clearly *Ioudaioi* means "Jews," and people who on religious grounds are opposed to Jesus. In a manner related to what we have already seen in chapters 3 and 5, Jesus anticipates the hostility and rejection of his hearers, telling them even before they have

---

[20] For example, Bultmann, *The Gospel of John: A Commentary*, pp. 209f.

responded to his "I am the bread of life" that they do not believe (verse 36). Then he goes on to speak of the salvation and assurance he brings to those who accept him, all under the symbolism of bread from heaven. The conflict underlying, and in a sense preceding, the narrative is clear enough.

Chapter 7 finds Jesus going once again to Jerusalem, not at his brother's bidding, but later (7:2–10; cf. 2:4). This is his third trip, and now he will stay there, or at least in Judea. Jesus' encounter with the Jewish authorities and their unsuccessful effort to arrest him (7:32,45–49) hint strongly of what is to come in the passion narrative. At this stage there is apparently potential support for Jesus among the citizens of Jerusalem; certainly not all have made up their minds against him, and many are positively impressed (7:12,15,25–26,31, 40,43,46). Yet the authorities are already dead set against him. Already they seek to kill him (7:19), although this is denied. These authorities who consistently oppose Jesus are called the Pharisees, with whom the chief priests are linked (verse 45). The chief priests were, of course, his antagonists in Jerusalem, according to both John and the Synoptics, particularly on the occasion of his arrest, trial, and execution.

The implacable hostility that manifests itself among the authorities in chapter 7 continues as the chief subject matter of chapter 8, although the connection between the chapters is otherwise quite loose. (Thus the story of the woman taken in adultery, which was no part of the original text of the Gospel, was inserted between them, 8:1–11 in the traditional versification.) Charges and countercharges are flung back and forth between Jesus and his opponents. Jesus in effect makes the Jews responsible for his death (8:28,40,59). The extremely hostile interchange ranges over such topics as who is Jesus' father, who is Jesus, who are the true descendants of Abraham, who is the Jews' father, Abraham or the devil, and whether Jesus has a demon. In conclusion, Jesus claims priority and superiority over Abraham (8:58). Although hopes for some rapprochement between Jesus and the Jews have occasionally been allowed at least to flicker up to this point, they now appear to go out. The Jews attempt to stone him – it is their form of execution – but he slips away and hides (8:59). In this chapter the harshness of the dialogue is matched by the roughness of the literary construction. Jesus makes several abrupt beginnings, after the initial "I am the light of the world," each of which makes only the loosest connection with what precedes. The reader is likely to be unsettled by the structure as well as the content of this bitter interchange.[21]

Chapter 9 is an entirely different matter as far as unity of composition is concerned, but this episode of the man born blind has only the loosest connection with what precedes. Briefly, Jesus encounters a man born blind, anoints his eyes with spittle, and gives him sight. The story is not without Synoptic precedents (cf. Mark 8:22–26), but as those questioning the man who was blind say, no one has ever heard of anyone opening the eyes of someone blind from birth (9:32). Emphasis falls, however, not so much on Jesus' unique deed as upon the blind man who has received his sight, the reaction of his neighbors, and, at length, of the Pharisees and Jews. Needless to say, their reaction is negative and hostile, both to Jesus and to the man healed. After failing to disprove the reality of the miracle, they revile, reject, and in effect excommunicate this man, who, left alone, is taken in by Jesus, whom he worships (verse 38). Jesus again states the purpose of his coming, this time in terms of sight, blindness, and seeing (verses 39–41). A familiar course is rerun, but on the basis of a different narrative episode.

There is now, however, a remarkable clue that may tell us something about the nature and purpose of this Gospel. In the course of their investigations the Jews call the blind man's parents to account (9:18–23) and ask them to certify that the man who claims to have been given sight by Jesus is really their son who was born blind. They give a minimal testimony, identifying the healed man as their son who was born blind;

---

[21] Bultmann's solution (*The Gospel of John: A Commentary*) was to reorder the "fragments" of the text of chapters 8 and 12 into a more intelligible arrangement on the theory that the original order of the Gospel had been lost (see pp. 342–357). Cf. D. Moody Smith, Jr., *The Composition and Order of the Fourth Gospel: Bultmann's Literary Theory* (New Haven, 1965), pp. 155–163.

but more than that they will not say, for fear of being put out of
the synagogue (9:22) – a strange punishment, one might think.
But more than once in this Gospel the threat of being put out of
the synagogue is mentioned as something that may dissuade
people from confessing belief in Jesus (also 12:45; cf. 16:2). It is
worth noting that such fear does not necessarily prevent faith,
but may prevent the confession of this faith in view of the likely
consequences.

How are we to understand this circumstance? Nowhere in
the other Gospels are people prevented from confessing Jesus
because of their fear of being expelled from the synagogue. (Of
course, believing and confessing faith in Jesus is not a subject
for such explicit discussion in the Synoptics as it is in John.)
Moreover, to this point of the narrative, hostility has been
directed against Jesus, not his followers. In the episode of the
lame man healed at the pool, there was the possibility that such
hostility might be incurred by the man cured, but that individual rather quickly got himself out of harm's way. Here,
however, the possibility of expulsion from the synagogue is first
mentioned (9:22); then the man healed is, in fact, condemned
and cast out (9:34–35); finally, Jesus finds him and that man
affirms faith in Jesus the Son of Man (verses 35–38). The
drama has centered not so much on Jesus as upon the one to
whom Jesus gave sight. Does he represent the members of the
Johannine church or the readers to whom the Gospel is
addressed?

In the next episode (chap. 10), however, Jesus returns to the
center of attention once more, with the congregation of his
followers. He presents himself as both the door of the sheep
(verse 7) and the good shepherd (verse 11), and although the
switch in imagery may be confusing, the centrality of Jesus and
his loyalty to the flock are clear. Other shadowy figures, the
thieves and robbers, the stranger, the hireling, and the wolf
obviously represent those who would mislead, abandon, or
attack the sheep. With whom they are to be equated among
Jesus' or John's contemporaries is not clear, but that question
need not detain us. Once again, followers of Jesus appear as
people threatened, but Jesus is their protector.

"The Jews," who have not yet been mentioned explicitly in this episode, now return to the center of the stage as Jesus' opponents, although even now there is a division of opinion among them (verses 19–21). Immediately, the interrogation and accusations against Jesus that were so prominent in chapters 5–8 resume, with the Jews again taking up stones against him. The Jews' initial demand that Jesus should not keep them in suspense but say whether he is the Christ (verse 24) is strange, and Jesus' response, to the effect that he has been telling them so all along, is not surprising. This could be just a literary device to get the dialogue going. Yet it also hints at a circumstance that doubtless pertained during Jesus' ministry, but that the Gospels, especially John, have painted over. Jesus' identity and role were not known and understood during his ministry (cf. Mark 6:14–16; 8:27; Matthew 11:2–6); and perhaps ironically, John, the most explicitly christological of all the Gospels, makes this fact clear (13:7,19; 16:12–13). When once again the Jews are about to arrest Jesus (10:39), he escapes from them, and retires "to the place where John at first baptized" (verse 40).[22]

From this vantage point in the Gospel, the conflict between Jesus and the Jews or Pharisees stands out as the dominant theme of chapters 2–10. The theological, or christological, issues that emerge in this section of the Gospel for the most part arise directly out of this conflict. In the latter part of this chapter we shall shift attention from the narrative development of this conflict, with which we have been engaged, to its historical setting and roots (see c, 1 below). Apparently, the author of the Fourth Gospel was very much of the opinion that the conflict was rooted in the ministry and controversies of Jesus himself, although it clearly also reflects the evangelist's own situation. In what sense this may be true is an important

---

[22] One might think that 10:40–42 represents the conclusion of Jesus' public ministry, and perhaps in an earlier recension of the Gospel the Lazarus episode was missing. See Raymond E. Brown, *The Gospel According to John: Introduction, Translation and Notes*, Anchor Bible 29 (Garden City, NY, 1966), p. 414; also Barnabas Lindars, *The Gospel of John*, New Century Bible (London and Grand Rapids, 1972), pp. 50, 377, 379–382.

question, which we shall have to consider, and this investigation will be not only interesting but rewarding.

4 *The culmination of the public ministry (11:1–12:50)*

The narrative of Jesus' raising Lazarus (11:1–44) from the dead may be anticipated by resuscitations in the Synoptic Gospels (Mark 4:35–43; Luke 7:11–17), but nothing quite like this is recounted there. Although such a resuscitation is unprecedented in the other canonical Gospels, there may be a closer parallel in the apocryphal Secret Gospel of Mark, in which Jesus raises a young man who has died to life.[23] The narrative drives home the distress of Lazarus' sisters and friends, as well as the gross physical reality of his death (11:39) in a way not paralleled in the rest of the New Testament. Jesus comes out of his self-imposed retirement to deal with this dreadful thing that has overtaken his friends. Only the most direct, miraculous intervention could save the situation. So Jesus, or God through Jesus' intervention (11:40–42), raises Lazarus from the dead. It is an utterly uncanny scene (11:43–44), and one wonders to what extent John believed that he was recording an historical event. Moreover, it is remarkable that such a deed should have been unknown to, or passed over by, the other evangelists.

However that may be, this culmination of Jesus' ministry leaves no doubt in the reader's mind as to who Jesus is. Jesus, like God, gives life to the dead (5:19–29). Indeed, this very resurrection of Lazarus seems to have been hinted at already (5:28–29). Earlier on, before the really harsh opposition between Jesus and the Jews had developed, his God-given mission was described as saving people from death for life (3:16). Thus now at the end of his public ministry Jesus gives life in a graphic, almost offensive, way. Whatever one makes of the raising of Lazarus, it is the evangelist's way of portraying in unmistakably realistic terms the fact that Jesus Christ gives life to the dead. The episode is a kind of parable of what Jesus does

---

[23] For the presentation of the text of Secret Mark and a full discussion, see Morton Smith, *Clement of Alexandria and a Secret Gospel of Mark* (Cambridge, MA, 1973).

not only for Lazarus, but for all who believe in him.[24] The reader learns what the Gospel message is and what God actually does through Jesus. Moreover, in the course of the narrative the evangelist corrects misunderstandings about Jesus' life-giving work, which occurs already, now and not just in the future, as many Christians, influenced by apocalyptic thought, had assumed (11:23–27).

The Lazarus story is then a fitting conclusion of the public ministry of Jesus, which has been so riven with controversy, for the ministry is finally not about controversy or even about death, but about the giving of life. Perhaps significantly, controversy recedes in this long episode, and the Jews (Judeans?) who appear here are sympathetic to Jesus' friends and misunderstand him no more or less than do Mary and Martha (cf. 11:24,32–33,37). In fact, they may even understand why Jesus himself is weeping: he loved Lazarus (verse 36). At the conclusion of the Lazarus episode, many of these Jews believe (verse 45), but others inform on Jesus to the Pharisees (verse 46); it is a division to which we have grown accustomed.

The chief priests or Pharisees then gather the council, the Sanhedrin, to deliberate and presumably take action against Jesus (verse 47). Such a meeting is barely reported in Mark (14:1–2), but here we have a rather complete account, as John's narrative begins to move into conformity with the Synoptics. Whereas Mark (with Luke 22:2) reports that the chief priests and scribes took counsel against Jesus, and Matthew (26:3) the chief priests and elders, John typically reports that the chief priests and Pharisees took the lead. The Pharisees are those Jewish authorities who since early in his ministry have been plaguing Jesus (cf. Mark 3:6). Typically John indicates that the signs Jesus is performing pose a problem for them. The expressed fear of Roman intervention is unique to the Fourth Gospel. So far, we have heard nothing even of a Roman presence in Palestine, but now the governing Roman authorities, soon to be represented by Pontius Pilate, enter the

[24] Cf. Luke 16:19–31, where a Lazarus who dies figures in a parable of Jesus. It is difficult, however, to derive the Johannine story from the Lucan parable, or vice versa.

picture as a decisive factor in the political and religious scene. Caiaphas counsels that because of the danger of their intervention Jesus should be put out of the way (verses 49–50). He couches his advice in terms the evangelist exploits for their irony, for his cynical counsel can, unbeknownst to him, be read as a prophecy of Jesus' redemptive death (verse 51).

Without commenting explicitly upon their theological relationship, the evangelist has juxtaposed two impressive narratives that convey profound truths about the revelation of God in Jesus Christ, and his saving work. In the first, Jesus gives life to a dead man and so his life-giving work, which is the work of God, is symbolized and epitomized. In the second, Jesus' own death is plotted and thus the one who gives life is to be done to death, or so his enemies intend. It is difficult to imagine that this juxtaposition was not intentional and pregnant with meaning for the author.

The conclusion of Jesus' public ministry (chap. 12) once again makes contact with the Synoptic Gospels. Jesus is a guest at a supper hosted by Mary, Martha, and Lazarus (John 12:1–8; cf. Mark 14:3–9; Luke 7:36–50). On this occasion Mary anoints Jesus' feet with oil and wipes them with her hair. Although the incident has parallels in the Synoptics, the Johannine account is distinctive in the people who are named. In John, as in Mark and Matthew, the anointing is closely associated with Jesus' imminent death, although the story occurs at a different point in the narrative. Following an aside about the chief priests' plot against the life of Lazarus, on account of whom many people believed (12:9–11), Jesus enters Jerusalem in a triumphant procession (12:12–19). Whether John relied on the Synoptics at this point or on his own traditions, either by his own intent or by the strength of tradition, or both, his narrative now begins to conform closely to that of the other Gospels. From the arrest of Jesus (18:1) onward the various narratives will show a closer conformity still.

Although the Jews, or Jewish authorities, with whom Jesus had the severest conflict during his ministry will if anything play a more active role in his trial and death than they do in the Synoptics, they now recede into the background. The Pharisees' parting word (12:19) is an expression of cynicism and despair at the prospect of stopping Jesus, so great is his popularity among the people. Their statement that "the world has gone after him" is a bit of sarcastic hyperbole, but in saying this they utter a truth more profound than they can realize (cf. 11:51), for Jesus, when he is lifted up, will draw all people to himself (12:32). In the remainder of chapter 12 Jesus is approached by Greeks eager to see him (12:20); he announces his hour has come (12:23); and he speaks of his approaching death before a crowd, who while uncomprehending are not hostile (12:24–36). Then the evangelist signals the conclusion of Jesus' public ministry, noting the rejection he has faced (12:37–43), and, as a kind of finale, Jesus himself summarizes the meaning of his mission and message (12:44–50). With 3:16–21, set toward the beginning of his career, this passage affords as neat a summary of the theology of the Fourth Gospel as one could ask.

5   *The farewell discourses (13:1–17:26)*

The Last Supper scene (chap. 13), clearly parallel to the Synoptic accounts, nevertheless displays striking differences, at least two of which are difficult to account for. In the first place, the meal takes place before the Passover feast begins and is therefore not, as in the Synoptics, a Passover meal. In the second, instead of presiding at the institution of the Lord's Supper, as he does in the Synoptics (and cf. 1 Corinthians 11:23–26), Jesus washes the feet of his disciples (13:1–20) – a unique act reported nowhere else. But as in the Synoptics, Jesus predicts that he will be betrayed (13:21–30) and that Peter will deny him (13:36–38). Between these two episodes Jesus speaks of his glorification and departure in an enigmatic but Johannine way (verses 31–33) and promulgates to his disciples a new commandment (verse 34), that they love one another. This commandment makes clear the meaning of the footwashing scene (13:12–17) and prepares for the teaching about love in chapter 15.

The overarching theme of the Johannine Jesus' final conversation is set out in the reassuring words "Let not your hearts be troubled" (14:1). Jesus addresses the fear and threat of loneliness among his disciples at his departure and prepares them to live with each other in the world afterward. Like the departing Moses of Deuteronomy, Jesus as he departs gives commandments to his followers (14:15), but in this case these commandments boil down to the one commandment of mutual love (15:12; cf. 13:34). Jesus also warns the disciples of the hatred of the world that will encounter them (15:18–16:4), which will take the form of expulsion from synagogues and perhaps even death (16:2). Again, we get a window on the life-setting of the church in which this Gospel was composed. The world's hatred assures these Christians that they are truly following Jesus, whom the world also hated (15:18–20). Out of this caldron of hostility emerged the Johannine dualism and theology, and into it the love commandment is set. The farewell discourses may, in fact, be a composite of materials arising out of such controversy, for at 14:31 the discourse seems to be drawn to a close by Jesus, but it nevertheless continues with no further indication of a change in setting.

Bereft of Jesus and beset by the world's hatred, how can the Johannine Christians live? In such a hostile setting their love for each other will be of immeasurable importance, but alone it will not suffice. They will need Jesus. The major message of the farewell discourses is that Jesus himself will come to them and abide with them. He will not leave them orphans (14:18; Greek: *orphanous*). The question, now more than a half-century after Jesus' death, is how this can be. John weaves together several motifs from the Christian tradition in answering this question: faith in Jesus' resurrection; hope for his return; and the experience of the Holy Spirit. One should add that the continued presence of Jesus is also contingent upon the disciples' mutual love. Chapter 15 makes this clear, and it is a recurrent theme of 1 John.

In a real and significant sense the farewell discourses in John replace the apocalyptic discourses of the Synoptic Gospels (Mark, chap. 13 parr.), where Jesus speaks to his disciples of historic, cosmic, obviously public events that will unfold before his return, which in turn will be a revelation for all to see. Finally, the Son of Man will be seen "coming in the clouds with great power and glory" (Mark 14:26). In all the Synoptics the character of this apocalyptic discourse is similar, for it is a revelation (Greek: *apokalypsis*) of the secrets of the future to the disciples, so that the faithful will understand when these events begin to unfold. One speaks then of apocalyptic literature and apocalyptic eschatology. In John also, if in a very different mode, Jesus reveals to his disciples what is to come.

The Fourth Gospel reinterprets such apocalyptic thought and speech (cf. 11:23–27), although traces of it are still found. Thus, Jesus is asked how he will manifest himself to the disciples and not to the world (14:22). This manifestation is something clearly different from the coming of the Son of Man in the Synoptic apocalypses, although not unrelated to it. In fact, John, and only John, speaks of the coming again (14:3; Greek: *palin erchomai*) of Jesus, evoking the conceptuality, if not the language, of the Synoptic apocalypses. Why this reinterpretation of Synoptic, and earliest Christian, eschatology? Is it a way of dealing with the fact that decades have passed, leaving Christians puzzled and disappointed that their Lord has not returned (cf. 2 Peter 3:4–7), so that John wants to set matters straight by removing the predictions and promises that evoked such expectations from the lips of Jesus himself? There may be an element of truth in such an assessment, but it would be a mistake to view John as struggling to explain a severe embarrassment that was threatening to undo the Christian faith. Unless his style and mood deceive us, he is leading from strength rather than weakness. In the appearance of Jesus as God's Son, the decisive event has already occurred.

The return of Jesus is also described with reference to his own resurrection (14:19–20; 16:16–24), of which again he speaks in a veiled or enigmatic way, and the coming of the Holy Spirit or Paraclete (14:15–17,25–26; 16:12–15). "I will give you another Counselor" (NRSV: "Advocate"), says Jesus (14:16), implying that he himself is the first (cf. 1 John 2:1). Clearly John is rethinking the meaning of the revelation of

Jesus Christ for the present and future of Jesus' disciples and for those who would come after. Certainly the resurrection of Jesus, which John reports in much greater detail and richness than the other Gospels, is for him the *sine qua non* of Christian faith, for without it the claims made for Jesus can easily be falsified. Yet the resurrection cannot be presented as some sort of empirical proof, subject to general observation, of the truth of the Gospel message. If there is such empirical, or experiential, proof, it is to be found in the work of the Paraclete or Holy Spirit, promised by Jesus to his disciples as the continuation and interpreter of his own ministry.

To go one step further, it is a reasonable and likely inference from John's description of the importance of the Spirit's ministry that the Gospel itself is somehow a product of it. Throughout the Gospel there are hints and indications of the living reality of the Spirit in the community of Jesus' disciples, and of the indispensability of the Spirit for understanding and appropriating the reality of God the Father in Jesus the Son. The Spirit is given only after Jesus is glorified (7:39), that is, crucified and raised from the dead. Thus the presentation of Jesus, replete with his theological significance, is not an historical given, in the sense that any observer might have seen Jesus and immediately become convinced that he was the Son of God. It is a retrospective, Spirit-inspired portrayal. Not only the opponents of Jesus, but also his disciples, are unable to grasp fully his being and meaning during his public ministry. And even after Jesus reveals himself during the farewell discourses, the disciples still lack comprehension and devotion to him, even though they recognize that Jesus is speaking plainly to them (16:29–30). They will abandon him and leave him alone (verses 31–32).

Nevertheless, in his final prayer (chap. 17), Jesus speaks of the disciples as if they were now his loyal, comprehending followers (17:6–8). "Now they know ..." (17:7). A subtle, but real and important shift takes place between chapters 16 and 17, as Jesus prays for his disciples, who will believe in him as risen Lord, and for the church that is to come after them (17:20). The prayer itself is a kind of last will, or testament, of

Jesus in which he summarizes his earthly ministry as obedience to God his Father.[25] The sharp and striking dualism, in which Jesus' obedience marks him off from the world, continues, and the disciples are included in it as the world now hates them (verse 14) as it hated Jesus (cf. 16:18). In all probability the Gospel of John is the product of a Christian community alienated from its environment because of its loyalty to Jesus, whose members find their security not in this world but in their community with Jesus. The community they have experienced with him, and continue to enjoy through the Spirit, in a very real sense extends into the future as well. Jesus prays that his disciples "may be with me where I am" (*egō eimi*) to behold his preexistent glory (17:24). This particular petition confirms the shift in perspective of which we have spoken: Jesus has already arrived at the place of glory for which his disciples are destined. Thus the community of his disciples is characterized by fulfilled hope, as well as faith and joy.

6 The passion and resurrection (18:1–21:25)

The Johannine passion narrative resembles the comparable Synoptic accounts more closely than does any other part of the Fourth Gospel, but it is still the distinctively Johannine Jesus who now moves toward death as one who wills and controls his own destiny in obedience to God. In this respect the Johannine account is unique as, for example, Jesus takes control of his own arrest (18:1–11) or of the trial before Pilate (18:28–19:16). Whereas in the Synoptic accounts (cf. Mark 15:1–15) Jesus is silent before Pilate (verse 5), in John he speaks out boldly and clearly. Yet there is not the sharp hostility between Pilate and Jesus that we observed between Jesus and the Jews, although Pilate remains clueless about who Jesus really is. And while Jesus is certainly not silent before Pilate, when Pilate asks him about his "whence," that is, "Where are you from?" (19.9), Jesus gives him no answer. Thus John preserves the *Leitmotif* we found in the Synoptics, while striking a characteristic note.

[25] See Ernst Käsemann's *The Testament of Jesus: A Study of the Gospel of John in the Light of Chapter 17* (Philadelphia and London, 1968).

As Jesus is in command of his arrest and his trial, so also he remains in control up to his death. There is no cry of dereliction (cf. Mark 15:34) in John (as there is none in Luke); Jesus announces the completion of the work the Father has given him to do and hands over the Spirit (19:30). While the narrative line is basically similar to Mark and to the other Synoptics, there are also some differences that on the face of it do not seem to be alterations of the Synoptics in light of Johannine theology. Thus, for example, only a brief hearing before the chief priest Annas is narrated, and while Jesus is reported to have been taken to Caiaphas the high priest, the Marcan account of a trial before him and the Sanhedrin (Mark 14:53–65) is not found. At the end, after Jesus has died, a detail of Roman soldiers is sent out to break his legs and those of the two criminals executed with him (19:31–37), a common practice to hasten death and something that might well have happened, although only John reports it, and of course he utilizes it to make theological points (verses 35–37).

Such unaccountable divergences from the Synoptic passion narratives suggest that John conveys, along with his intense theological purpose and preoccupation, a tradition somewhat different from the Synoptic, although obviously related to it. The account of Jesus' burial (19:38–42), also closely parallel to the Synoptics with Joseph of Arimathea taking the lead, has its distinctively Johannine hallmark as well: Nicodemus reappears to assist with the burial. Whether or not Nicodemus was a specific individual, he represents the learned, Pharisaic leadership, those Jewish authorities who for the most part rejected Jesus' claims. Yet Nicodemus' presence here implies that even this aspect of the Johannine mission was not without success, for even if Nicodemus has remained within the Jewish community until now (cf. 12:42), he here comes out of the closet, so to speak, in order to serve Jesus. What more could one do at this point? It is, after all, a public act that he performs.[26]

---

[26] The burial of Jesus may actually have been carried out by people unfriendly to him: cf. Acts 13:29 and Raymond E. Brown's article, "The Burial of Jesus (Mark 15:42–47)," *CBQ* 50 (1988), 233–245. Nevertheless, it is clearly portrayed in the Gospels, and particularly in John, as an act performed by friends or disciples.

The Johannine resurrection narratives (chaps. 20 and 21), richly diverse as they are, also give valuable clues about the character of the community in which the distinctly Johannine theology was formed. The risen Jesus' first appearance is to a woman, Mary Magdalene, about whom we know little enough, except that in all the Gospels she is named as visiting Jesus' tomb. In the Gospel of Luke (8:2), Jesus is said to have driven seven demons from her. That she was one of the early female disciples is clear enough, and the prominence she receives in John suggests that the evangelist, and perhaps his community, had a particular interest in her.

The appearances of Jesus before his disciples (20:19–23, 24–29) find a close parallel in Luke (24:36–43), so that it is sometimes suggested that John here employed that Gospel. If so, the two renditions now differ significantly, for in Luke the point seems to be the continuity between Jesus' earthly and resurrection bodies: the risen Jesus eats fish as he makes this point explicitly. In John, however, the invitation to Thomas to touch Jesus goes unanswered, and the final blessing (verse 29) upon those who have not seen, and yet believe, calls into question Thomas' desire to obtain tangible proof of the reality of Jesus' resurrection, not to speak of the Lucan narrator's desire to prove that Jesus' resurrection body is the same as his physical body (contrast 1 Corinthians 15:35–45).

However that may be, it is clear enough that the band of the twelve, to whom Jesus appears on successive Sunday evenings, represent the church *in nuce*, and the fact that the disciples gather behind closed or locked doors "for fear of the Jews" (20:19) may well reflect the situation of the specifically Johannine community at, or for some period before, the writing of the Gospel. What the message of the Gospel is intended to effect (faith in Jesus) is made explicit in the colophon of 20:30–31, which looks very much like the original conclusion of the Gospel. The final scene in which doubting Thomas appears (20:24–29), concluding as it does with a blessing upon those who will believe without seeing, thus addresses a question or problem that loomed large in the farewell discourse, the absence of Jesus from his disciples. Of course, they have now

received the gift of the Holy Spirit (20:22), which will con-
tinuously convey his heavenly presence to them as it reminds
them of his earthly words and work. (The fact that 20:30–31
has the ring of a conclusion, while a new scene, in a different
setting, begins abruptly in chapter 21 suggests that this chapter
has been appended to the Gospel later, perhaps by another
hand. Yet there is no manuscript evidence for an edition of the
Gospel without chapter 21.)

Chapter 21 presents another cycle of resurrection stories,
beginning with a scene by the sea, probably once a first
resurrection appearance (cf., however, Luke 5:1–11). Peter has
decided to go fishing, i.e., to resume his old occupation; hardly
likely if he had just twice seen the risen Jesus in Jerusalem.
Moreover, such a first resurrection appearance in Galilee is just
what the Gospel of Mark leads us to expect. This scene actually
continues in the conversation between Jesus and Peter. Mark
already hints that Peter will be restored to the fellowship of
Jesus (16:7), and here we have what amounts to a narrative
account of that restoration (21:15–23). Moreover, it finally
introduces once again the Beloved Disciple (21:20–23) and
seems to deal also with the question of Peter's relationship to
him. Clearly Peter is not to worry about this enigmatic figure,
who is so close to Jesus himself, but to look to his own discipleship (verse 22), in the course of which he will suffer martyrdom
(verses 18–19). Incidentally, only here in the New Testament
is the martyrdom of Peter acknowledged.[27]

Exactly what are the implications of this long closing scene
with Peter for our understanding of the setting and circumstances of the Gospel? In the first place, it serves to rehabilitate
Peter and in that sense allows the narrative, which has raised
serious and disturbing questions about his loyalty, to come to
rest on a happy note. But why should this Gospel be interested
in Peter's fate? Elsewhere in John, where Peter appears
alongside the Beloved Disciple, he definitely comes in second
best. Peter scarcely comes off worse in the Gospel of John than
in Mark, and the fourth evangelist shows no inclination to

---

[27] On the martyrdom of Peter (and Paul) see *1 Clement* 5:2–7 for the earliest reference
outside the New Testament. See also Eusebius, *Ecclesiastical History* II.25.5–8.

denigrate him, but it is not immediately obvious why John goes out of his way to show him reinstated, when none of the other Gospels do so. In all probability Peter's appearance has something to do with what or whom he represents, for there is no doubt that Peter was an important leader in the early church, as apparently he had been among Jesus' disciples. The Beloved Disciple, the truth of whose witness is strongly attested (21:24; cf. 19:35), is, so to speak, the patron saint of the Fourth Gospel and the representative of the Johannine community and tradition. Does this final scene represent some sort of rapprochement between the two, in which Peter and Petrine, or "apostolic," Christianity are recognized, but the Beloved Disciple retains pride of place?[28] Probably the intention is to honor Peter and the Christian tradition he represents, while simultaneously underscoring the value and truth of the Johannine witness and its Gospel (21:24).

At the same time, and in a unique way, John draws together the threads of the resurrection traditions as they are represented in the other Gospels, and even in Paul. Each of the Johannine resurrection stories finds a related account in other Gospels. Even John's story of the visit of Peter and the Beloved Disciple to the tomb (20:3–10) has a brief counterpart (Luke 24:12,24). The fact that alone among the Gospels, John places Peter at the beginning of the resurrection occurrences (20:3–10 and again in 21:1–14) draws a parallel with Paul's traditional testimony that Peter was the first to see the Lord risen (1 Corinthians 15:5). The Johannine story of Mary Magdalene's encounter with Jesus in the garden has a relatively colorless counterpart in Matthew 28:9–10. As has already been observed, John's story of Jesus' meeting with the twelve (20:19–23,26–29) is paralleled in Luke 24:36–43, and his account of the group of disciples, including Peter, encountering Jesus at the Sea of Galilee is just the appearance story the Gospel of Mark leads us to expect. Moreover, the fragment of the apocryphal *Gospel of Peter* that we possess breaks off at the point where Peter, who has not yet seen the risen Jesus, is

---

[28] This is the view of Raymond E. Brown, *The Community of the Beloved Disciple* (New York, 1979), pp. 161–162.

heading back to the Sea of Galilee to resume fishing. Almost certainly *Peter* next recounted a resurrection appearance of Jesus there.

The Synoptic Gospels show broad agreement in the account of Jesus' public ministry, but John is strikingly different. Yet in the preparation for the passion and especially in the passion and resurrection narratives themselves, John draws close to the Synoptic accounts. Still, there are differences. John departs at a number of points from Mark's passion, as do Matthew and Luke, but his departures are larger in scope than theirs, and he does not presuppose, or seem to be based upon, the Marcan narrative in the way that Matthew and Luke are. What is more, the Johannine Jesus, who strides so sublimely through his public ministry, behaves in exactly the same way as he turns to the cross. In the resurrection narratives, however, the pattern of similarity to the Synoptics is quite different. The way in which John gathers up the threads of the resurrection traditions has a kind of parallel in the specious longer ending of Mark (16:9–20), which almost certainly betrays knowledge of the resurrection stories of Matthew and Luke, and perhaps John 20. John's rendition can be understood as his conflation and redaction of the Synoptic accounts, but whether or not this is the case remains a matter of some dispute.

As we surveyed the Gospel of John, we have found it necessary and important to emphasize that we are dealing with a narrative of Jesus' ministry rather than a theological treatise, although theological themes certainly emerge. For all the abruptness, or even lacunae, of the narrative at certain points, the author demonstrates that he is capable of telling a good story and telling it well.

Moreover, the Gospel claims for itself a first-hand authority (21:24), although the identity of the Beloved Disciple, who is said to be the Gospel's source, remains unclear. There is an aura of independence and authority about the Gospel from the beginning (see 1:14), however, so that the reader is not astonished that it goes its own way, differing as it does from the others. As we have seen, the nature of the author's sources and his relation to the actual events and earliest tradition are difficult to establish or confirm. Nevertheless, it is likely that the evangelist had independent sources of tradition, which he used freely to express his own theological insights.[29]

C   THE SETTING AND SOURCES IN JUDAISM AND EARLY CHRISTIANITY

1   *The setting in Judaism*

All along we have observed the debates between Jesus and his opponents, called "the Jews" and "the Pharisees," and found that it is precisely in those debates that the theological themes of the Gospel emerge. Moreover, we have seen repeatedly that these debates are quite divisive. They either create divisions or exacerbate divisions already present. Typically, the divisions are along what we now call Jewish–Christian lines. (The term *Christianoi*, Christians, does not appear until the Book of Acts, 11:26.) In the questioning of the man born blind, his antagonists accuse him of being a disciple of Jesus rather than Moses (9:28), as if the two were mutually exclusive alternatives, and thus reveal that for John, as well as these opponents, that was actually the case.

a   *"The Jews" in John*
In fact, just the use of "Jews" (Greek: *Ioudaioi*) for Jesus' opponents is strange. Were not Jesus and his first disciples themselves Jews? Nevertheless, being a Jew, or a Pharisee, is not a good thing. ("Jew" and "Pharisee" seem to be virtual synonyms.) The hostility between Jews and Jesus' followers is epitomized in the threat to expel followers of Jesus from synagogues (9:22; 12:48). Yet this is rather strange too, for other-

---

[29] Quite possibly the Gospel incorporates a primitive narrative source consisting of miracles and passion. This is the view of Robert T. Fortna, *The Fourth Gospel and its Predecessor: From Narrative Source to Present Gospel* (Philadelphia, 1988). Cf. his earlier work, *The Gospel of Signs: A Reconstruction of the Narrative Source Underlying the Fourth Gospel*, SNTSMS 11 (Cambridge, 1970). In principal agreement with Fortna on the unity of miracles and passion in such a primal Gospel is Urban C. von Wahlde, *The Earliest Version of John's Gospel: Recovering the Gospel of Signs* (Wilmington, DE, 1989).

wise there is no evidence for such expulsion during Jesus' ministry. Moreover, if followers of Jesus are Christians, why should they fear expulsion from the synagogue? They belong to the church – or do they? That is the crux of the matter, and we may find here an important key to understanding the theological controversy that produced the Fourth Gospel and therefore to understanding its theology.

Before inquiring further into the question of what that key might be, or how it might function, it is important to underscore the anachronistic character of John's view that Jesus is opposed to "the Jews." In the first place, the evangelist knows very well that Jesus was a Jew; in fact, he knows that Jesus was from Nazareth and was the son of a certain Joseph (1:45). In the Synoptic Gospels, of course, there is no indication that Jesus was not a Jew. Quite to the contrary, and the Gospels of Matthew and Luke underscore his Jewishness by presenting him as the scion of Jewish ancestors going back to David and Abraham (Matthew 1:1–2,6; Luke 3:31,34). John, on the other hand, seems to ignore matters of Israelite genealogy (7:40–44), whether deliberately or not. Moreover, the separating of Jesus from his ethnic and religious context is something historically misleading, indeed false, if we have in view Jesus' historical ministry. Jesus was a Jew who was very much concerned with his ethnic and religious heritage, if we are to believe the Synoptic tradition at all, and its portrayal of Jesus is in this respect intrinsically probable. The Synoptic Gospels present a picture of Judaism that includes scribes, Pharisees, Sadducees, Herodians, even Zealots, followers of John the Baptist, and Jesus and his disciples. The Gospel of John tends to reduce these to Jesus and his disciples, on the one hand, and Jews, who can also be called Pharisees, on the other. Is John guilty of a sheerly arbitrary distortion of history, or is there a setting within the first century, or in the history of Christianity and Judaism, within which such a dichotomy makes sense? In all probability the latter is the case.

That Sadducees, the high priestly party, Zealots, Herodians, and Essenes, along with scribes, are not found in the Gospel of John tells us something about the time and circumstances of its origin. After the disastrous Roman war (66–70) and the destruction of the Jerusalem temple, most of the Jewish parties or groups that are not mentioned in the Fourth Gospel would have disappeared from the scene.[30] For example, the high priestly function and party would have dissolved after the destruction of the temple, while the Essene monastery of Qumran was destroyed in that war. Scribes are seldom if ever mentioned in Jewish sources after the New Testament period.[31] Thus the term would seem to fall out of common usage after the Roman war, and the Gospel of John follows suit. The Pharisees, or the Pharisaic point of view, then developed into the dominant form of Judaism, one centered upon the Bible understood as law. (This fact is reflected in the Fourth Gospel, in that "Jew" and "Pharisee" appear to be virtual synonyms.)

b   John, Paul, and Judaism

A generation earlier the Apostle Paul had strongly dissented from such an understanding of scripture as law, but had intended to remain within the community and tradition of Israel, albeit reinterpreted in light of the coming of the Messiah (cf. Romans 4 with 7:7–12). Yet he saw that most Jews were not accepting the Christian interpretation of Jesus (Romans 9:1–5), and the cracks that would lead to schism are already visible. In the Gospel of John there are some notable similarities to Paul, as well as differences. On the one hand, Jesus can speak of the law as "your law" (8:17; 10:34), as if it belonged to or pertained to the Jews, but not to his followers. On the other, he can say in almost the same breath, "Scripture cannot be broken" (10:35), and go on to quote the Bible (Psalm 82:6). Obviously John's scriptural interpretation, like Paul's, was influenced by his belief that Jesus is the Christ, the Son of God.

---

[30] See Shaye J. D. Cohen, *From the Maccabees to the Mishnah*, Library of Early Christianity (Philadelphia, 1987), p. 224: "In the first century CE Judaism was marked by numerous sects and groups: Pharisees, Sadducees, Essenes, the Jews of Qumran, Zealots, Sicarii, 'the Fourth Philosophy,' Christians, Samaritans, Therapeutae, and others. Judaism after 70 CE, in contrast, was not marked by sectarianism."

[31] See the article on *grammateus*, scribe, by J. Jeremias, *TDNT*, I, pp. 740f.

Nevertheless, the fact that John holds on to what Christians came to call the Old Testament, while later gnostics abandoned it, is quite significant.

Paul differs from John in that he still argues theologically about the place and status of the law and how the coming of Christ fits within a reasonable understanding of it from what he assumes to be a Jewish perspective. For John, however, that issue seems settled and he does not argue, or describe arguments, about it. Scripture (if not law) has a legitimate status as witness to Christ, and specific directives can even be cited in a positive way (7:23). Nevertheless, midrashic argument cannot in John's view validate belief in Jesus: that is a given of revelation.[32] Although the givenness of the revelation is also axiomatic for Paul, he is still trying to present Jesus, and argue for Christian claims on his behalf, out of a scriptural and Jewish tradition that he thinks should stand.

Because of these differences between John and Paul, it has frequently been assumed that John represents a theological development beyond Paul, and so to speak stands on Paul's shoulders. Yet the theological, terminological, and conceptual agreements between Paul and John do not go beyond what could have been established on the basis of widely held early Christian emphases and beliefs.[33] In other words, it is a dubious procedure to attempt to understand the theology of John as if it were a development on the basis of, and beyond, Paul.

Like Paul, John also reflects a debate with, or within, Judaism, but one differently focused. In John the question is not the law, but the Messiah himself and the claims made for him. Paul is trying through scriptural and other arguments to

---

[32] See J. Louis Martyn, *History and Theology in the Fourth Gospel*, rev. ed. (Nashville, 1979), p. 128: "John allows Jesus paradoxically to employ a form of midrashic discussion in order to terminate all midrashic discussion!"

[33] As Rudolf Bultmann recognized, *Theology of the New Testament*, ii (New York, 1955), p. 7: "Nor is it surprising that Paul and John agree to a certain extent in the use of *common-Christian terminology.*" C. H. Dodd, *The Apostolic Preaching and its Developments* (London, 1936), seems in light of later scholarly developments to overstress the unity of the early Christian preaching. Yet his basic point was not invalid and is still relevant.

show why the death of Christ, an anomaly to the Jews, was not only necessary according to scripture, but also of salvific benefit. While the death of Jesus is still an important theological theme for John, he does not argue about it in the same way. Perhaps this is why he seems less deeply involved than Paul in the use of sacrificial, temple imagery to explain Christ's death. John is concerned not so much to explain and expound upon Christ's death, understood as personal and liturgical sacrifice, as to expound upon his dignity and even divinity. Thus, while Paul's arguments met resistance and rejection among his Jewish colleagues, John's aroused the most vehement opposition and outrage. There is then a sense in which this theological aspect of John's Gospel seems to be beyond Paul, but in many respects John represents simply an alternative form of the conflict between what we were later to call Judaism and Christianity.

John knows, or knew, Christians who were Jews and wanted to remain Jews in good standing, who therefore feared the prospect of being put out of the synagogue because of their belief in Jesus (9:22; 12:42). John is thus rooted in Jewish Christianity. Paul, on the other hand, although he was very much a Jew, was by his own claim Apostle to the Gentiles. For most of Paul's career he had to contend with the questions and charges of other Jewish Christians rather than Jews about the premises and practices of his predominantly Gentile churches. Frequently in the Book of Acts but only rarely in his own Letters do we find Paul in conflict with, or entertaining the prospect of conflict with, Jewish authorities (see Romans 15:31; 2 Corinthians 11:24). It is understandable that for Paul the issue was what should be expected of believers in Christ who were not, and had never been, Jews, and quite naturally his questions centered about the law. For John, who had in view people who were or had been Jews, the issue very quickly became Jesus himself and the claims made for him. The problem was not the status of the law so much as the implications of the claim that Jesus, whose life and death scarcely met Jewish messianic expectations, was both Messiah and Son of God, with those terms implying more and more about his divine status as his proponents vigorously pursued a campaign of mission and conversion among their fellow Jews.

c   The parting of the ways

If the claim that Jesus, the crucified one, was the Messiah gave offense (1 Corinthians 1:22) because it contradicted the basic idea of what the Messiah was to be and do, the belief that he had been raised from the dead and seated at the right hand of God probably seemed even more obnoxious or outlandish. In principle, little or no limit was set on the power or dignity that could be accorded him. Thus the limits of Jewish messianism were being transcended in more ways than one simultaneously in the seemingly opposing directions of humiliation and exaltation. Against such a background the Jewish reaction to the claim made by Jesus that he was working along with his Father (5:17) is understandable, and we no longer wonder why it so quickly reaches a furious pitch. The Jews seem to respond not so much to what is claimed as to what might be claimed, and to where this kind of claim could lead – and perhaps had led by the time these words were written.

In the aftermath of the Roman war, there was a period of retrenchment, renewal, and realignment within Judaism. The old faith in God and belief in his favor toward Israel remained, but aspects of religious practice had to change. With the temple in ruins and the priestly royal establishment that had governed at the behest of the Romans now dissolved, the Pharisees and people of similar outlook and intent, whose interests had always been important, moved into the vacuum and assumed the central role. Judaism as a religion, as opposed to a national ethnic entity, was emerging as very much a religion of the book, scripture and its interpretation. The book had long been regarded as Torah, law, divine revelation. The early Christians were also interpreters of a book, the same book, but they presumed to understand it on the basis of their faith in Jesus. They were much less interested in applying its commandments to the various contingencies of life, although they could at points do that. Moreover, other Jews had probably not forgotten that this Jesus, of Davidic lineage, had been executed by the same Romans who had destroyed Jerusalem and the temple, and that his followers had harbored hopes of a supernatural, apocalyptic restoration of the people of God with his return. If these Christians, as they came to be called, were looked upon as an aberration and a danger, this would not be surprising. Why not exclude them from the synagogue, or from the Jewish community? Some such circumstances and mind-set must underline the fear of being put out of the synagogue, expressed in the Fourth Gospel, and this fear could only have arisen at a time when the earthly Jesus had passed from the scene. That this is the case accords entirely with the impression given by the other Gospels, as well as what we know of the history of Judaism.

Is there more precise evidence of such a state of affairs in Jewish sources? This is difficult to say, for much of the Jewish material going back to this period, especially rabbinic sources, has been subject to repeated editing and the addition (and deletion) of material in later times. A most ingenious suggestion, argued with strength and perspicuity by J. Louis Martyn, is that the Twelfth Benediction of the standard Eighteen Benedictions of the synagogue service was composed, or amended, to facilitate the dismissal of such troublesome sectarians, particularly Christians, from the synagogue.[34] Suspected Christ-confessors would be appointed to lead the Benediction, and if they refused would reveal themselves as such. Martyn gives the following, ancient version of the Twelfth Benediction:

> For the apostates let there be no hope
> And let the arrogant government
> be speedily uprooted in our days.
> Let the Nazarenes [Christians] and the Minim [heretics]
> be destroyed in a moment

[34] Martyn, *History and Theology in the Fourth Gospel*, esp. pp. 50–62. But see also W. Schrage, *aposynagogoi*, *TDNT*, vii [German original, 1964], pp. 848–852, who links the term with the *birkat ha-minim*, as well as Brown, *The Gospel According to John* (i–xii), pp. LXX–LXXV, LXXXV.

And let them be blotted out of the Book of Life and not be
   inscribed together with the righteous.
Blessed art thou, O Lord, who humblest the proud![35]

In Martyn's view, the Benediction was revised so as to
include (and exclude) *notzrim* (Nazarenes = Christians) and
minim (heretics) by Samuel the Small, who flourished ca.
80–90.[36] If John was written toward the end of the first
century, as on other grounds seems likely, the coincidence of
dates would be almost perfect. Martyn and others have linked
this evidence with statements of Justin Martyr, *Dialogue with
Trypho* (16, 95, 110, 133), about Jews cursing Christians in
their synagogues.

   Since Martyn published the comprehensive statement of this
thesis, which defines the setting and, to a considerable extent,
the purpose of the Fourth Gospel, there has been a renewed
discussion and debate about the purpose and date of the
Twelfth Benediction. Martyn's proposal about how the Benediction functioned to identify Christians is suggested, but not
demanded, by the Talmudic evidence. While Martyn has
conceded that the evidence supporting his early dating of the
birkat ha-minim is less secure than he might wish, for good reason
he continues to look in that direction for the background of the
controversy reflected in the Fourth Gospel. That there was a
real controversy behind the Gospel is clear, and if the controversy can scarcely be dated in Jesus' own time, we must look
for an alternative setting. That the controversy was with Jews,
initially among Jews, can scarcely be doubted. Biblical religion

---

[35] Martyn, *History and Theology in the Fourth Gospel*, p. 58. Martyn's rendition is
obviously based upon the version of the Eighteen Benedictions discovered in the
Cairo Geniza and published by Solomon Schechter in 1898. Whether it represents
Samuel the Small's emendation of the Twelfth Benediction or whether there was
only one version in the first century is a good question (see n. 36). See E. Schürer,
The History of the Jewish People in the Age of Jesus Christ (175 B.C.–A.D. 135), vol. ii,
ed. G. Vermes, F. Millar, and M. Black (Edinburgh, 1979), pp. 455–463, on the
Eighteen Benedictions.

[36] Martyn, *History and Theology in the Fourth Gospel*, pp. 53–54. In the report of the
Babylonian Talmud (*Berakoth* 28) only the *minim* are mentioned, and it provides the
basis for Martyn's description of how the Benediction was used to smoke out
suspects. But Martyn believes, following the Cairo Geniza text (above), that
Samuel introduced the *notzrim* into the Benediction as well.

was the soil from which Christianity, even the Johannine version, grew and we are hardly justified in looking elsewhere for the Gospel's setting, especially in view of the evidence of the Gospel itself and our knowledge of the Judaism contemporary with it.[37]

That Jesus' opponents are called "the Jews" makes of them symbols of human rejection of God's revelation in Jesus.[38] So they become representatives of the world in a negative sense. On the one hand, they symbolize all rejection of Jesus, but, on the other, they do not in the evangelist's view represent all Jews contemporary with Jesus. No doubt the separation, and often hostility and persecution, that has characterized Jewish–Christian relations is adumbrated in the Fourth Gospel. Nevertheless, it is an understandable but unnecessary mistake of tragic proportions to assume that "the Jews" in the Gospel of John means all Jews in every time and place (see below, pp. 169–173).

2   *The setting in the New Testament and early Christianity*

In discussing the background of the theology of the Gospel of John, it has seemed appropriate to refer to Paul and the Synoptic Gospels. While it may be less than clear that John assumes or uses the other Gospels or the Pauline Letters in their canonical form, there is no doubt that he is dealing with the same subject matter, namely, the historical ministry of Jesus, his death, and belief in the resurrection. Moreover, eschatology remains a fundamental concern for John, although he has reinterpreted the apocalyptic categories common to Paul, the

---

[37] See D. Moody Smith, "The Contribution of J. Louis Martyn to the Understanding of the Gospel of John," in R. T. Fortna and B. R. Gaventa (eds.), *The Conversation Continues: Studies in Paul and John in Honor of J. Louis Martyn* (Nashville, 1990), pp. 275–294, esp. 279–284, and on the Twelfth Benediction n. 17. For a more detailed assessment of the Jewish setting of John, see also James D. G. Dunn, *The Partings of the Ways Between Judaism and Christianity and their Significance for the Character of Christianity* (London and Philadelphia, 1992), pp. 220–229.

[38] See Bultmann, *The Gospel of John: A Commentary*, pp. 86f., and compare John Ashton, *Understanding the Fourth Gospel* (Oxford, 1991), pp. 131–137, who cites Bultmann to good effect. See also Paul S. Minear, *John: The Martyr's Gospel* (New York, 1984), p. 34.

Synoptics, and presumably Jesus. Not surprisingly, John is often treated as the pinnacle of the development of New Testament theology.

a   The Johannine Epistles and Revelation

The Gospel of John does not stand alone in the New Testament. Not only are there other Gospels, but four other books that are attributed to John, traditionally the Apostle of that name. In fact, the three Epistles of John do not identify their author by name, but in the Book of Revelation, or the Revelation to John, the author several times says that his name is John (1:1, 4, 9). Nevertheless, Revelation exhibits a number of sharp stylistic and theological differences that set it apart from the Gospel, so that even in antiquity their common authorship was questioned. A consensus of modern scholarship assigns Revelation to another author.

Of course, the Johannine Epistles are so closely related to the Gospel in vocabulary, style, and theology that it has long been assumed that they too were written by the same Apostle John who wrote the Gospel. And even when critical questions were advanced against Johannine authorship, many exegetes continued to espouse the common authorship of Gospel and Epistles, whoever the author may have been. Moreover, Rudolf Bultmann, though he doubted common authorship, could entitle one of the four major parts of his *Theology of the New Testament* "The Theology of the Gospel of John and of the Johannine Epistles," using the Epistles to illuminate the theology of the Gospel.

Despite the close similarities, there are nevertheless some important differences that loom even larger on close inspection. For one thing, the author(s) of the Epistles seem(s) to fight on a different front. The Jews, who were the chief opponents in the Gospel, have disappeared. The word *Ioudaios*, which is found scores of times in the Gospel, occurs not at all in the Epistles. Nor are there any Old Testament quotations in the Epistles, as one would expect if they were to, or about, Jews. Efforts to argue that the opponents who deny Jesus are nevertheless Jews face an uphill struggle against such stubborn facts. In some contrast to the Gospel, where Abraham, Moses, and Jacob have a certain prominence, the only biblical figure mentioned is Cain (1 John 3:12), who otherwise seldom appears in the New Testament. The absence of "the Jews" from the Epistles, like their prominence in the Gospel, says something significant about the setting, and opponents, of each.

The opponents in the Epistles are apparently other Christians, who nevertheless are guilty of serious error, an inadequate christology. Seemingly, 1 John (4:1–3; cf. 2:18–23) and 2 John (verse 7) are combating a form of that heresy that denies the humanity of Jesus. Called *docetism*, because it maintained that Christ only seemed (Greek: *dokein*) to be human, this doctrine was closely tied to the rejection of creation as a work of the God who is the Father of Jesus Christ the Son. To what extent a full-blown docetism is in view remains a debated question, but that something like it has caused the Epistles' author to write as he did remains quite likely. Aspects of the Gospel of John, its stress on the divinity of Jesus as it distinguishes him from other human beings, could encourage a move in the direction of docetism, even if the Gospel does not itself represent a kind of incipient docetism.[39] That "the word became flesh" (1:14) implies all that is said in 1 John (1:1–4, esp.) may have seemed obvious to most Christian readers through the centuries, but perhaps that is because they have read the famous statement from the Gospel's prologue in light of 1 John, a reading that the author of the Epistle would have approved and likely wanted to encourage.

Moreover, the theological differences between Gospels and Epistles are also not insignificant.[40] As we have seen, the Gospel places heavy emphasis on the present apprehension of

[39] Ernst Käsemann pointed to the Fourth Gospel's incipient docetism in *The Testament of Jesus*; Raymond E. Brown has, in effect, countered by arguing that the Johannine Letters, particularly 1 John, were intentionally crafted to head off such a reading of the Gospel. See Brown's *Epistles of John*, Anchor Bible 30 (Garden City, NJ, 1982), as well as his *Community of the Beloved Disciple*, pp. 93–144.

[40] The differences were already noted by C. H. Dodd, *The Johannine Epistles*, Moffatt New Testament Commentary (London, 1946), pp. xlvii–lvi. See now the work of Judith M. Lieu, *The Theology of the Johannine Epistles*, New Testament Theology (Cambridge, 1991).

eternal life and downplays traditional apocalyptic eschatology. In 1 John particularly, although eternal life seems to be possessed already, there is a still very lively expectation of the imminent return of Jesus (2:28; 3:2; contrast John 21:23). The Gospel makes relatively little of the death of Christ as sacrifice in correspondence with the cultic imagery of the Bible and Jewish temple practice (but cf. 1:29,34), while this conceptuality and set of ideas is prominent in 1 John (esp. 1:7,9; 2:1–2). The Gospel has Jesus promise the Spirit or Paraclete as the virtual continuation of his own ministry (for example, 14:26; 16:12–15), and the Spirit assumes an almost personal form. In the Letters, although the Spirit is certainly mentioned, this distinctive, characteristically Johannine, aspect of his characterization and ministry is overlooked. In light of 1 John 4:1–3 the interpreter wonders whether this emphasis on the new and, in a sense, innovative work of the Spirit has not created some problems in the community. Apropos of this, it is striking that the Gospel presents the historic ministry of Jesus, but relates it, as we have seen, to his and his community's present experience, while the Epistle's author addresses a church in the present but insists through his emphasis on what was in the beginning on its rootage in the past, that is, in Jesus.

Because 1 John particularly seems to uphold more primitive ideas about eschatology, the work of Christ, and the Spirit, it has been proposed from time to time that it was actually written earlier than the Gospel as a kind of first attempt to set down what would later be developed more fully.[41] Nevertheless the view that the Epistles presuppose the Gospel and are really only intelligible on the basis of it, or something very much like it, seems preferable to most interpreters and is more widely held. We shall assume that position, and this means that 1 John will not be taken to be the traditional, theological basis on which the Gospel was developed. Nevertheless, 1 John can be used in a cautious and critical way to illumine wherever possible the theology of the Gospel. Whether by the same author or authors or not, they are very closely related.

[41] For example, by Kenneth Grayston, *The Johannine Epistles*, New Century Bible Commentary (London, 1984), pp. 7–9.

On the other hand, that the Revelation to John has any direct or significant relation to the Gospel of John is now widely contested or doubted. Already in the third century Bishop Dionysius of Alexandria pointed out the significant differences of style and theology between Revelation on the one hand and the Gospel and Epistles of John on the other, and expressed his opinion that Revelation could not be the work of the Apostle who, he assumed, wrote the other four.[42] Dionysius' basic arguments have held up remarkably well, and while most critical scholars are unwilling to ascribe the Gospel and Epistles to John the son of Zebedee, they agree that Revelation must be the work of someone other than their author(s). Perhaps ironically, the only one of the five Johannine books to mention any John (other than the Baptist) is the Book of Revelation, which claims to have been written by John of Patmos. But this John never claims to be an apostle or eyewitness and distances himself from those who were (Revelation 18:20; 21:24). The Apocalyptic eschatology of Revelation seems far removed from what one finds in the Fourth Gospel; the tenor of the book is completely different from the Gospel, conceptual and theological issues aside. While Gospel and Epistles share much common ground, so that the burden of proof lies on the contention that they are not by the same author, Revelation is so fundamentally different that common authorship seems a matter scarcely worthy of discussion.

Nevertheless, there are some significant points of contact. For example, only in Revelation, aside from the other Johannine books, is Jesus called the word (19:13: "the Word of God"). Only in Revelation (1:7) and the Gospel of John (19:37) is Zechariah 12:10 applied to the crucifixion of Jesus. Revelation, as well as the Gospel and 1 John, speaks frequently of witnessing and of conquering or overcoming (*nikān*, the same Greek word). The Spirit-Paraclete, who Jesus promises in the Gospel will continue and explain his revelatory mission, appears in the first three chapters of the Book of Revelation, mediating the word of Jesus to the seven churches of Asia. It is

---

[42] The relevant passages of Dionysius are quoted by Eusebius, *Ecclesiastical History* VII.25.

this Jesus who says (Revelation 3:20), "Behold, I stand at the door and knock," sounding very much like the Jesus of the Gospel of John. One would not want to claim too much common ground in view of their wide-ranging differences, but the similarities that are distinctive and not widely shared by other New Testament books suggest that the communities (or individuals) that produced the Gospel and Revelation had some overlap or area of contact. Indeed, like the Gospel of John and unlike the Letters, Revelation refers to *Ioudaioi*, and in a negative way (Revelation 3:9). But the appellation "those who call themselves Jews but are not" looks like an attempt to preserve the positive sense of the term "Jews" that we find still in Paul (Romans 2:17–29). The overlap or area of contact of Gospel and Revelation may then extend to their setting.

The Epistles of John suggest the existence of a circle of Christian communities toward which the Elder (2 John 1; 3 John 1) has a sense of responsibility. That this is the case is implicit in 1 and 2 John and becomes quite explicit in 3 John. The letters to the seven churches (see Revelation 1–3) attest a similar, if not the same, circle of churches in Asia Minor, not too far from the Island of Patmos, where the Revelation to John was written (1:9). Of course, the traditional site of the Gospel's origin is the great Asian city of Ephesus, one of the seven churches of the letters of Revelation. Something can be said for the Ephesian origin of the Johannine literature (see above, pp. 6–7), but that is not the principal point. More important is the evidence of a community, or community of churches, that produced the Johannine literature. Moreover, insofar as the Gospel itself shows signs of having used independent traditions or sources, as well as indications of editorial development, it too provides subtle, if elusive, evidence of its communal origin.[43] In fact, the view of the Gospel of John's character and interests espoused in this book quite strongly suggests a community setting and purpose: there was first one

---

[43] D. Moody Smith, *Johannine Christianity: Essays on its Setting, Sources, and Theology* (Columbia, sc, and Edinburgh, 1984), pp. 1–36, esp. 18–19. Cf. "Johannine Christianity: Some Reflections on its Character and Delineation," *NTS*, 21 (1976), 222–248.

community, the synagogue, which was then divided over the status to be accorded Jesus as what we call the church emerged from it. That rupture had already taken place by the time the Gospel was written, but it has left very clear marks in that document. The history of community and controversy that lies behind the Gospel of John goes a long way toward accounting for its distinctive character and its wide differences from the Synoptic Gospels.

b   The Synoptic Gospels

The relationship of John to the Synoptic narratives is a fascinating and puzzling problem, which has intrigued and frustrated exegetes not only in modern times, but also in antiquity. Clement of Alexandria's statement to the effect that John, realizing that the other evangelists had recorded the historical facts, wrote a spiritual Gospel has long seemed an adequate and accurate understanding of the relationship of the Fourth Gospel to the other three.[44] But Clement's assessment of this relationship works much better, so to speak, on the macro-level than on the micro-level. That is, it seems an adequate account of the relationship generally, but breaks down repeatedly when specific aspects of John are compared with the other Gospels.

For example, in John the public ministry of Jesus is not a Galilean ministry of the sort we find in the Synoptics. Rather, Jesus moves back and forth among Galilee, Judea, and Samaria. Although in all the Gospels Jesus is crucified on a Friday at the beginning of the Passover, in John that Friday falls on Nisan 14, just before Passover begins that evening, while in the Synoptics it follows the beginning of Passover the previous Thursday evening. Thus in the Synoptics Jesus and his disciples celebrate the Last Supper as a Passover meal, while in John they do not. In the Synoptics, Mark and Matthew particularly, there seems to be a formal trial of Jesus before the Jewish authorities, the Sanhedrin (Mark 14:55–65), while in John there is only a kind of informal hearing before

---

[44] Clement's famous dictum is quoted by Eusebius of Caesarea, *Ecclesiastical History* VI.14.7. On the modern scholarly discussion see D. Moody Smith, *John Among the Gospels: The Relationship in Twentieth-Century Research* (Minneapolis, 1992).

Annas (John 18:19–23), who is called the high priest, although elsewhere that title is given Caiaphas (18:24; cf. Matthew 26:57). The fact that the Marcan trial scene accords so closely with John's view that the Jews condemned Jesus for blasphemy because of his claims for himself (Mark 14:63–64; cf. John 10:33–36) renders John's omission of it puzzling if he knew Mark.

Moreover, why John omitted the account of Jesus' institution of the Lord's Supper, the tradition of Jesus' public teaching, as well as all his parables and the Lord's Prayer (missing also from Mark), the birth narratives (again, also missing from Mark), the temptation by Satan, Gethsemane (cf. John 12:27), all Mark's healing narratives, and, indeed, most of the Synoptic accounts of the public ministry has been a source of continuing puzzlement to exegetes. In some cases, for example, the account of Jesus' agony in Gethsemane, the episode flies in the face of John's portrayal of Jesus as one neither stymied nor perplexed by any opponent or circumstance, and John may have omitted it for that reason. In fact, in this particular instance there is evidence that John knows a tradition he does not narrate (John 12:27; cf. Hebrews 4:14–16; 5:7–9). But often when a Johannine account is compared with an episode found also in the Synoptics, John differs in unaccountable ways. Thus the feeding of five thousand people by Jesus (John 6:1–15; cf. Mark 6:32–44; 8:1–9) is obviously the same episode in John as in Mark, but John's version differs not only in typically Johannine ways (6:5–6), but in such a detail as the small boy with five barley loaves and two fish (John 6:9), which does not advance the Gospel's obvious theological interests. Similarly, the story of the woman anointing Jesus (John 12:1–8; Mark 14:3–9) is more eloquently and economically told in Mark than in John, and it is hard to understand why John would have altered Mark's account as he did.

Yet, at another level, the assumption that John wrote with Mark or the Synoptic Gospels (indeed, the entire New Testament) in view works rather well in interpretation. This is the so-called macro-level. At this level the statement of Clement of Alexandria still seems valid. That the Synoptic Gospels or the whole New Testament lead up to the pinnacle of Johannine thought is the premise of many a modern, critical New Testament theology,[45] and there is an important element of truth in the view that John clarifies or makes explicit what is implicit or inchoate in the other Gospels or elsewhere in the New Testament.[46] Probably the majority of careful Christian readers of the New Testament have viewed John as this sort of culmination of early Christian theology or witness; or, readers who view the New Testament negatively may well have seen in John's Gospel the nadir of what is wrong or perverse about it.[47]

Nevertheless, it would be a mistake to think that the essence of John's theology could be arrived at by simply observing and measuring its distance or differences from the Synoptics – to use the most obvious comparison – on specific points or items. Attempts to interpret John on the basis of its specific differences from the Synoptics tend to break down precisely because on major theological points John stands in general agreement with them. Thus with some reason John Calvin, the great sixteenth-century Protestant reformer, could see in the Fourth Gospel the key to the other three, for it seems to say explicitly what the others suggest or call for.

The theological difference between John and the Synoptic Gospels lies not so much in what their authors may have

---

[45] Bultmann's *Theology of the New Testament*, Part III, is only the leading example. (Of course, the final part of Bultmann's *Theology*, "The Development toward the Ancient Church," is clearly presented as anticlimactic, and judgments about this development are made on the basis of theological criteria derived from Paul and John.) One might note also, by way of example, Hans Conzelmann, *An Outline of the Theology of the New Testament* (New York, 1968), "Part Five: John," pp. 321–358; and W.-G. Kümmel, *The Theology of the New Testament According to its Major Witnesses: Jesus—Paul—John* (Nashville, 1973).

[46] See the important conclusions of James D. G. Dunn, *Christology in the Making: A New Testament Inquiry into the Origins of the Doctrine of the Incarnation*, 2nd ed. (London, 1989), pp. 248–250, esp. p. 249: "Certainly therefore the Fourth Gospel can properly be presented as the climax to the evolving thought of first-century Christian understanding of Christ: whether that climax is simply the outworking of the inherent logic of God's (final) revelation in and through Christ, or reflects something of wider developments of thought in the Hellenistic world of the late first century AD is an issue we will explore further in the final chapter."

[47] See the remarkable introductory essay of the well-known literary critic Harold Bloom (ed.) in *The Gospels*, Modern Critical Interpretations (New York, 1988), pp. 1–15. He writes, "To my reading, the author of the Gospel of John was and is a more dangerous enemy of the Hebrew Bible than even Paul, his nearest rival" (p. 1).

believed about Jesus as in the way, or the extent to which, they set forth that belief. Despite their significant differences, the Synoptic Gospels' picture of Jesus – not only what he did but the issues he addressed and the kinds of things he said about them – is generally coherent and self-consistent, although based on several sources (Mark, Q, the special materials of Matthew and Luke). The Synoptic tradition (or traditions), influenced though it may be by later Christian interests, allows the historical Jesus to speak in idioms characteristic of him (parables, kingdom proclamation, etc.). The Gospel of John, however, presents Jesus speaking to christological issues, and to them almost exclusively. Thus historical criticism has rightly preferred the Synoptic account for historical purpose. Yet the other evangelists clearly understand Jesus to be Son of God as well as the Messiah of Israel, that is, their christologies already expand the boundaries of traditional messianic expectation. Mark is as interested in christology as John, for at Jesus' baptism, transfiguration, and death he has him hailed as Son of God (Mark 1:11; 9:7; 15:39), and at his trial the high priest wrings a messianic confession from Jesus' lips (Mark 14:61–63); but in Mark the christological question is dealt with as a question, so that Jesus does not immediately provide the answer as in John. The same is more or less true of Matthew and Luke, who augment Mark with the tradition of Jesus' sayings but do not have obviously higher christologies. There is a sense in which John too may be understood as augmenting Mark with Jesus' sayings, but how different are those sayings! Moreover, the evidence of John's use of Mark is much sparser and more ambiguous than in Matthew and Luke. As we have already observed, there is little enough evidence of literary relationships between any of the Johannine writings and the rest of the New Testament, even though their substantial agreement with other expressions of early Christian faith and ethics is clear.

c Pauline Christianity

The relationship between John and the Synoptic Gospels is once again a matter of scholarly discussion, but the question of Paul and John has lain dormant for years. Early in this century it was widely assumed that the Fourth Gospel was based upon Pauline Christianity,[48] probably for two basic reasons. First, given John's much later date (by a half-century or so), it seemed unlikely that John would not have known Paul, or his Letters. Second, their theologies, with their intense concentration upon christology and therefore on faith issuing in participation or union with Christ, seemed quite similar, particularly when put over against Jesus, the Synoptics, and the Synoptic tradition. But the sheer historical probability that John would have known Paul's Letters fades before the fact that Paul was not in the first century the universally revered figure of Christendom he is today and that in any event his Letters were not collected and circulated until toward the end of the first century. The author of Acts apparently did not know them. As to the theological agreement between Paul and John, it is at one level clear enough, but this does not necessarily mean that they were historically related in the sense that John was derivative from Paul.

Recent interpreters have observed that their common theological interests are expressed in quite different ways. The christological title "Lord" (*kyrios*), Paul's favorite, is rare in John, as is Paul's characteristic opposition of flesh (*sarx*) and Spirit (*pneuma*). "If it be said that both writers are preoccupied with the relation between Christianity and Judaism, the answer must be that the focus is completely different in the two cases. John shares none of Paul's obsession with the law; he never speaks of the righteousness of God, or sees human history in terms of God's plan for the world."[49] Or as Rudolf Bultmann put it, despite the use of common Christian terminology, John lacks specifically Pauline terms, and particularly the terminology relating to the history of salvation. Thus "grace" (Greek: *charis*), the characteristic Pauline term for describing God's disposition and action, is seldom found in John (but see

---

[48] See, for example, Albert Schweitzer, *The Mysticism of Paul the Apostle* (New York, 1931), esp. pp. 371–372. Schweitzer's argument that John's mysticism differs decisively from Paul's in being truly Hellenistic takes for granted John's knowledge of Paul, which was a given in the exegesis of the time.

[49] Ashton, *Understanding the Fourth Gospel*, p. 51.

1:14). Moreover, the concept of God's covenant with his people Israel, his election of them, plays no explicit role (cf. Romans 9–11).[50] Bultmann thought that one could account for their central common christological motif of the sending of the Son into the world by recourse to a prior gnostic redeemer myth, which they independently shared. The existence of such a pre-Christian myth in sources earlier than the New Testament cannot be shown, and this has put Bultmann's thesis in doubt. Subsequent research has shown that the notion of God's sending his emissary from heaven is suggested in relevant Jewish sources, which may point to John's background.[51] In any event, Bultmann took the common christological motif for a given of early Christianity, rather than something distinctive of Paul and John to be explained by the dependence of one on the other, and in this he would find broad agreement among subsequent interpreters.

d Hebrews

At the edge of the Pauline corpus stands the Epistle to the Hebrews, which does not claim to have been written by Paul but probably gained canonical status because of its association with him. Although Hebrews shows little or no evidence of knowledge of the Fourth Gospel (or vice versa), there are nevertheless some interesting similarities or points of contact. As to background, Philo of Alexandria and more recently Qumran have been thought important for both, but the more remarkable parallels are in certain christological perspectives and motifs. For Hebrews as for John, Jesus Christ was pre-existent, the agent of God in creation (Hebrews 1:2) as well as the Messiah of Jewish expectation. Moreover, in quite different ways Hebrews and the Gospel of John emphasize Jesus' exaltation. Although Hebrews never mentions the resurrection, it focuses upon Jesus' death, exaltation, and his high priestly

[50] Bultmann, *Theology of the New Testament*, II, pp. 7–8.
[51] See, for example, Peder Borgen, "God's Agent in the Fourth Gospel," in the collection of his essays, *Logos Was the True Light and Other Essays on the Gospel of John* (Trondheim, 1983), pp. 121–132, as well as "The Son of Man Saying in John 3:13–14," pp. 133–148 in the same volume.

ministry before God. In a real sense John also presents Jesus as one already ascended and transcendent, and it is this exalted Jesus who not only moves across the plane of his earthly ministry but ministers through the Spirit to his church in this world. Obviously, although they share important motifs, Hebrews and John are focused in different directions. Hebrews gives an account of Jesus' heavenly ministry, John of his earthly.

Yet for Hebrews as for John the reality of the earthly ministry of Jesus remains quite important, and the incarnation is for Hebrews as important as it is for John.[52] The explanation of the significance of Jesus' real humanity, suffering, and sacrifice is underscored in Hebrews (4:14–5:10) in what became for later Christian theology a classic expression of the meaning and necessity of the humanity of Jesus. Here Hebrews (5:7) like John (12:27) betrays knowledge of Jesus' trial and anxiety in the face of death, the Gethsemane tradition (cf. Mark 14:32–42), without telling the story. At this point there is also the greatest difference between Hebrews and John, because while John knows but makes little of the explicitly cultic, sacrificial terminology and conceptuality in explaining Jesus' death, Hebrews exploits it to the full: Jesus is the great high priest who brings the present sacrificial system to an end by offering himself.

Just at this point, however, there is a marked similarity or parallel in the concept of supersession. Jesus Christ is both the fulfillment of the old and its successor. In Hebrews this is stated in terms of the temple cult and sacrificial system, in John in terms of the scriptures and Moses (1:17,45; 5:45–47), but also, if more subtly than in Hebrews, the temple. Jesus replaces the temple as the place of God's revelation (1:14; 2:19–21; 4:21–24). The fact that in John "the Jews" are no longer Jesus' people but his enemies is clear evidence of the prominence of the supersession motif. The difference in terminology from Hebrews is here most striking, for the word *Ioudaios* occurs not

---

[52] On the relationship of John and Hebrews, and the danger of indiscriminately mixing the two, see Barnabas Lindars, *The Theology of the Letter to the Hebrews*, New Testament Theology (Cambridge, 1991), pp. 32–35, 121f.

at all in Hebrews. Therefore, while the parallels between John and Hebrews are notable and important they seem to be just that, parallels that do not represent direct, or literary, relationships. There is no more reason to suppose that John knew Hebrews than that the author of Hebrews knew John.

e Other early Christian writings

The relationship between John and the other New Testament writings is obvious, even though it is not easy to explain. As we have seen, it is possible that the fourth evangelist did not know or use any of the other New Testament books *per se*. A similar relationship, real, but difficult to explain, exists between the Fourth Gospel and certain other early Christian writings, even writings subsequently adjudged gnostic and heretical.[53]

For example, the second-century *Gospel of Truth* shares much of the theological vocabulary and dualism of the Gospel of John. Yet its interests and theological atmosphere or aura seem quite different, and this is not merely a reflection of the fact that the *Gospel of Truth* is not a narrative, while John is. The narrative character of John is, however, importantly related to the historical character of revelation. The word was not only made flesh, but his deeds, words, and death are intrinsic to the meaning of the gospel message. In the *Gospel of Truth* a narrative of Jesus' ministry may or may not be presupposed; there are possible allusions to the canonical Gospels. But the author's interests obviously lie elsewhere, in theological and cosmological speculation about the relationship of the Son to the Father and in the cosmology and psychology of salvation as it affects the individual believer. The significance of the death of Jesus, which seems to be acknowledged as an historical fact, nevertheless is not basic to the theological system, but is subsumed in it. Moreover, while in the Gospel of John there is a tension between the dualism and doctrine of election on the one hand and the importance of a meaningful decision of faith on the other, in the *Gospel of Truth* dualism and the predesti-

---

[53] For Christian gnostic documents see especially Robinson (ed.), *The Nag Hammadi Library in English*.

nation of the elect seem to be basic and immutable categories. Possibly the author of the *Gospel of Truth* knew the Gospel of John and used its language for his own purposes. Whether or not this is the case, the two writings, different as they may be, are somehow related in their conceptual world or milieu.

Among extra- or post-canonical Christian books, John has closer affinities with the *Odes of Solomon*, an ancient collection of odes or poems which, if they were not originally Christian (rather than Jewish), were soon adopted and presented as such. Their Christian character is often quite evident, and they sometimes reflect the language or conceptuality of the Gospel of John, at just those points at which there is also an affinity with the sectarian documents of Qumran.[54] In Ode 7:6–7 we read:

> Like my nature He became, that I might understand Him.
> And like my form, that I might not turn away from Him.
> The Father of knowledge is the Word of knowledge.

Or in Ode 8:8, 12:

> Hear the word of truth, and receive the knowledge of the Most
>   High ...
> For I turn not my face from my own, Because I know them.

While Jesus is not mentioned by name, there are clear allusions to his death and to the Virgin, his mother, while the term "Messiah" occurs more than once. The passage about the incarnation in Ode 7 recalls John 1:14, of course, and almost seems to be an interpretation of it, while the statements of Ode 8 are much like those of Jesus about his disciples in John 6:37,45 and 10:14–15. Equally impressive is the way the risen Jesus himself speaks in the *Odes*, presumably through the mouth of an inspired prophet. Indeed, he seems to say explicitly how this comes about (Ode 42:6):

---

[54] See the translation and notes of James H. Charlesworth, *The Odes of Solomon: The Syriac Texts*, Society of Biblical Literature Texts and Translations: Pseudepigrapha Series (Missoula, MT, 1977), from which the following quotations are taken; also the article by Charlesworth, "Qumran, John, and the Odes of Solomon," in the collection he has edited, *John and the Dead Sea Scrolls* (New York, 1990), pp. 107–136.

> Then I arose and am with them,
> And I will speak by their mouths.

Such Spirit-inspired prophecy may well account for the distinctive character of the self-proclamation of Jesus in the Fourth Gospel (cf. John 14:26; 16:12–14).[55]

These evocations of the Gospel of John are reminiscent of those found in Ignatius of Antioch,[56] and the problem of whether Ignatius knew the Gospel or only antecedent traditions is quite analogous. An eastern origin of the *Odes* is likely, and it is certainly not impossible "that Qumran, and possibly, early pre-Johannine traditions current in Syria, were entangled in their roots."[57] While there are similarities to gnosticism, in their frequent reference to knowledge, as well as their mysterious and enigmatic tone, the *Odes* appear to differ sharply from gnosticism in at least a couple of crucial points: the biblical doctrine of creation is embraced, as is the death of Jesus, who is taken to be genuinely human. The question of whether the *Odes* are fundamentally Jewish with a Christian overlay or originally Christian is related to the question of whether they belong to the background of the Fourth Gospel or to its sphere of influence, and neither is easy to decide. In any case, there seems to be a real relationship between the *Odes* and Johannine Christianity, however it may have been mediated. With the *Odes* we are perhaps closer to the ambiance of the Fourth Gospel than with the other, gnostic texts.

In the case of the *Odes of Solomon* or of the *Gospel of Truth*, our quandary is not unlike that over the New Testament books: it is difficult to determine the nature of their relationship to the Fourth Gospel. Possibly there is direct knowledge and literary dependence, but the evidence is by no means so unambiguous

---

[55] On the relation of the *Odes* to the phenomenon of Spirit-inspired, or charismatic, utterance, see the important article of D. E. Aune, "The Odes of Solomon and Early Christian Prophecy," *NTS*, 28 (1982), 435–460.

[56] C. K. Barrett, *The Gospel According to St. John: An Introduction with Commentary and Notes on the Greek Text*, 2nd ed. (London and Philadelphia, 1978), p. 113. In his *The Gospel of John and Judaism* (London, 1975), pp. 52–55, Barrett makes noteworthy observations about parallels between John and Ignatius in their relation to Judaism and gnosticism.

[57] Ibid., p. 54.

as to be compelling. One must reckon at least with a broad base of early Christian tradition in which the author of the Fourth Gospel shares. Nevertheless, when John reflects ideas, vocabulary, or even events found in other New Testament writings, his individual and distinctive character is such as to call into question the assumption that he must have used other early Christian writings, or have been used by them. We can neither explain the Gospel of John as the redaction of other early Christian writings nor explain it without reference to them.

D   SUMMARY AND CONCLUSION

In examining the setting and sources of Johannine theology we have of necessity reviewed the question in relationship to the character, origin, and movement of the Gospel as a whole. In pursuing this task a more or less inductive procedure has been followed. First to be considered were representatives and representative texts of the broader cultural and religious world of which John was a part. A crucial decision in utilizing such materials is, of course, which part or aspect of that world is most closely related or pertinent to the Fourth Gospel. John's possible relations, points of contact, or parallels with ancient sources and texts are so many that one might think the evangelist was deliberately casting the nets broadly in order to attract and interest as many readers as possible. Clearly John drew upon theological ideas and vocabulary that were widely used in antiquity, but the impression gained from surveying the evidence is that the closer one gets to Judaism, as well as early Christianity, the closer one is to John.

Rather than select one or more of these backgrounds as paramount as a source or setting of Johannine theology, however, the next logical step seemed to be to make a survey of the Gospel itself, asking what is most distinctive, most clearly Johannine. Such a survey led quickly to certain observations and conclusions. In the first place, the narrative character and setting of Johannine theology is most important: we are dealing not with a theological treatise but with a story, and this fact must not be lost from sight in any treatment of it. But while the narrative is significant as narrative, it may and does point away from itself, and this is also important in grasping Johannine theology. The narrative is about Jesus, and as theologically freighted and obviously selective (20:20; 21:25) as it may be, the author repeatedly calls attention to this fact (for example, 1:14) and obviously believes it to be of great importance.

Yet, there are not only anachronistic aspects of the Gospel's narrative, such as the dichotomy between Jesus and the Jews, but also clear indications that the evangelist himself wrote with knowledge that was not possible or accessible while the events of Jesus' historic ministry were taking place (16:12–13). As we probe the text at just such places as contain anachronisms and other indications of a later perspective, the possibility arises that the evangelist has not been careless, but has deliberately cast his narrative so that it reflects at least two historical perspectives.[58] The drama transpiring on the stage, or on the page before the reader, has two levels, that of the historical Jesus and his contemporaries and that of the evangelist, the Johannine community, and their Jewish adversaries. The heat of the polemic arises not just out of the past, but from the evangelist's present, and Jesus continues to battle, now with his disciples of a generation or two later, against opponents who represent the forces of darkness and disbelief.

The critical orthodoxy of the earlier part of this century found the source of John's narrative in the Synoptic Gospels and the inspiration of his theology in Paul, and this was not an unreasonable view. John's narrative is obviously related to the Synoptic, more closely at some points than at others, and his christological focus is strikingly like Paul's, especially in contrast to the Synoptic tradition and, presumably, Jesus. But we have seen that the differences from the Synoptics and Paul are not easily accounted for simply on the basis of John's theo-

---

[58] So also Ashton, *Understanding the Fourth Gospel*, pp. 419f.: "Had Martyn [*History and Theology in the Fourth Gospel*] noticed the evangelist's careful explanations of the necessary gap between hearing and seeing on the first level of understanding and full comprehension on the second, he would surely have revised his opinion that John was not 'analytically conscious' of his own procedure. On the contrary, he gave considerable thought to the theological implications of the Gospel genre."

logical purpose or agenda, given the other writings as his sources. The view that John wrote with the Synoptics in view, either to supplement or to correct them, risks distorting the interpretation of the Fourth Gospel. Something similar must be said about the possible danger of interpreting John over against the background of Paul or Paul's Letters. For example, to attribute John's conception of the incarnation to Paul or to attribute Paul's view of the salvific effect of the crucifixion of Jesus to John results in misinterpretations of either or both. In the words of a perceptive interpreter, in this and other respects the wiser course is to let John be John.[59] Doubtless John owes something to his Jewish, Christian, and other predecessors, but the lack of exact parallels or models for his distinctive theological thought and christological conceptuality suggests that "John" is, after all, an original thinker, whose genius shines through his writings, especially the Gospel.

[59] Cf. James D. G. Dunn, "Let John Be John: A Gospel for its Time," in Peter Stuhlmacher (ed.), *The Gospel and the Gospels* (Grand Rapids, MI, 1990), pp. 293–322.

CHAPTER 3

The themes of Johannine theology

A PRESUPPOSITIONS

Every theology or system of thought takes for granted presuppositions or axioms that are regarded as generally held or
uncontestable. In John certain inherited beliefs are treated as
givens. That is, they are regarded as true, even if their meaning
must be debated, inasmuch as the coming of Jesus Christ has
upset all human presuppositions, axioms, and expectations.
For John, Jesus Christ is the negation and judgment of this
world insofar as it is independent of, and over against, God.

1 God

To mention God invites the question of the sense in which the
existence and rule of God are axiomatic for the Fourth Gospel.
Obviously, if the fourth evangelist were asked whether he
believed in God, he would affirm such belief, but might
counter by asking the questioner what God he or she believes
in and how that belief could be validated. The fundamental
question of the Fourth Gospel is the question of God, not
whether a god exists but who is God and how God reveals
himself. Thus the fundamental question or issue of the Gospel
can be stated as the nature of revelation.[1] What God is
revealed, and how is God revealed?

---

[1] J. Ashton, *Understanding the Fourth Gospel* (Oxford, 1991), p. 62f. In Ashton's view,
Bultmann correctly saw the centrality of the concept of revelation: "His fundamental
insight, from which he never wavered, was that the central theme of the gospel is
revelation" (p. 63). On literary-critical grounds a similar position is taken by

Should one answer for John that the God revealed is the God of Abraham, Isaac, and Jacob, as well as Moses and David, that answer would be correct as far as it goes. Again, however, the counter-question might be: How is that God known? The traditional biblical, Jewish, and even Christian answer is that God is known first of all through scripture, and, indeed, scripture is one of the givens of Johannine theology.

2 *Scripture*

Early on, John says that the law was given by Moses (1:17), and even though he continues that grace and truth came by Jesus Christ, it is not obvious that Jesus Christ simply negates Moses. In fact, Jesus is the one of whom Moses in the law and also the prophets wrote (1:45), the Messiah of biblical expectation (1:41). Really to understand Moses is to see that he wrote about Jesus (5:45–47), for the scriptures testify to him (1:39). Jesus can refer to the scriptural law of Moses as "your law" (8:17), as if it were a law that applied to the Jews, or his opponents, but at the same time recognize its validity, if in a provisional or penultimate sense. Indeed, he can say that "scripture cannot be broken" (10:35). In considering John's christology, we shall entertain the question of whether or in what sense Jesus was the Messiah of Israel, but for the moment it is sufficient to recognize that he is presented as the one spoken about, prophesied, in scripture. The intelligibility of the Christian revelation then depends on scripture, but at the same time the intelligibility of scripture depends on the revelation of God in Jesus Christ. It is a reciprocal matter.

By the same token, the God of the Gospel of John is the God of Israel and Israel's scripture, but God as known from scripture now becomes intelligible only as the Father of Jesus Christ, so that a radical reappraisal of who that God is is called for in light of Jesus' appearance. Scripture and the God of scripture are axiomatic for John's theology, but they are never-

Gail R. O'Day, *Revelation in the Fourth Gospel: Narrative Mode and Theological Claim* (Philadelphia, 1986).

theless not static or fixed concepts over against which the Christian revelation must be made to fit, for that revelation becomes determinative of how scripture and God appear and are to be understood. At the same time God's positive and fundamental role in creation is strongly affirmed, as well as his speaking to and through the founders and prophets of Israel.

3 Jesus

Presupposed also by John is the advent of Jesus Christ as a human being (1:14), a man, a native of Nazareth and the son of Joseph (1:45); therefore a Jew (4:9,22). Despite the critical problems connected with the Gospel's authorship, it wishes to be understood as based upon eyewitness testimony to the historical figure of Jesus. Yet John does not present itself as the reader's first encounter with Jesus or the gospel message about him. Thus the account of Jesus' encounter with the Baptist is narrated by John the Baptist himself, retrospectively, so that although the reader is not told of Jesus' baptism, he will likely presume it and read the Gospel's account with it in mind. The resurrection of Jesus is referred to as something the reader would already know about (2:22), as is the coming of the Spirit (7:39) and the existence of an inner circle of twelve disciples (6:67), whose appointment is never recounted. Moreover, the recurrent references to Jesus' hour as not yet having arrived (for example, 2:4) would be intelligible only to a reader who knew Jesus' earthly destiny. Indeed, Jesus Christ himself is first mentioned as someone already known (1:17). The point is that John seems to presuppose familiarity with important aspects of Jesus' ministry and fundamental tenets of early Christian belief about him. One might say then that he knows Gospel tradition and the early Christian *kērygma* or credo. The form in which he knew them is, however, a matter of dispute.

The question of John and the Synoptics is a large and complex one, which cannot be resolved here. Although John at some points strongly evokes the Synoptics, his narrative so frequently ignores theirs or even collides with it that the Fourth Gospel can scarcely be regarded simply as a supplement of, or midrash upon, them. While it would be infelicitous to claim that John presupposes the Synoptics, the two colophons intended to conclude the Gospel (20:30–31; 21:25) clearly indicate that it presents only a selection of what was known and could have been narrated. The second even hints that other such "books" (i.e., Gospels) are known. The fourth evangelist clearly knows more than he narrates, and it is arguable that he wrote with something like the Synoptic tradition, if not the Synoptic Gospels, in view.[2]

4   Kerygma, church, and Spirit

More than a half-century ago, C. H. Dodd, the eminent British New Testament scholar, published a brief book in which he maintained that the major New Testament writers presuppose a pattern of early Christian preaching that set the Gospel message in the context of scriptural prophecy and expectation and was centered in the crucifixion and resurrection of Jesus.[3] He called this the *kērygma* (Greek for proclamation), in part to distinguish it from *didachē* (teaching). Although subsequent research has suggested there was greater variety in such preaching and teaching than Dodd's thesis allowed, what he proposed seems to correspond with beliefs widely, if not universally, accepted among early Christians, even if some of the details may be contested.

Certainly such diverse documents as 1 Corinthians, Mark, Hebrews, and Revelation agree on the salvific and theological importance of Jesus' death and resurrection (or exaltation), even if they did not share a common kerygmatic outline. Similarly, Mark and John seem to presuppose remarkably similar convictions about the theological significance of Jesus, which are all the more surprising in view of the astonishing differences in their Gospels. Significantly, both undertake to

---

[2] See Edwyn C. Hoskyns, *The Fourth Gospel*, ed. F. N. Davey, 2nd ed. (London, 1947), passim, who argues this position strongly. On the question of John and the Synoptics in recent research, see D. Moody Smith, *John Among the Gospels: The Relationship in Twentieth-Century Research* (Minneapolis, 1992).

[3] See above, Chapter 2, n. 33.

write a narrative of Jesus' ministry and death. Presumably John knows and assumes something approximating an early Christian credo or *kērygma*, whose elements can be traced in major New Testament writings.

Johannine theology presupposes God, scripture, Jesus, tradition about him, and a distinctly Christian understanding of who he was. There is a sense in which all these factors are axiomatic for the fourth evangelist. In addition, there are a couple of presuppositions that are probably not best understood simply as theological axioms, or at least they have other dimensions. First, as we have seen in Chapter 2, the Gospel of John presupposes a distinctively *Christian community*, a church, that stands over against the synagogue, having in all likelihood emerged from it. While the church is perhaps not aptly described as an axiom, what is axiomatic is its distinct character, independence of, and opposition to, the synagogue. In other words, Christianity has become something separate and different from Judaism, and the origins of that difference are made clear in the Gospel itself.

This Christian community is not, however, defined only or primarily by its opposition to Judaism, or even by its beliefs. It is a community in which the *Spirit* continues the presence and ministry of Jesus (20:22; 14:16–17). The vitality of the Spirit, as well as the church's reliance upon the Spirit, was a hallmark of Johannine Christianity, although the Spirit was certainly a prominent reality in the Pauline churches as well. Exactly how the Spirit made its presence felt is impossible to say, but it is likely that Spirit-inspired prophets spoke in the name of Jesus to the gathered congregation (cf. 1 John 4:1–3; 1 Corinthians 12:3; Revelation 3:20).[4] Be that as it may, the community of

---

[4] Ashton, *Understanding the Fourth Gospel*, pp. 181–189. Cf. M. E. Boring, "The Influence of Christian Prophecy on the Johannine Portrait of the Paraclete and Jesus," *NTS*, 25 (1978/79), 113–123. On the possible significance of similar prophetic speech *ex ore christi* ("from the mouth of Christ") in the *Odes of Solomon*, see D. E. Aune, "The Odes of Solomon and Early Christian Prophecy," *NTS*, 28 (1982), 435–460. The question of the Spirit-Paraclete's authority, particularly in relation to Jesus, has been subjected to probing examination by D. Bruce Woll, *Johannine Christianity in Conflict: Authority, Rank, and Succession in the First Farewell Discourse*, SBLDS 60 (Chico, CA, 1981).

the Fourth Gospel was one in which the presence and activity of the Spirit must have loomed large, and the experience of the Spirit with all its spontaneity and the problems that could arise from it was nevertheless the basis for the Christian doctrine of the Holy Spirit as a member of the Trinity.

The purpose of this major chapter of the book is to see how the presuppositions of the Fourth Gospel unfold in its under-standing of faith and life. We shall not proceed chrono-logically, or even by the progression of the narratives, although either way might be possible. Instead we shall attempt to unfold the logic of faith's understanding of revelation, in order to see how the revelation itself is perceived and in what terms it is presented. Although God is the ultimate source of revelation, it would be a mistake to begin a presentation of Johannine theology with the doctrine of God, for that doctrine is formed, or reformed, on the basis of the revelation of God in Jesus Christ. Therefore, the only viable beginning point is Jesus Christ himself, or the presentation of him in the Gospel of John. We shall be interested in asking: Against what background of expectation is he understood? How are such expectations ful-filled, contravened, or revised? What are the implications of belief in the revelation (i.e., faith in Jesus Christ) for the believer's faith and life?

B   THE REVELATION OF THE GLORY TO THE WORLD

Traditionally, Christian theology has as one of its major head-ings or subjects anthropology, a consideration of the human condition. The Johannine view of the human condition is summed up in the term *world*. John can use "world" (Greek: *kosmos*) as a virtual synonym for creation, "all things" (cf. 1:1,10), with no negative connotation whatsoever. There is, however, another and more typical use of *kosmos* that occurs already in the prologue, where the evangelist writes (verse 10): "He was in the world, and the world was made through him, yet the world knew him not." The first occurrence of "world" in this passage is neutral; it simply signifies the place where Jesus appeared. The second is positive; the world is God's creation through the word. The third is negative; the world as such rejects God's revelation in Jesus. Thus the world in the negative sense defines itself precisely by rejecting or refusing to know Jesus Christ. The world then is opposed to God and takes its place as the primary antipode in the Johannine dualism: God and world. Yet in the Fourth Gospel the dualism of God and world is not absolute: the world was not only created by God, but is also the object of his love and salvation (3:16–17; 12:46).

As the object of God's salvation, however, the world presently stands in a state of alienation and condemnation characterized by darkness (1:5; 12:46), death (5:19–27; 8:37,44), sin (8:21,34), slavery (8:34–36), and falsehood (8:44). The portrayal of the world, and thus of the human condition, not only accords with what we find in the New Testament generally, but summarizes and, indeed, accentuates its desperate quality. It seems to agree most closely with what is found in Paul, whose probing of the depths of human depravity is profound (cf. Romans 1:18–3:20; chaps. 5–7). Both Paul and John agree that the human plight is desperate, indeed, hopeless apart from God's initiative in salvation through Jesus Christ. Both see the salvation wrought by God through Jesus Christ as centered, or culminating, in his death and resurrection, although they understand and interpret Jesus' death in different ways.

How humanity reached such a hopeless condition is also understood somewhat differently. Paul devotes a good deal of attention to human *sinfulness* or what one might call the history of *sin* (Romans 1:18–3:20; chaps. 5, 7, cf. chaps. 9–11), but John seems to assume the human condition as a given. At points John can sound quite Pauline, as he has Jesus speak of slavery to sin and of salvation as liberation from bondage (8:31–36), although the familiar Pauline polarity of righteousness and sin, or human sin versus God's righteousness, is not found in John. John knows and uses the terms for sin (*hamartia*) and righteousness (*dikaiosynē*), although they are many times less frequent than in Paul, but the typical Pauline verb *dikaioun*, to justify in the sense of make or pronounce righteous, does not occur at all in the Fourth Gospel or Johannine Epistles. Thus it is unsafe to assume that Paul's struggling with the history of the human condition really underlies John's assessment of it.

In the case of Paul it is certainly justifiable to speak of human sin as the presupposition of God's salvation understood as the revelation of his righteousness, for the Apostle devotes a great amount of attention to the development of these themes. While it is arguable that Paul's thought really moves from solution to human plight, so that he could scarcely have imagined the former apart from the latter, at the same time his painstaking reconstruction of the human condition suggests that for him it becomes quite intelligible and indeed important as the prolegomenon of the Gospel.[5] With John, however, the situation is somewhat different in that the Gospel almost goes out of its way to indicate that the seriousness of the human plight would not even have been known apart from the revelation of God in Jesus Christ, which is not, as in Paul, described as the revelation of God's righteousness. (Moreover, the role of the law in relation to consciousness of sin receives no attention in John, as it does in Romans 7.) The Johannine Jesus says, "If I had not done among them the works which no one else did, they would not have sin; but now they have seen and hated both me and my Father" (15:24). And again: "For judgment I came into this world, that those who do not see may see, and that those who see may become blind" (9:39). When the understandably perplexed Pharisees ask whether they are then blind, Jesus continues: "If you were blind, you would have no guilt; but now that you say, 'We see,' your guilt remains" (9:41). Obviously, the advent of Jesus as God's word, his revelation, creates a new situation. It is not that God in no way revealed himself or acted in the history of Israel – what is now called the Old Testament period. John assumes the reality of God's revelation to Abraham, Jacob, and Moses. But someone greater than Jacob or Abraham has now come (4:12; 8:53).

---

[5] On the priority of plight to solution, see Ed P. Sanders, *Paul and Palestinian Judaism: A Comparison of Patterns of Religion* (Philadelphia, 1977), esp. pp. 442–447.

Not Moses but Jesus gives the true bread from heaven (6:32–35), and Moses wrote about Jesus, if only he were properly understood (5:45–47). Now, whether or not one even believes in God will be decided on the basis of the response made to Jesus, so that those who do not believe in Jesus also reject God (5:37–38).[6]

Obviously John does not envision a situation in which all was well until the appearance of Jesus, who upset all previously held standards and expectations; therefore, the view that John must have presupposed something like the Pauline accounting for sin, even if he did not know or make use of Paul's Letters, makes a certain sense. "He came to his own, but his own received him not" (1:11), but why should they have not received him if all has been well? Of course, the continuing assumption of Jesus' Jewish opponents is that all is well (cf. 8:33), and precisely for that reason Jesus' coming and claims constitute an unnecessary interruption and disturbance of their ordered universe. But for John the givenness of a human situation characterized essentially by death, darkness, falsehood, and sin is axiomatic: "The light shines in darkness and the darkness has not overcome it" (1:5). Whoever believes in the Son does not perish, which would otherwise be his or her fate, but has eternal life (3:17). The "which would otherwise be his or her fate" is not explicitly said, but is the proviso, and the only one, that makes sense of what is said.

That grim proviso should, however, be seen in the likely historical setting of the Fourth Gospel, which is the conflict between Jewish adherents of Jesus and those who oppose that claim. This conflict has led to increasingly negative views of the opposition on either side, so that we have "the Jews" represented as vehemently rejecting Jesus and heaping opprobrium upon him, while Jesus, who clearly represents the Johannine

---

[6] The KJV translation of John 14:1, "Ye believe in God, believe also in me," although grammatically possible, is hardly possible theologically. In Johannine thought, belief in Jesus is not something merely to be added to belief in God. Most modern translations rightly construe this as a double imperative: "Believe in God; believe also in me." The command to believe in God becomes the command to believe in Jesus.

Christians, responds in kind. Given the Johannine view of the Jewish authorities, presumably the heirs of the Pharisees, who are his chief opponents, it is not surprising that the Gospel portrays the world into which Jesus came as one of falsehood, sin, darkness, and death. Whether that is an accurate portrayal remains a question for the open-minded reader. But suffice it to say that the evangelist does not wish his reader to remain open-minded, but to take sides. In fact, he anticipates a sympathetic audience for his Gospel. At the same time he does not doubt that the facts bear him out. Of course, the question that must be decided is what are the facts.

It would be unfair to the evangelist, however, to characterize the view of the world or of the human situation as simply a by-product of a religious struggle with social overtones and implications (i.e., being put out of the synagogue). The fact that subsequent generations of readers, who have no direct relation to that ancient struggle, have resonated to the evangelist's description of the world and of the bleakness of human existence strongly implies that John's perception of the forces threatening human blessedness and life is widely shared. Whether Jesus affords the answer to such threat and the possibility of life is a matter of faith, for it cannot be proved that he does, except, of course, in the experience of those who share that faith as they face life and death. Moreover, the Fourth Gospel presupposes a history of God's standing over against the world, particularly as it is represented in scripture, that is, the Old Testament. Such an assessment of the tension in the relationship between God and world as we find in the Gospel would appear extreme, but not unprecedented against that background.

Toward the end of the biblical period, in books like Daniel, Zechariah, and Isaiah 24–29, Old Testament *prophecy* gives way to *apocalyptic*, a view of the world and its history that distinguishes sharply between good and evil, sees the world as dominated by the latter, and looks only to God's intervention for redemption. Characteristic of apocalyptic is the revelation itself, mediated from a heavenly or supernatural figure through a human recipient. While the prophetic literature generally anticipates an historical future in which God's judgment will be made manifest as life goes on, apocalyptic literature characteristically anticipates God's intervention in history to change it radically from the history of sin to the time of God's rule. Such an apocalyptic view of history underlies much of the Synoptic tradition, as well as Paul's theology, and is, of course, the subject of the Revelation to John. While the Gospel of John does not share the expectation of a future, cataclysmic resolution of world history in favor of God's people, its view of the world and God is quite similar to that of apocalyptic.[7] The Qumran War Scroll is an account of the apocalyptic conflict between the Sons of Light and the Sons of Darkness. Such light/darkness dualism in the Scrolls, and probably also in John, is rooted in an apocalyptic world-view. In John the character of the future expectation has changed because of the past, historic advent of Jesus Christ and the presence of the Spirit in the community, but the view of the nature of the world and its continuing bondage in darkness has not.

Into the world of darkness and death, God sends his Son Jesus Christ in order to save it (3:16–17). Thus Jesus is not only the light of the world (1:5; 8:12), but also the resurrection and the life (11:25), the one who has descended from God and ascended to God (3:13; 6:38; 17:13). He is the revealer who contravenes and overrules all human expectation. Yet at the same time he is the expected one, the Messiah of Israel, the Christ, and the fulfillment of deep human need.

1 Jesus as Messiah or Christ

All the Gospels are based upon a fundamental conviction of faith that Jesus is the Christ, the Son of God, and that to follow him is to attain life (see John 20:31), but only John formulates

[7] On the origins and characteristics of apocalyptic literature and thought, see John J. Collins, *The Apocalyptic Imagination: An Introduction to the Jewish Matrix of Christianity* (New York, 1984), pp. 1–32 ("The Apocalyptic Genre"). On the relationship of apocalyptic thought to the Fourth Gospel, see Robert G. Hall, *Revealed Histories: Techniques for Ancient Jewish and Christian Historiography*, Journal for the Study of the Pseudepigrapha Supplement Series 6 (Sheffield, 1991), esp. pp. 209–236.

this conviction so explicitly and only John puts the character and content of this faith on the lips of Jesus himself, so that Jesus talks continually about christology, often in debate with opponents. All the Gospels, as well as the rest of the New Testament, take Jesus to be the Messiah, the Christ of biblical and Jewish expectation. While no Gospel makes the element of fulfillment more explicit than John, in no Gospel is this expectation more fully transcended and transformed. Perhaps John recognized most clearly that the crucifixion of Jesus spelled the end of any traditional messianic conception.

Although Jewish expectations of God's redemption were not uniform, the Messiah, literally the anointed one, seems to have been the expected monarch of Davidic lineage who was to "restore the kingdom to Israel" (Acts 1:6).[8] With the land of Israel under Roman control and the province of Judea ruled directly by a Roman prefect, the hope of restoration must have been alive in Jesus' day. There are hints here and there in the Gospels that some of his compatriots believed that Jesus would be the answer to such hopes (John 6:15; Luke 24:21; as well as Acts 1:6). The fact that Jesus himself was of Davidic lineage (Romans 1:3; Matthew 1:6–17; Luke 1:27) would in all probability have encouraged them. No Gospel stands at a greater remove from such hope and expectation than John; but at the

---

[8] The New Testament applies the title Christ (Messiah) to Jesus with such consistency that one naturally assumes that the Judaism of his day was rife with expectation of the Messiah's advent. When one probes behind the New Testament into biblical and ancient sources, however, this turns out to be not so obviously the case. There is ample precedent and basis for New Testament affirmations, but no uniform picture. The breadth and variety of ancient Jewish and Christian messianic concepts are richly displayed in the essays of a number of scholars in the Princeton Symposium volume edited by J. H. Charlesworth and others, *The Messiah: Developments in Judaism and Christianity* (Minneapolis, 1992). For an excellent, succinct treatment of this important matter, see M. de Jonge, "The Earliest Christian Use of *Christos*: Some Suggestions," *NTS*, 32 (1986), 321–343. The centrality of the concept of the Messiah in the Fourth Gospel, as well as its complexity, is a recurring topic of the important work of John Painter, *The Quest for the Messiah: The History, Literature and Theology of the Johannine Community* (Edinburgh, 1991), esp. pp. 7–25. Also relevant is Donald Juel, *Messianic Exegesis: Christological Interpretation of the Old Testament in Early Christianity* (Philadelphia, 1988), who carefully defends a critical version of the traditional view that the earliest Christians understood Jesus, who had been crucified as a messianic pretender, as the kingly, Davidic Messiah. Nevertheless, by means of scripture they reinterpreted both the traditional expectation and its fulfillment.

same time no Gospel is more clearly in touch with Jewish, traditional roots. Only in John's Gospel does the transliterated Hebrew term *messias* actually occur (1:41; 4:25) (a fact obscured in the NRSV, where *christos* is in the Gospels frequently translated "Messiah"). Elsewhere we find the Greek translation *christos*, Christ, and in Paul and elsewhere in the New Testament, "Jesus Christ" seems more a proper name than a title. Perhaps not surprisingly, John knows the traditional expectation that the Messiah would be born in Bethlehem of Davidic lineage (7:42; cf. 2 Samuel 7:12–13; Micah 5:2), although he makes nothing of it and never refers to Jesus as the Son or progeny of David.

But as far removed from traditional messianic expectation as John may seem, the Gospel makes contact with such expectation in a significant way. The appearance of Jesus is presented by John as the eschatological fulfillment of biblical expectation, even though it is not the fulfillment of traditional messianic hopes for the restoration of Israel's kingship and independence. Thus, at the beginning of the Gospel, John the Baptist denies that he himself is the Christ (1:20) and hails Jesus as the lamb of God (1:29,36) and Son of God (1:34). After John sends two of his disciples to follow Jesus, one of them, Andrew, finds his brother Simon (Peter) and identifies Jesus to him as the Messiah or Christ (1:41). Jesus then gives the name Peter to Simon as he does in the Matthean account of Peter's confession of Jesus as Christ (Matthew 16:18). Shortly thereafter the author makes clear that this Messiah is the figure spoken of in scripture (Moses and the prophets; cf. 1:45), and Nathanael calls him the king of Israel.

The motif of kingship then recurs later on, as Jesus withdraws from a crowd for fear they will seize him and make him king (6:15). Then he enters Jerusalem as a messianic, kingly figure (12:13), and finally the issue of his kingship becomes a major theme of the passion narrative and is developed there much more fully than in the other Gospels, particularly in the interchange between Jesus, Pilate, and the Jews (18:28–19:16). At the culmination of the trial scene Pilate shrinks back from crucifying the king of the Jews, but they renounce Jesus, saying that only Caesar can be their king (19:15). Pilate then hangs upon the cross of Jesus the inscription "Jesus of Nazareth, the King of the Jews" (19:19), similar to that reported in the other Gospels, but only in John do the Jews protest (19:20–22). (Only John reports it was written in Hebrew, Latin, and Greek, underscoring the universal importance of what is said.) Jesus is executed as the king of Israel, or of the Jews, depending on one's point of view. The title "King of Israel" is clearly preferred by the evangelist, for "King of the Jews" reflects the perspective of foreigners, like Pilate.

In John's view, Jesus dies as the rightful king of Israel, rejected as he may have been by the people. Thus the word of the Gospel's prologue is fulfilled: "He came to his own home, and his own people received him not" (John 1:12, RSV). Still, throughout Jesus' ministry the question of whether Jesus is the Christ, the Messiah of Israel, keeps coming up. The Samaritan woman slowly comes to the conclusion that he is (4:29), inchoate as her faith may be. The Jerusalem crowd of chapter 7 puzzle over the question of whether Jesus is the Christ, and some believe (7:31,40), although the authorities sharply reject him (7:45–49). Later on, however, they can still ask him whether he is, in fact, the Christ (10:24), but at this point Jesus will not give them a direct answer, but alludes to his previous statements. On the one hand, the Jews, the authorities, threaten to expel from the synagogue any who confess Jesus to be the Messiah (9:22); but on the other, his friend Martha forthrightly expresses her belief that Jesus is the Christ (11:27). When it is said that many of the authorities believed in Jesus, but did not confess him for fear of being put out of the synagogue (12:42), they may be presumed to have believed that he was the Jewish Messiah. So even toward the end of the Gospel, in what was once intended as its conclusion, the purpose is stated as evoking belief that Jesus is the Christ, the Son of God (20:31). No Gospel shows as great an awareness of the nature of the issue of messiahship and whether Jesus could legitimately claim it than the Fourth. Other claims made for Jesus appear to be rooted back in this claim, as even the Son of

God title, which has many other ramifications, is closely linked
to it (1:49; 20:31). (For the attribution of divine sonship to the
king – i.e., the Messiah – see 2 Samuel 7:14 and Psalm 2:7, both
of which are applied to Jesus in Hebrews 1:5.)

Needless to say, the question of whether Jesus was, or
claimed to be, the Messiah reaches a critical point with his trial
and death, as John particularly makes clear. A crucified claimant to the throne of David would scarcely have qualified as the
one designated and accepted by God as the king of Israel
on any conventional view, for the crucifixion would have
rendered that claim null and void. Yet the earliest Christians
insisted that precisely this crucified Jesus was the Messiah, all
appearances to the contrary notwithstanding, and this in itself
implied a thoroughgoing revision of the concept of messiahship, which John carries through with a vengeance. It is
significant that this crucified Messiah is explicitly said to be the
king of Israel (1:49), and that a discussion of his kingship
dominates the trial of Jesus before Pilate. Such a discussion is
unique to the Fourth Gospel. More than any other evangelist,
John is aware of, and makes explicit, the role of the Messiah as
king of Israel. In all the Gospels Jesus dies on a cross under the
title "king of the Jews," but in John he dies as the king of
Israel, albeit rejected by the Jews. John, unlike Mark (15:32)
and Matthew (27:42), does not have Jesus mocked as the king
of the Jews, or of Israel.

As we have seen, "the Jews" in John's view are not simply to
be equated with Israel. Israel plays a positive role, although
the Jews do not. John came baptizing in order to manifest Jesus
to Israel (1:31). There are obviously people in Israel who
accept and believe in Jesus, namely, his disciples, among whom
is Nathanael, "truly an Israelite in whom there is no guile"
(1:47; cf. 21:2). Moreover, Nicodemus, ignorant though he
may seem (chap. 3), is nevertheless a teacher of Israel (3:10)
who returns to defend Jesus (7:50–52) and finally to help bury
him (19:13). Being a teacher of Israel is a good thing. In the
course of the Gospel story many other Jewish people are said to
believe, and if their belief is inadequate, so is Jesus' disciples'

faith until after the resurrection. Traditional Christian interpretation might infer that with the Jews', i.e., Jewish, rejection
of Jesus, the Christian church becomes the New Israel. This is
not an unreasonable inference or conclusion, but it is one
which the Fourth Gospel itself (which never uses the terms
"Christian" or "church") does not explicitly draw. The question who will be truly an Israelite, or a teacher of Israel,
remains open, although rejection of Jesus excludes that possibility.

Although not afraid of anachronism, John seems aware of
the impropriety of heaping upon Jesus titles or accolades that
were not accorded him until after his death and resurrection.
Thus "Lord" (Greek *kyrios*) is seldom applied to Jesus during
his public ministry, but is reserved for the period of the resurrection, although the vocative *kyrie*, with the meaning "sir,"
appears frequently. This is a striking reticence, particularly
in view of the fact that *kyrios* is after *Christos* itself the most
common christological title in Paul's Letters. The title
"savior," which is, surprisingly, not so common in the New
Testament, occurs only once of Jesus, on the lips of heterodox
Samaritans (John 4:42). It is, of course, a postresurrection
title (cf. 1 John 4:14), and it is perhaps appropriate that it
should be used by heterodox Samaritans among whom the
Gospel was apparently preached at a point quite early in the
spread of the Christian mission (cf. Acts 1:8; 8:9–25). When
John pushes beyond the historical limitations of Jesus' ministry
in interpreting his role christologically, he does so with an
apparent awareness of what he is doing and why. Thus while
enlarging greatly upon what we might properly call Jesus'
christological role, he anchors that role where on historical,
theological, and semantic grounds it is most naturally
anchored, namely, in the claim that Jesus of Nazareth is the
Messiah of Israel, a claim that he regards as true, even if it
requires elaboration and alteration because of what Jesus was
and is. This insistence on the messiahship of Jesus corresponds
well with what we can discern about the setting and development of the Fourth Gospel and its traditions in a Jewish, or
Jewish-Christian, milieu.

2   *The role of Jesus, the question of his origin, and how one comes to believe*

a   The role and origin of Jesus

Despite John's insistence on Jesus' messiahship, Jesus' revelatory and salvific role is not related to it in any traditional way. Rather that role is fundamentally shaped by Jesus' death: "If I be lifted up from the earth, I will draw all peoples to myself" (19:32). The death of Jesus raised in an acute way the question of his origin. Therefore, for John Jesus' origin, and what view of his origin is adequate to explain him, becomes fundamental in the narrative development of John's christology. The worldly view of Jesus' death does not disclose his true origin. Only with his resurrection can it be discerned that all along he had come from God.

Before Jesus is ever named in the Gospel he is identified with the word (*logos*) of God in the prologue, and before he is addressed as the Messiah he is called first of all "rabbi." These two terms nicely bracket Johannine christology, in the sense that everything else falls between them. To human eyes, even friendly ones, Jesus appears as a rabbi, that is, a teacher (as the term is translated in 1:38). Indeed, he is a teacher sent from God (cf. 3:2). But this teacher seen from the side of God is the *logos*, the agent of God in creation as well as redemption, so that he can himself be called *theos*, God (1:1,18; 20:28). By juxtaposing *logos* and "rabbi," we establish a framework within which to understand Johannine christology, because the terms represent two poles, divine and human.

As *logos* Jesus Christ is anchored in God. As rabbi he appears as a man among other human beings, and other rabbis like John the Baptist (3:26). As soon as the appearance of Jesus in human form is mentioned, he ceases to be called *logos*, but his God-given role and authority are not thereby diminished. When that role is truly recognized, he is no longer called a rabbi, for even when his disciples call him rabbi, they thereby signal that they do not really understand him. The term attempts to explain Jesus in terms of a worldly function or origin, and that is precisely why it fails to do him justice. The

Fourth Gospel is full of either well-meaning or hostile efforts to define or understand Jesus genetically, by reference to origins. And such efforts, confined as they are to this-worldly origins, always fail. Thus Nathanael at first says, "Can anything good come out of Nazareth?" (1:46); and later on Jesus' messianic status is denied precisely on the basis of his origin in Galilee (7:41,52). He is Jesus of Nazareth, the son of Joseph (1:45), but he is at the same time the Messiah of whom Moses and the prophets wrote.

Despite the fact that John is quite convinced of Jesus' messianic status, he does not spend a great deal of time and effort arguing for it on exegetical or traditional grounds. In contrast to the Gospel of Matthew, for example, John does not accept the premises necessary to establish Jesus' messiahship within Judaism by means of exegetical and traditional discussion (see 7:42). Consequently, when Nicodemus approaches Jesus in a friendly way, apparently to carry on such a discussion (3:1–2), he is greeted by the sharpest rebuff (3:3), being told that he must be born again, or from above, and the ensuing conversation takes place like ships passing in the night. The statements of Nicodemus seem altogether unexceptional and natural, given his presuppositions, while Jesus either does not answer Nicodemus or responds in a puzzling or riddling way.[9] The question of Jesus' origins and his rebuffs to Nicodemus are integrally related. To know Jesus' origin rightly is to know that he comes from God. His divine origin is then the only adequate, and indeed the only relevant, basis for understanding him. Once one understands him, the scriptures may be helpful for illuminating his mission and ministry, but in themselves they do not account for him. Until one is open to receive the revelation of God in Jesus, the scriptures remain a closed book (John 5:39–40; cf. 2 Corinthians 3:14–16).

Paul is portrayed in the Book of Acts as arguing in the

---

[9] See the penetrating discussion of the Nicodemus discourse and the issues it raises regarding the social setting of the Fourth Gospel and its language in Wayne A. Meeks, "The Man from Heaven in Johannine Sectarianism," *JBL*, 91 (1972), 44–72. The essay has been reprinted in John Ashton (ed.), *The Interpretation of John*, Issues in Religion and Theology 9 (Philadelphia and London, 1986), pp. 141–173.

synagogue, on the basis of scripture, that Jesus was the Christ and that he suffered according to God's will (for example, 17: 1–3). Possibly the earliest use of scripture was apologetic, particularly with reference to Jesus' suffering and death, intended to prove to a Jewish audience that this central event did not contradict, but rather proved, that he was the Messiah. Alternatively, the earliest Christians' exegetical efforts were devoted to making Jesus' messiahship intelligible to themselves in view of the crucifixion. Ultimately, the cross confirmed their messianic faith.[10] In either case the famous Suffering Servant passages of Isaiah were adduced in order to make this point (1 Peter 2:18–25), and the Gospels' passion narratives are full of Old Testament quotations, testimonies, used for the same purpose. The Gospel of John too shares in this passion testimony tradition (19:24,28,36–37). Quoting a very ancient kerygmatic tradition, the Apostle Paul says of Jesus that "he died for our sins according to the scriptures" (1 Corinthians 15:3); and to this general statement there is a close parallel in John: as they stand in the empty tomb, Peter and the Beloved Disciple are said not yet to know the scripture, "that he must rise from the dead" (20:9). In neither case is the scripture cited, but its existence is assumed.

b   How one comes to believe

It seems entirely likely that the apologetic use of such scriptural arguments lies behind John's view of the way people come to belief in Jesus, and there is an important sense in which the intelligibility of such arguments is acknowledged. At the same time, it has apparently become clear to John that no amount of scripture proof or scripture learning can in itself initiate belief in Jesus Christ, if such belief is at bottom belief in him as the

---

[10] The apologetic thesis is found in the important work of Barnabas Lindars, *New Testament Apologetic* (London, 1961). Against Lindars, Juel, *Messianic Exegesis*, argues that the earliest Christians engaged in messianic exegesis of scripture to clarify for themselves the meaning of Jesus' messiahship, particularly in view of his crucifixion (see esp. p. 1). But is the alternative as posed by the theses of Lindars and Juel a necessary one? At least in the early Johannine synagogal context Christian hermeneutical and apologetic purposes would have been opposite sides of the same coin. One would clarify Jesus' messianic role as one argued for it.

one sent from God, the final revelation of God. Jesus is said to be the Messiah of Jewish or biblical expectation, but such expectation did not entail the Messiah's inaugurating a radically new understanding of who God is. The Messiah fit a set, or different sets, of criteria and expectations. The Johannine Jesus, however, defies and shatters traditional criteria or expectations, although if one believes in him, the pieces of such traditions can be reassembled in a new way. The pieces will remain recognizable, but the new configuration will not be. How, then, does one come to the fresh insight that Jesus, the crucified messianic claimant, is the Messiah of Israel, but more than that, the one sent from God, God's word, God's Son, the savior of the world?

To do so is not just a matter of believing the Bible or of being persuaded intellectually. It is a matter of faith, believing the word of Jesus or the word about Jesus, which in John's view amounts to the same thing. John can talk in two different, and apparently contradictory, ways about how one comes to Jesus. In addition to the language of faith, which implies a meaningful human decision to believe in Jesus, a decision that expresses one's conviction and moral intent (3:16–21), John can also speak of being born again or, better, from above (3:3–8). Indeed, these two ways of coming to Jesus, believing and being born from God, are placed side by side in the prologue (1:12–13), as if the decision of faith, believing, could only be explained as a new birth. It will be necessary to return to the related questions of faith, rebirth, knowledge, and union with Jesus to discuss them more fully, but at this point it is important to observe how they are related to the questions of messianic expectation and tradition. Christian faith takes up older traditions and sees them in a new light, the light of the coming of God to humankind in the man Jesus, and the decision to see them in this way is itself viewed as a gift, a birth from God. Here John is again remarkably close to Pauline theology (cf. Romans 8:28–39).

Whatever John's actual historical connections to other New Testament writings or early traditions may have been, his way of viewing human response to Jesus as entailing an act of faith that can only be explained as a gift from God, for it is life itself, has struck a deep chord of resonance with Christians and Christians-to-be through subsequent centuries. Thus the phenomenon of conversion has never been far from the center of Christian experience, and talk of being born again, however easily it may be trivialized, expresses an important aspect of that experience. Being Christian, as it has since been called, involves a reorientation of life and thought on the basis of the coming of God to humankind in the crucified Jesus. John's perception of the radical nature of this event for human experience of the past, as well as hope for the future, has made his Gospel a classic of Christian experience and spirituality.

By putting it in terms of being born again, John poses the alternative of believing or not believing in the sharpest possible way. There can be no fence straddling; one is either in or out. Such a sharp drawing of the alternatives corresponds to the Johannine dualism and may, in fact, have the same basis or background in a distinct set of historical circumstances. In the previous chapter, the relationship of the Gospel of John to a conflict, first among Jews, then among Jews and Christians, became evident. The language and conceptuality of John fits a setting in which Jews and Christians, or Christ-confessing Jews and others, have come to a parting of the ways over the question of whether or not Jesus is the Messiah. Jesus predicts to his followers that they will be expelled from synagogues and even put to death (16:2). Moreover, during the course of Jesus' ministry (9:22) and at its end (12:42) it is said that people fear to confess Jesus lest they be put out of the synagogue. Apparently a situation is envisioned in which people believe in Jesus but do not confess that belief for fear of the consequences in the Jewish community. Not only is believing in Jesus important: one must also be willing to confess that belief publicly, an idea that, beginning in the Johannine literature, has important implications for the stance Christians later assumed in the face of Roman persecution.

The fissure in the Jewish community that began with belief and confession that Jesus was the Messiah continued to grow as Christ-confessors emphasized just those aspects of their faith that departed from or clashed with traditional Jewish mess-ianism and even monotheism. Not surprisingly, their strong affirmations were followed by an equally strong negation and in some cases at least, exclusion from the synagogue. From the point of view of the Christ-confessors, the members of the Johannine Christian community, the resistance they en-countered could only be explained as having the darkest, most Satanic origins. The Johannine Jesus denounces his adversaries as children of the devil, and by implication murderers and liars (8:43–47). The Jews, who are Jesus' adversaries, reply in kind. Jesus is a Samaritan and demon possessed (8:48,52). Polemic cannot become any sharper than this. Jesus later refers to the Jews', and the world's, hatred of him and his disciples:

If the world hates you, you know that it has hated me before you. If you were of the world, the world would love its own. Because you are not of the world, but I chose you out of the world, on account of this the world hates you. Remember the word that I said to you, "A slave is not greater than his Lord." If they persecuted me, they will persecute you; if they kept my word, they will keep yours also. But all these things they will do to you on account of my name, because they do not know him who sent me. If I had not come and spoken to them, they would not have sin; but now they have no excuse for their sin. The one who hates me hates my Father also. (15:18–23)

The Jews are, for John, representative of unbelief, but as the story of Jesus' own ministry nears its end, the evangelist con-templates a broader hostility and rejection of the Gospel. In 1 John, where the Jews have entirely disappeared, the sharp antinomy between Jesus and his followers and the world is maintained (see 1 John 2:15–17). Here the representatives of the world are misguided or disobedient Christians.

To come to Jesus in faith out of the world that so sharply rejects and condemns him is too much for any one person to accomplish as an independent, autonomous act. As Nicodemus is told, unless someone is born from above, he or she cannot see or enter the kingdom of God; he or she cannot believe in Jesus. Not coincidentally, Jesus immediately thereafter (3:8) begins to speak of the unfathomable work of the Spirit. The sharp antinomy between belief and unbelief in Jesus that pervades the Fourth Gospel doubtless reflects the antipathy between Christ-confessors, whose messianic expectations had been radically revised, and Christ-rejecters, who adhered to traditional messianic expectations and conventional religious standards. Understandably, "the Jews" respond by strongly rejecting Jesus, his followers, and the claims made for him. Because the standards and criteria of Judaism were so thoroughly negated by the preaching of Jesus the crucified as Christ, "the Jews" became for John the primary, but not the only, representatives of the world's unbelief, or, to put matters more accurately, of the unbelief that constitutes the world. But Jesus overcomes the world (16:33) in the sense that through him God begets faith and the prospect of new life. Nevertheless, to share in such faith and life one must confess, and suffer the pain and opprobrium of the world's rejection (12:42).

The coming of Jesus as God's word of salvation and judgment is with good reason referred to by modern exegetes and theologians as an eschatological event, for it is God's decisive intervention in human history and life, resulting in a division or sunderance between those who believe and follow and those who will not. In other words, it is in effect the execution of judgment or condemnation for those who reject it, but life eternal for those who believe – and are born into this new life. This understanding of the crucial significance of Jesus' coming and its appropriation through conversion or rebirth is correlative with the overturning of earlier expectations and traditions and the effecting of a new beginning in the history of salvation. As St. Paul wrote (2 Corinthians 5:17): "If anyone is in Christ it is a new creation; the old things have passed away; behold the new have come into being." The difference between Paul and John is that John has thought through in an even more radical way the meaning of the New for the status of the Old.

There is also a cognitive side of believing in Jesus (or being born from above). To believe in Jesus is to know him, and, in particular, to know his origin in God (17:7–8,25). Those who truly know Jesus know God (14:7), and the opposite is equally true: those who do not know Jesus do not know God (8:19). Knowledge of Jesus, and of God, is not an external, objective, cognitive relationship, however, but a more intimate and personal one. Such knowledge assumes or implies acknowledgment and belief. Knowing is not, however, a step beyond believing, but the correlate of believing. "Only in cases where 'believe' means a first turning toward Jesus not yet developed into full faith, can 'know' be distinguished from 'believe' as a distinct act."[11] Yet Jesus himself is said to know the Father as well as his own disciples (19:14f.), although he is not said to believe. This is because Jesus himself is the object of faith; only through believing in him does one believe in God (14:6) and know God (14:7). Believing, trusting, is the proper attitude of a mortal, human being before God. God does not believe, for God knows. On this crucial point Jesus is on the God side rather than the human side. He knows, and does not need to believe. (John uses two Greek verbs for "to know" interchangeably: *ginōskein* and *eidenai*.)

Elsewhere in the Bible knowing and knowledge play similar and fundamental roles. "Before I formed you in the womb I knew you," says the Lord to the prophet Jeremiah (1:5). Isaiah describes the state of the generation to which he prophesies (1:3): "The ox knows its owner, and the ass its master's crib; but Israel does not know, my people do not understand." Jeremiah, however, foretells a day when "no longer shall each man teach his neighbor and each his brother, saying, 'Know the Lord,' for they shall all know me, from the least of them to the greatest ..." (31:34). To know the Lord is to honor and obey him (cf. the Book of Ezekiel, where knowing the Lord is a continuous refrain); it is the essence of a proper relationship to God. This is also true for John, for whom knowledge of God can only be attained by a proper response to Jesus Christ (14:6).

Such knowledge can never be divorced from faith or be played off against faith, for it belongs to the very nature of faith in Jesus Christ to know the one who is believed and trusted. The later, gnostic subordinating of faith to knowledge, so that

[11] R. Bultmann, *Theology of the New Testament*, II (New York, 1955), p. 74.

those who only believe are inferior to those who have knowledge, is totally foreign to the Fourth Gospel.

3 The sending of the Son

John describes the eschatological event of Jesus' coming as the
sending or giving of the Son (for example, 3:16–17) or as the
Son's descent into the world (3:13; 6:38), from which at the end
of his mission he ascends to the Father, first of all by means of
his death (12:32). John's statements that Jesus came to his own
(1:11) and that the word became flesh (1:14) are to be understood against the background of the descent – ascent motif.
Whereas in Mark Jesus is said to be the Son of God, and
obviously enjoys great dignity and plays the central role, his
being sent by God is not described in terms of descending and
ascending, and the same may be said of the other Gospels.
Perhaps closer to John in this connection is Paul's statement in
Galatians (4:4) that when the fullness of time had come, "God
sent forth his Son." Paul also can talk in terms that suggest
Jesus' descending and ascending (Philippians 2:5–11), but this
is not his usual way of describing Christ's mission. In later,
deutero-Pauline formulations, however, there are hints of
such a concept (Ephesians 4:8–10; 1 Timothy 3:16; 1 Peter
3:17–22).

It has been argued that the descent and ascent of the
redeemer is a motif taken by Paul and then by John from
gnosticism, but evidence of such a redeemer myth does not
antedate the New Testament, although the motif of gods'
descending to earth and ascending again is very ancient.[12] The
affinities between John and gnosticism are, however, extensive,
for in both there is a sharp dualism between this world and the
above, which is breached and bridged by the redeemer's
coming. The question remains, of course, whether the Gospel
of John is the product of such a gnostic view or rather represents the first major step in that direction. For our purposes,

---

[12] On earlier precedents see Charles H. Talbert, "The Myth of a Descending –
Ascending Redeemer in Mediterranean Antiquity," *NTS*, 22 (1976), 418–440.

however, the meaning and function of this redeemer myth are more important than its origin. Moreover, it is certainly the case that the epoch-making character of the coming of Jesus into the world, his advent as eschatological event, is well conveyed by the descent – ascent motif, which as it is used in John underscores Jesus' uniqueness.

The exaltation or translation of righteous men to heaven is a biblical idea going as far back as Elijah, and even Enoch. Elijah is said to have ascended in a whirlwind into heaven (2 Kings 2:11). It is said of Enoch that he was no more, for God took him (Genesis 5:24), which opened the door for speculation about his ascension. Thus we have the pseudepigrapha books of Enoch. The fact that Moses' tomb was unknown (Deuteronomy 34:6) apparently led to similar speculation about him.[13]

Furthermore, the descent – ascent motif is closely intertwined with early Christian belief about Jesus' fate and destiny. After his death and resurrection Jesus was raised to God's right hand (Acts 2:33). In the Gospel of John, Jesus already in his death returns heavenward, to the Father (12:32), so that his death can be called his being lifted up (Greek: *hypsoun*) and alluded to as the hour of his glorification (12:23). Apparently with forethought and intention John refers to Jesus' death with language that is ordinarily used of eschatological or apocalyptic victory.

The idea of Jesus' descending is obviously also related to his preexistence (John 1:1; Colossians 1:15–20; Hebrews 1:1–3), which is a logically prior idea, if not chronologically prior in its development. The one who is already in heaven must come down, as the Nicene Creed says: "Who for us human beings and for our salvation came down from heaven ..." While individual human beings do not come down from heaven in the Bible, or for that matter in later Jewish thought, personified wisdom – as we have seen – does. Not only is wisdom preexistent with God, and active in creation, but she descends from God to dwell among humankind (Sirach 24:1–34;

---

[13] On the death of Moses and speculation about his ascension see W. A. Meeks, *The Prophet-King: Moses Traditions and the Johannine Christology*, Supplements to Novum Testamentum 14 (Leiden, 1967), pp. 209–211.

Wisdom 9:9–10). Thus, as is frequently said by commentators, the prologue of the Gospel of John looks like the adaptation of a wisdom hymn for christological purposes. Also, while the idea of a human being descending from God to earth is at best extremely rare in Judaism, that of God's commissioning and sending forth a prophet is not. God's word, of course, typically comes to prophets in the Bible (Jeremiah 1:4), while in John's prologue Jesus himself appears as the incarnate word. Yet the difference only underscores how the prologue is enmeshed in biblical and Jewish thought, even as John 1:1 clearly begins in such a way as to evoke the first line of the Book of Genesis (1:1). Given the Jewish and Jewish-Christian milieu that has become increasingly evident as the background of the Gospel, it is altogether likely that its major christological motifs somehow originated there, perhaps to some degree in forms of thought or speculation later regarded as dangerous or heretical.[14]

The concept of the sending and the descent of the Son is closely paralleled by what is said of the word in John's prologue, even though the exact language of sending and descent – ascent is not found there. (Only the Baptist in verse 6 is said to be sent by God.) The word as light shines in darkness (verse 5), comes into the world (verse 6), comes to his own home (verse 11), and becomes flesh (verse 14). Therefore, when we read in the Gospel that God has sent his Son, who has descended from heaven, we are not at all surprised. The Jesus who appears in the Gospel narrative is entirely like the word who is made flesh in the prologue. In fact, the word or *logos* of the prologue is replaced by the Son of God in the body of the Gospel, as *monogenēs* (literally, "only begotten") in 1:18 already hints will happen.

4   *The character and theological significance of Jesus' ministry*

In John at least three temporal perspectives merge, yet are discernible and distinguishable. The revelation of God in Jesus

---

[14] In this connection one should consult the work of Alan F. Segal, *Two Powers in Heaven: Early Rabbinic Reports about Christianity and Gnosticism*, Studies in Judaism in Late Antiquity (Leiden, 1977).

is first presented in a *cosmic*, eternal dimension in the prologue. Yet the entire Gospel is written, and could only have been written, from the standpoint of a distinctly Christian and *postresurrection* perspective. But the interpreter should not lose sight of the *historical* perspective of this highly theological Gospel, if for no other reason than that the author emphasizes its importance. This last perspective has, however, two dimensions, the obvious one of the earthly, historical Jesus, but also the no less important historical dimension of the Johannine community, represented by Jesus' disciples. Thus the historical and postresurrection perspectives actually merge. Jesus, who was historically real, is now truly known only in light of his death and resurrection and in the struggles of the community of his followers. That is, the struggle of the Johannine (or Christian) church with its enemies is a continuation or broadening of the conflict in which Jesus ultimately laid down his life (cf. 15:18–19; 17:14). But the life of the disciples, or followers, of Jesus is assured. As he was with God in the beginning (1:1), so he is and will be with God eternally (17:24; cf. 14:1–3), and his disciples will be with him. He has overcome the world (16:33). The disciples are told that Jesus will lay down his own life to secure life for them (3:16; 6:51; 10:11; 11:50; 13:1; 15:12–13), and the evangelist clearly believes that he has now done this.

The Gospel of John then narrates the ministry of Jesus from the standpoint of his death and resurrection, as well as his cosmic role, and therefore with full knowledge of what we might call his theological significance. In this John does not so much differ from the other Gospels as it allows this Christian theological perspective to pervade the deeds and words of Jesus himself. We shall now consider the major aspects or themes of the Johannine account of Jesus' ministry, as well as what is missing from it, with a view to assessing their significance for the theology of the Fourth Gospel. John's characterization of Jesus' ministry might be described in the same general terms that would cover the Synoptics as well: Jesus gathers disciples, performs miracles, teaches, engages in conflicts with opponents, and is ultimately condemned to death and crucified. But the way in which John describes and nuances these activities and events is distinctive of his narrative style and theology. Theological themes arise from, but are inseparably related to, the account of Jesus' ministry. Earlier we observed how the distinctiveness of the Gospel of John and its theological interests emerge in the narrative (Chapter 2, B). Now we concentrate more directly on those interests and the theological themes themselves.

It is sometimes observed that there is no transfiguration scene in the Gospel of John because throughout this Gospel Jesus appears transfigured. This transfigured Jesus is, after all, the incarnate word of God. The prologue, particularly the statement that "the Word became flesh and dwelt among us" (verse 14), prepares the reader for the portrayal of Jesus and his ministry found in the Fourth Gospel. Thus, while this Jesus differs from the figure we encounter in the Synoptics, he differs in ways we have already been led to anticipate. In fact, the fourth evangelist is willing to identify Jesus not only with the word of God and to call him God's Son, but to say that he is himself *theos*, God (20:29; cf. 1:1,18). By identifying Jesus not only with the purpose and mission of God, but with his being, John goes a step beyond the other Gospels, and, indeed, the rest of the New Testament. Yet John does not allow the man Jesus, that is, his humanity, to fall out of sight. Nevertheless, his purpose is not simply to present or advocate Jesus' humanity, but to argue that in this man God was uniquely present.

a   John the Baptist and the gathering of Jesus' disciples
We have already observed that in John as in the Synoptic Gospels, Jesus' ministry begins with his encounter with the Baptist (always called simply "John"), who is less an eschatological figure (cf. his denial that he is the Christ, Elijah redivivus, or the prophet in 1:20–21) than a sheer witness to Jesus as Son of God (verse 34). Jesus can, if rarely, speak of himself as the Son in the Synoptics (Mark 12:32; Matthew 11:27), and the other evangelists describe him as Son of God (for example,

Mark 1:1,11; 9:7; 15:39), but only in John does Jesus repeatedly present himself as the Son of God or the Son, the latter usually a shorthand way of referring to the full title. Before the Baptist sends two of his own disciples to Jesus, he tells them – and the readers of the Gospel – that he is the "Lamb of God who takes away the sin of the world" (1:29; cf. verse 34) in what is probably an allusion to Jesus' coming death.

At the instance of the Baptist, Jesus begins to gather his disciples around him, but we are never given a list of who they are, and only later do we learn that they are twelve in number (6:67; but cf. Mark 3:16–19 parr.). Already the fact that the twelve are not named puts some distance between John and certain views of apostolic authority vested in a corps, and a core, of such disciples (cf. Acts 1:12–14,15–26). John will maintain the importance of a believer's direct and unmediated access to Jesus (4:42; 20:29). Nevertheless, for John, as for the other evangelists, the existence of this inner group of Jesus' disciples is an historical fact to be conjured with. Moreover, for John also the twelve constitute the core of the postresurrection church, even though Jesus apparently had other disciples (6:66).

The gathering of the disciples is tied into Jesus' encounter with the Baptist in a way that is unique to the Fourth Gospel, for only here does the Baptist send his own disciples over to Jesus (1:35–37). More attention is paid the Baptist in the Fourth Gospel than in any of the others, if only to make sure that the reader keeps him in his proper, subordinate place. Indeed, the fourth evangelist finds it necessary to declare at the outset that John was not the light, but came to bear witness to the light (1:8) and to have John, in his very first words, subordinate himself to Jesus (1:15, cf. verse 30). The concern to keep the identity of the Baptist in proper perspective accords with John's concentration upon the true and proper confession of Jesus as Messiah and Son of God. The Baptist, in fact, becomes the first human witness to Jesus as lamb of God (1:29,36) and Son of God (1:34), the one upon whom the Spirit of God has descended and remained (1:32), who himself baptizes with the Holy Spirit (verse 33).[15]

b Temptation and kingdom

John's account of the beginning of Jesus' ministry omits two features that characterize the Synoptic portrayal. Jesus is not tempted by the devil or Satan, and he does not announce that the kingdom of God is at hand. Both omissions are significant in that they say something about John's theology and christology, whether he omitted them knowingly or did not have them in his tradition.

The Jesus of John's Gospel cannot be tempted by Satan or anyone else. He will not even take cues provided by his mother (2:3–4) or his brothers (7:2–10), but marches to his own drumbeat. As far as Jesus is concerned, the ruler of this world (Satan) has already been cast out (12:31; cf. Mark 3:27; Luke 10:18). Even as Jesus is not tempted by the devil at the beginning of his ministry, so at the end he is not tempted to escape the trial and death set before him (but cf. 12:27). We do an injustice to the Gospel if we think that this Jesus is simply God striding across the earth. Nevertheless, the evangelist's postresurrection perspective, and the inspiration of the Spirit, authorize him to present the theological truth about Jesus as he was in his relationship to God.

There is also no reason for the reader to be surprised at the lack of any forthright proclamation about the onset of the kingdom of God, for John transposes the apocalyptic hopes and categories of Paul and the other Gospels into another key. Moreover, eschatology understood as God's acting in history with a view to bringing it to a culmination still provides the conceptual framework for the theology of Paul and the Synoptic authors, while with John there has been a fundamental

---

[15] Jesus had likely been baptized by John even as the Gospel witnesses assert. Interestingly, the Gospel of John does not report this baptism directly, and in Matthew the Baptist at first demurs from baptizing Jesus, suggesting that he himself needed to be baptized by Jesus (3:14). This actual relationship makes the Fourth Gospel's attempt to get the priorities straight quite intelligible and understandable.

change. No longer is christology interpreted with reference to an eschatology oriented toward the future. Rather eschatology is subsumed under christology, for the decisive, eschatological event, the coming of Jesus, has already occurred. The meaning of Jesus is not worked out against an apocalyptic, eschatological scheme, but rather the meaning of eschatology is redefined in light of the coming of Jesus.[16] Thus John's two departures from the Synoptic tradition at the beginning of Jesus' ministry are not only typical but pregnant with significance as keys to the Gospel's theology, and particularly its christology.

c *Signs*

As in the Synoptics Jesus comes forward doing mighty works, healing sickness and casting out demons, so in the Gospel of John he performs signs upon the sick, lame, blind, and dead. As he feeds a multitude and is seen walking on the water, the portrayal is very familiar; the chief difference is that the Johannine Jesus seems larger than life. Is Jesus now after all God striding across the earth? There is a sense in which he is, but again the interpreter must be careful not to read John in a one-sided way or, better, not to read only one side of the Johannine Jesus. Jesus performs astounding miracles, giving sight to a man who has been blind from birth and life to Lazarus, who has been entombed long enough for his body to decompose. This in addition to the fact that he is obviously in control of every situation, apparently omniscient and omnipotent. Yet this is only part of the story, for despite his performance of such deeds, Jesus does not win universal approval and acceptance as the emissary of God. The reality of his signs is sometimes contested (chap. 9), but even those who believe he performs such deeds and that they authenticate his claims (3:2) are not able to assess and appreciate him adequately.

The Johannine use of miracle tradition differs from the

---

[16] See E. Käsemann, *The Testament of Jesus: A Study of the Gospel of John in the Light of Chapter 17* (Philadelphia and London, 1968), p. 16: "Christology determines eschatology and eschatology becomes an aspect of christology."

Synoptic in a number of ways, and these differences are bound to have significance. Most important, the very designation of mighty works or miracles as signs suggests that they are intended to signify who Jesus is, as is indeed the case. Thus, after his first sign, Jesus' disciples believe in him (2:11). When he performs signs at a feast in Jerusalem, many believe in him (2:23). But at the end of his ministry, despite his signs, people are said not to believe in him (12:37). Near the end of the Gospel the reader learns of other signs Jesus did that are not recorded in it, and is told that these are recounted in order that the reader may believe that Jesus is the Christ, the Son of God, and in believing have life in his name (20:31). By way of contrast, in the Synoptic Gospels Jesus rejects the request for signs (for example, Mark 8:11–12), evidently as misplaced and misguided; and occasionally such a view of signs appears even in the Gospel of John (for example, 4:48). For the most part, however, John presents the signs of Jesus as if they ought to evoke belief in him. Indeed, the enigmatic prophecy of 1:51, which corresponds to no episode recounted in the Gospel, nevertheless prepares the reader for astounding events to come, principally the signs. Although John differs from the Synoptics in this respect, his use of signs is not entirely opposed to the Synoptic presentation, for in Mark, for example, the mighty deeds of Jesus clearly raise for his contemporaries, as well as for the reader, the question of who Jesus is.

The fact that the signs of John for the most part do not correspond to those in the Synoptics is surprising and doubtless significant. Most of the healing stories of Matthew and Luke correspond to, and are apparently the same as, the stories of Mark, from which they are probably drawn. Those in John are by and large different, with only the healing of the official's son (4:46–54) having a Synoptic parallel, but in Matthew (8:5–13) and Luke (7:1–10) only (seemingly a parallel from the Q source). One finds Marcan parallels only in the feeding of the multitude and the walking on the water, neither of which is a healing story. Although it has sometimes been thought that all John's healings are based on Mark or the

Synoptics, however much they have been transformed or rewritten, this is not obviously the case.

Did John use another, "sign," source? If so, what theological significance was attached to these miracles in the source? Such a source might have served originally as a kind of text for missionary preaching within the synagogue.[17] Perhaps the source represented a simple miracle faith, which John has seriously modified, if he did not oppose it. However that may be, if John did not modify Synoptic episodes beyond recognition, he evidently did draw these tales of Jesus' miraculous signs from some alternative narrative tradition or source. Curiously, this source would have contained no cleansing of a leper and no demon exorcism, or John decided not to use them. Avoiding demon exorcism stories may have been John's way of avoiding the charge that Jesus effected exorcisms by the power of Satan (Mark 3:22; cf. John 8:48–49). It is less obvious why there are no cleansings of lepers, except that they involve questions of ritual purity according to the law, in which John does not seem to be overtly interested (cf. Mark 1:40–45, especially 44).

Whatever their origin, the signs of the Gospel of John play a positive theological role in calling attention to Jesus' origin, power, and purpose. The very term "sign" recalls the Exodus tradition and the role of Moses, whom God empowered to work signs before Pharaoh. While merely to believe in the signs as miraculous deeds is not enough (2:23), to reject them is to reject Jesus' divine mission. In the Gospel of John no one who rejects Jesus' signs comes to him in faith. Anyone who believes the testimony of Jesus' signs (5:37) may go forward to deeper and theologically indispensable faith in him as God's Son, God's revelation. Jesus' signs are in this sense a preliminary revelation, for they require interpretation and understanding, which are given and made possible by Jesus' words.

The signs are also preliminary in another sense, for their

---

[17] This has long been the position of Robert Fortna, most recently set forth in *The Fourth Gospel and its Predecessor: From Narrative Source to Present Gospel* (Philadelphia, 1988), pp. 219–220. See also J. L. Martyn, *History and Theology in the Fourth Gospel*, rev. ed. (Nashville, 1979), pp. 12, 24, 65, 93f., 164–166.

proper and full interpretation waits upon Jesus' death and exaltation. The presentation of them in the Gospel is given from a postresurrection perspective, as Jesus' words are words of the risen and exalted Christ. Not that the evangelist manufactures them out of thin air. The only safe assumption is that he regards them as deeds Jesus actually performed, or at least as representative of deeds Jesus actually performed. Nevertheless, the evangelist was anything but naive about them. This is obvious not only from the substance and tenor of the Gospel, but from the intentional use of symbolic language to describe the revelation that the disciples will perceive in Jesus' historic ministry (1:51).

The sequence or arrangement of the signs clearly bespeaks a deliberate purpose and intention. The first, the wine miracle at the wedding feast in Cana of Galilee (2:1–11), is strange in that it differs from other miracles of Jesus in its character and setting and mysterious in that it seems to take place when no one is looking. The steward's reaction is to attribute unusual resourcefulness to the bridegroom (2:10), a typically Johannine misunderstanding in which a common-sense, worldly explanation overlooks the true, theological meaning. Moreover, that the best wine is kept until last says something about the appearance of Jesus in the economy of salvation. Toward the conclusion of the sequence of signs, Jesus gives sight to the man born blind (chap. 9) and raises Lazarus from the dead (chap. 11). In both cases Jesus' deed surpasses anything we read about in the Synoptic Gospels, but the reader misses the point if only their stupendous character is noted. These deeds are pregnant with salvific and theological meaning, for Jesus gives sight to people who do not see, but are not physically blind, and renders blind those who can still see with their eyes (cf. 9:39–41). He gives life to those who are in the tombs literally, while at the same time making it available to those who while alive physically are fated for death (5:24). That Jesus' gift of life to Lazarus (11:1–44) then leads directly to his enemies' plotting his own death (11:45–53) cannot be coincidental. The giver of life will be done to death. Thus Jesus' signs are rich with a symbolic meaning which the evangelist must have intended.

d   Words

The meaning of Jesus' deeds is made clear by Jesus himself: his words expand upon and reveal their meaning. Typically, Jesus declares who he is and debates with opponents his own status and role. That is, he makes straightforward christological assertions and defends them against attack. This is John's major departure from the Synoptic portrayal of Jesus, and indeed from the practice of the historical Jesus, insofar as we can recover it. Yet it is theologically significant that these christological words are placed on the lips of the earthly Jesus and integrally related to his deeds. This is John's way of anchoring christology in Jesus' ministry and affirming that this human Jesus really was the Son of God. (Later, gnostic gospels tended to put such revelatory words on the lips of the risen Christ.)

Typically, a sign of Jesus is followed by a dialogue between Jesus and interlocutors, usually opponents, and the dialogue often gives way to a monologue of Jesus. Thus in 5:1–9 Jesus heals the lame man and there follows a conversation between them (5:10–18), with the Jews' persecution of him noted at the end; whereupon Jesus launches into a long discourse (verses 19–47). In chapter 6 there is a much longer dialogue (verses 25–52) with a much briefer concluding discourse by Jesus (verses 53–58). The pattern has numerous variations, but with Jesus invariably having the last word, and Jesus' word is always about himself, his relationship to God and his work. While Jesus' works, particularly his signs, are greeted by amazement, and often by perplexity and disbelief except among his disciples, his words almost invariably lead some to hostile rejection, although the evangelist often goes out of his way to note that some believe (see, for example, 7:40–41).

Jesus creates division among people, and this division extends also to his disciples, some of whom fall away (6:66). Moreover, of those who do believe, some do not dare confess this openly for fear of the Jews (12:42). Therefore, the sharp dualism of the Gospel should not lead the reader to infer that people immediately fall into two well-defined camps of faith and unbelief. Ultimately they do, or they will, but John's

narrative reflects a more complex empirical situation. Nevertheless, the coming of Jesus is the judgment of this world (9:39;
12:31), even though salvation rather than judgment was the
purpose of his being sent (3:17; 12:47). So ultimately people go,
or are drawn, one way or the other. Clearly Jesus' true disciples
are understood to be the nucleus of the church that is to follow
him, and that later church occasionally breaks into view
(17:20; 20:29).

Jesus' words during the public ministry are for the most part
uttered in the presence of opponents who are identified as Jews
or Pharisees. They respond at best by puzzlement (2:20;
6:412–442), at worst by so sharply rejecting what Jesus has to
say that they seek to kill him (5:18; 7:19; 8:37,40; 10:31,39).
During his earthly public ministry, the disciples are at most
bystanders, and Jesus does not teach them at all. Any such
teaching is reserved for the Last Supper and farewell discourses. At the same time, his public words are directly relevant to
his disciples and carry a message for them, as well as for the
interlocutors in the narrative. Thus the great bread discourse
of chapter 6 is an exposition of Jesus as the bread from heaven
and the bread of life. Although given before Jews, who become
increasingly perplexed and even hostile, the discourse describes
the nature and benefits of salvation for Jesus' own followers.
Indeed, words of reassurance for the disciples are embedded in
this discourse (for example, 6:35–40). Typical of the relevance
of Jesus' words throughout the Gospel to the disciples is the fact
that the portentous "I-am" sayings are uttered during his
public ministry as well as in his private discourses.

The "I-am" sayings are distinctive and typical of the Fourth
Gospel, contrasting strongly with the sayings tradition in the
Synoptics, according to which Jesus was quite reticent in
discussing his own dignity and role. The Johannine Jesus
openly proclaims himself as "the bread of God ... who comes
down from heaven and gives life to the world" (6:33), as he
says, "I am the bread of life" (verse 35). By such I-am sayings
he also announces himself as the light of the world (8:12), the
door of the sheep (10:7), the good shepherd (10:11), the resurrection and the life (11:25), the way, the truth, and the life

(14:6), and the true vine (15:1). He implies, although he does not explicitly say, that he is the good wine (2:10), and announces that he is the source of living water (4:10–14). The predicates of such I-am sayings either name or symbolize the salvation that Jesus brings or his own salvific role. For the most part they draw upon biblical (Old Testament) imagery, although the symbols employed (bread, light, water, etc.) are so widely known and used in various religious traditions that it is difficult to identify a precise source. By the same token, they do not really need exposition or explanation. Each presupposes a human longing or need, for which Jesus is presented as the answer or fulfillment. Probably for this reason, because the symbols resonate so fully to human need, the I-am and related sayings have long captured the imagination of readers, who often have found, or seek to find, in Jesus the answer to their deepest needs and most profound questions.

In addition to the predicative I-am sayings, at several points the Johannine Jesus uses "I am" without qualification.[18] Sometimes it seems simply to mean "It is I" (6:20), as Jesus identifies himself, walking on the sea, to disciples in the boat. In response to the Samaritan woman's statement about the Messiah, Jesus answers, "It is I who am speaking to you," and thus identifies himself. The question arises, however, whether this solemn phrase means more than that, as when Jesus says, "Before Abraham was, I am" (*egō eimi*). Who is he? The *egō eimi* does not have an obvious antecedent in the immediate context, and it seems likely that the phrase itself, if not a title, implies a distinct role and dignity. Probably one should look to scripture, to the Old Testament, in order to understand what is implied about Jesus. Basically, two Old Testament backgrounds have been proposed, in each of which God identifies himself by saying "I am" (Septuagint: *egō eimi*). One is the Exodus scene in which God reveals himself to Moses at the burning bush as "I am that I am" (3:14; LXX: *egō eimi ho ōn*), a crucial point in the saga of Israel's Exodus tradition, the

---

[18] On these I-am sayings particularly, see Philip B. Harner, *The I-Am of the Fourth Gospel: A Study in Johannine Usage and Thought* (Philadelphia, 1971).

central event of deliverance in the Old Testament. The other is the recurring refrain of Second Isaiah in which the Lord identifies himself as the redeemer of Israel, evoking the atmosphere and imagery of the Exodus tradition. The Septuagint of Second Isaiah employs the same Greek phrase as the Fourth Gospel and the Book of Exodus, *egō eimi* (Isaiah 41:4; 43:25; 47:10; 48:12; 51:12; cf. 46:9; 48:17).

The redemption of Israel *per se* is not an explicit theme of the Fourth Gospel, not even in the sense in which it occurs at the end of the Gospel of Luke (24:21) and the beginning of the Book of Acts (1:6, where it is alluded to as a forlorn hope). As it stands, the Gospel of John has a distinctly individual and Christian focus. Nevertheless, certainly the major figures and also the themes of Israelite history play in the background, so to speak, as a kind of orchestral setting for the christological librettos and arias of the main theme of the Gospel's narrative and discourses. Thus the predicative *egō eimi* sayings draw upon Old Testament images, themes, and concepts to say who Jesus is: bread from heaven; the light of the world; the good shepherd; the vine.

The message that Jesus announces, his word or words (5:47), reveals the meaning of his coming and his deeds, but this meaning is in a very real sense retrospective, that is, one could not have known it prior to or apart from Jesus' death and resurrection. Thus the disciples, while they truly believe in Jesus during his earthly ministry (2:11; 6:67–68) and follow him (11:16), cannot understand him fully, as becomes apparent continually right up to the end of Jesus' farewell discourses (16:31f.). Obviously Jesus possesses the postresurrection knowledge that his disciples cannot have until "afterwards" (13:7). This is the knowledge that Jesus is not only the Messiah of Israel, but the Son of God, and that indeed he can and should be called *theos* (God). Thus not only Jesus' opponents, but his disciples repeatedly misunderstand him in a similar worldly or natural way, the former often with hostility, the latter simply with perplexity.

The typically Johannine *misunderstanding* of Jesus is more than a literary or rhetorical technique of the evangelist. It manifests in a dramatic way the world's inability to understand Jesus on its own terms. Thus the Jews reasonably think that Jesus means the temple building when he is really speaking of the temple of his body (2:20–21); Nicodemus takes Jesus to call for a natural rebirth, when he actually means being born from above (3:4); the woman of Samaria thinks that by living water Jesus is offering her a natural alternative to Jacob's well (4:15). In a more hostile vein, Jesus' Jewish opponents ask whether by his statement that where he is going they cannot come he means that he is going to kill himself (8:22). Obviously, in the Gospel's scenario, it is the Jews themselves who will do Jesus in. During the period of his public ministry Jesus' disciples, while sympathetic, do not fare much better. As yet they cannot really understand Jesus because the Spirit has not yet been given. The misunderstandings perhaps more than any other feature illustrate the evangelist's use of irony and its relationship to the Johannine conception of revelation.[19] Jesus, the evangelist, and the knowledgeable reader know who Jesus is and what he means in a way his own disciples – much less his opponents – during the period of his historic ministry cannot. As insiders to the distinctive message and language of the Gospel, they understand, while outsiders, however well-meaning, do not.[20] The reader (like Jesus and the evangelist) can see the message and ministry of Jesus from its end point and fulfillment and truly knows where Jesus has gone, and thus where he has come from.

So at the end of the main body of the Gospel, Thomas, who has doubted the testimony of his colleagues about Jesus' resurrection (20:24–26), when confronted with the risen Jesus who

---

[19] See especially O'Day, *Revelation in the Fourth Gospel: Narrative Mode and Theological Claim*, who emphasizes the importance of irony in the Johannine presentation of revelation.

[20] Perhaps the closest New Testament analogy to the insider–outsider language of John is Mark's parable theory (Mark 4:10–12). In Mark the disciples (and reader) are given the secret of the kingdom of God, while to those outside everything is in parables or riddles. See Werner H. Kelber, *The Oral and Written Gospel: The Hermeneutics of Speaking and Writing in the Synoptic Tradition, Mark, Paul and Q* (Philadelphia, 1983), pp. 211–220. With some reason, Kelber contends that the parable is the key to the Gospel genre – a view that the Gospel of John apparently supports.

possesses the stigmata, hails him not only as Lord but as God
(20:29, *Kyrios* and *theos*). The other disciples, having already
seen Jesus and received the Spirit (verses 19–23), already
possess this knowledge and can make this fully adequate confession of Jesus. As far as the disciples are concerned, they now
meet the description of them in Jesus' Great High Priestly
Prayer (chap. 17), a description for which their previous
behavior had not prepared the reader. As for Jesus himself, the
confession of him as God means that the narrative and the
reader have now come full circle, for what was said of the *logos*
in 1:1, namely, that the word was with God and the word was
God, is now confessed by Thomas as representative of the
disciples. The reader may infer, moreover, that Thomas' confession in 20:29 is prior to, or the basis for, the quasi-liturgical
statement of 1:1. That is, what is said in 1:1 about the word is
based on postresurrection knowledge and confession of Jesus.

e Death as glorification

The resurrection of Jesus, which of course presupposes his
death, is the precondition and basis of revelatory knowledge
about him. But apart from the death of Jesus there is no
resurrection, and therefore no revelation of God. The death of
Jesus is of crucial importance for John, as it is for Paul, Mark,
and the earliest Christian preaching, but in a somewhat different and distinct way.[21]

Paul, in citing an early kerygmatic formula, says that Christ
died for our sins according to the scriptures (1 Corinthians 15:3).
Mark's account of the eucharistic words of institution, followed
by Matthew and Luke, portrays Jesus speaking of his blood as
poured out for many (or for his disciples), an obvious allusion
to his death upon the cross, understood in cultic sacrificial
terms (Mark 14:24). Paul's tradition of the Lord's Supper has a
similar cup word (1 Corinthians 11:25), showing again that the

---

[21] On the death of Jesus in John, see J. Terence Forestell, *The Word of the Cross:
Salvation and Revelation in the Fourth Gospel*, Analecta Biblica 57 (Rome, 1974);
Donald Senior, *The Passion of Jesus in the Gospel of John* (Collegeville, MN, 1991);
and Godfrey C. Nicholson, *Death as Departure: The Johannine Descent – Ascent Schema*,
SBLDS 53 (Chico, CA, 1983).

interpretation of Jesus' death as a *vicarious sacrifice* was quite primitive. Paul, of course, develops the idea of Jesus' death as sacrifice in his own theological terms (cf. Romans 5; 1 Corinthians 1:18–25), while not concealing its more ancient, traditional basis (cf. Romans 3:24–25, as well as 1 Corinthians 15:3). We find this cultic sacrificial concept of the effect of Jesus' death also in 1 John (1:7; 2:2), as well as in the Revelation to John (1:5; 5:9; 7:14). Therefore, it is all the more surprising that such an understanding and interpretation of Jesus' death does not find a larger place in the Gospel of John. Yet several passages in the Gospel clearly allude to the primitive Christian interpretation of Jesus' death as a vicarious sacrifice: he is greeted as the lamb of God who takes away the sin of the world (1:29; cf. verse 34); out of his love God *gave* him (3:16; cf. Romans 5:8); Jesus gives his flesh for the life of the world (6:51); Jesus is said to die for the people (*hyper tou laou*), that the nation (*ethnos*) not perish (11:51). Moreover, the eucharistic language in 6:52–58 strongly suggests the participants' partaking of the redemptive benefits of Christ's death, and thus of his real humanity. It is noteworthy, nevertheless, that this language does not occur in the context of the passion narrative, as in the Synoptics and even Paul (1 Corinthians 11:23). Also in John's chronology alone, Jesus dies the afternoon of Nisan 14, while the Passover lambs are being slain. In the other Gospels, Jesus eats the Passover with his disciples. Yet John does not explicitly develop the idea of Jesus as Passover sacrifice (cf. 1 Corinthians 5:7).

Because John's interpretation of the death of Jesus does not develop the cultic sacrificial imagery more explicitly, it may seem that for the evangelist the death is not as important theologically as it is for Paul, Mark, and other New Testament writers. Nevertheless, in a somewhat different way and for different reasons, the death of Jesus is of fundamental theological importance in the Fourth Gospel. The Fourth Gospel seems to presuppose the more primitive view of the vicarious sacrificial effect of Jesus' death, as the related Epistle and Revelation suggest, but to express the vicariousness of that death by different means (see below, pp. 118–120). Compared to Paul, John focuses less upon issues having to do with how the specific mode of Jesus' death effected salvation on the analogy with cultic sacrifice, and more upon the nature of that salvation as revelation made possible through Jesus' death. Here John differs not only from Paul, but from the Letter to the Hebrews, which in important ways has affinities with, but differs from, both. Hebrews, more than any other New Testament book, explains *how* the death of Jesus is analogous with, but displaces, the sacrificial cult.[22] For John it is also important that Jesus displaces this cult, but this motif appears in the Fourth Gospel as Jesus' displacement of the temple generally (1:14; 2:19–22; 4:21–24), without specific mention of the cult or use of the sacrificial terminology.

John's perspective on, and presentation of, Jesus' death is directly related to his understanding of it as the key to the revelation of God in Jesus, the acceptance of which effects life eternal for the believer. John views that revelation as principally complete, seeing it in its totality and not focusing specifically on the mechanics (or, to a later perspective, mythology) of how that salvation took place. John's perspective, in which the revelation is complete, is at the same time an aspect of his so-called realized eschatology. For Paul, the believer is justified, but must await salvation (note the future tenses in Romans 6:5 and cf. 1 Corinthians 15:12–28); for John the believer has passed from death to life (John 5:24).

What, then, is the distinctive role of Jesus' death in the Fourth Gospel, and how does the evangelist express and underscore its importance? On the one hand, although it is evident that the evangelist knows the more ancient and traditional vicarious, sacrificial interpretation of Jesus' death, he accomplishes a representation or reminting of this perspective. On the other hand, the death of Jesus is important for John as the moment of his glorification, and this view of his death is quite different in purpose and function, while at the same time fundamental for John's understanding of revelation. Through

---

[22] See Barnabas Lindars, *The Theology of the Letter to the Hebrews*, New Testament Theology (Cambridge, 1991), pp. 86–98 especially.

his death Jesus brings life, but only after his death is its significance known.

The vicarious nature of Jesus' death, in the sense that he died for, and instead of, his followers, is more than once made clear. At his arrest Jesus identifies himself to the arresting party and tells them to let the others, his disciples, go (18:8). Presumably he will die in their stead. As Jesus instructs his disciples to love each other as he has loved them (15:12), he gives concreteness to the nature of this love by defining its extremity as laying down one's life for one's friends (verse 13). This, of course, is exactly what Jesus himself will do. Probably the basic, salvific meaning of Jesus' washing of his disciples' feet is that it symbolizes his vicarious death for them.[23] The footwashing is the most humble service, usually performed by a slave, and certainly not performed by the superior upon his inferiors or servants. Nevertheless, Jesus performs this humble service for his disciples. Peter cannot abide this seeming status reversal, and his initial rejection of Jesus' offer requires the Lord's stern remonstrance to be overcome (13:6–10). There is a remote, but nevertheless striking, affinity between this episode and the confession of Peter in Mark's Gospel (8:27–33), for there Peter recoils from Jesus' prophecy of his coming death and Jesus rebukes him sharply.

John's most extensive presentation of Jesus' death as a vicarious sacrifice occurs in the so-called parable (Greek: *paroimia*) of the good shepherd (10:1–16), which culminates in Jesus' identification of himself with this figure. Of course, this good shepherd is the one who lays down his life for his sheep. The discourse is typically Johannine, not only because it contains the predicative *egō eimi* saying ("I am the good shepherd": verses 11,14), but because it is at first cast in enigmatic language that only the insider could understand. Of course, the Johannine Christian, or anyone with knowledge of the Christian message, would know that Jesus is here not talking about a

---

[23] See now John Christopher Thomas, *Footwashing in John 13 and the Johannine Community*, JSNTSS 61 (Sheffield, 1991), pp. 94f., citing C. K. Barrett, *The Gospel According to St. John: An Introduction with Commentary and Notes on the Greek Text*, 2nd ed. (London and Philadelphia, 1978), p. 441.

mere willingness to sacrifice his life. Rather, these statements
are made with his specific sacrificial death in view. By the time
the Gospel was written Jesus had already died for his sheep.
The vicarious, self-sacrificial character of Jesus' death is clear
enough; what is missing is the cultic language of the sacrificial
altar. Apparently, John has chosen to present the old message
in a new and different mode. Possibly he does this because at
the time of his writing the temple was already gone from the
scene, destroyed by the Roman army in AD 70. Whether or not
this was the case, both the traditional roots of John's thought
and his imaginative reworking of them are very much in
evidence.

John's distinctive understanding of Jesus' death comes most
clearly to expression in his presentation of it as Jesus' being
glorified (*doxazein*) and lifted up (*hypsoun*). Jesus' death is the
hour of his *glorification* (7:39; 12:16; 12:23; 13:31, etc.), in which
his glory and the glory of God are revealed. Glory is an
eschatological theme in the New Testament: "When the Son of
Man comes in his glory, and all the angels with him, then he
will sit on his glorious throne" (Matthew 25:31). That is, it is
associated with the end-time as conceived in apocalyptic
thought. The idea of being lifted up, exalted, is in John
integrally related to glorification. Instead of saying repeatedly
that the Son of Man must suffer, as the Synoptic Gospels do,
John speaks to the same purpose of the Son of Man's being
lifted up (3:14; 8:28; 12:32). Thus the concepts of glorification
and exaltation are used of Jesus' ignominious death in a
manner that can only be called paradoxical. This is altogether
typical of the insider language of the Fourth Gospel: the
Christian reader will understand Jesus' or the evangelist's
references to the hour of his glorification or exaltation as
allusions to his approaching death. When this is understood,
the theme of Jesus' death, far from being a mere vestige of
tradition, is seen to pervade the Gospel (cf. 1:11; 1:29; 2:4;
2:17–22; 3:14–16, etc.).

The traditional term for the time of Jesus' death, the "hour"
(Greek: *hōra*), recurs throughout the Gospel (2:4; 4:21; 5:25,28;
7:30; 8:20; 12:23). In the Synoptic tradition Jesus in Geth-

semane prays that he may be delivered from "the hour" of his coming trial (Mark 14:35), but with the approach of the arresting party, he knows that the hour has come (verse 41). Later, as the moment of the actual crucifixion arrives, the third, sixth, and ninth hours are tolled (Mark 15:25,33,34). The term "hour" is not, however, used in Mark of Jesus' death until the Gethsemane scene. By way of contrast, its use in John from the very opening episode of Jesus' ministry is a means of narrating the whole ministry from the perspective of Jesus' death, or with the death in view.

While it is true that John does not describe Jesus' death as his suffering (cf. Mark 8:31; 9:12; Hebrews 12) or humiliation (cf. Philippians 2:6–11, especially verse 8) any more than he makes use of the sacrificial language of the altar, the evangelist's presentation is best understood as assuming such a natural human understanding but going beyond it, because he intends to present Jesus' death as the revelation of God's glory. Theologically perceived, Jesus' death is the crucial moment of God's revelation and judgment in and through him, shedding light upon his own ministry, so that it can be properly understood, even as it opens the way to the future as the time of the risen and ascended Christ (cf. 20:17) and of the Spirit-Paraclete who continues and extends his revelation. It is no happenstance that John's precise description of the moment of Jesus' death differs from the Synoptics by virtue of its deliberate ambiguity. In a neat play on words Jesus is not said simply to expire or breathe his last (Mark 15:37; Greek: *exepneusen*), but to give up (or give over) his (or the) Spirit (John 19:30; Greek: *paredōken to pneuma*). The allusion to the coming of the Holy Spirit can hardly be missed.

The early traditional and Pauline theological theme of the crucifixion of Christ as the point and means of God's redemption of humanity is then not lost in John. Rather, it becomes an underpinning of his distinctive view and presentation of Jesus' whole ministry as the revelation of God's judgment and of his gift of eschatological life: judgment against those who reject him (chaps. 2–12; cf. especially 1:11; 3:19; 9:39; 12:37–41, 48), but life for those who believe (1:12–13; 3:16–18; 12:44–47, 49–50).

As we have already noticed, it is certainly not by coincidence that Jesus' restoration of Lazarus to life (11:1–44), anticipated in Jesus' earlier eschatological discourse (5:25), is followed immediately by the priests' plotting against Jesus' own life (11:45–53). By this narrative connection the Christian conviction of the life-giving character of Jesus' own death is subtly but unmistakably suggested. Jesus' life and his life-giving work culminate in his own death, but only because of and through that death is Jesus able to give life. Moreover, that death is the prism through which Jesus' life and work can be seen for what they are, and thus it is the critical point of the revelation of God through Jesus Christ his Son. The description of Jesus' death as exaltation and glorification is a way of underscoring its revelatory character.

Thus the concept of glory (Greek: *doxa*) in the Fourth Gospel is intimately connected with revelation and with Jesus' death. Of course, in the Bible generally, glory is an attribute or quality that belongs to God. Isaiah is said to have seen the divine glory (12:41), obviously an allusion to the theophany scene of Isaiah 6:1–13.[24] When John writes of the incarnate word (Jesus Christ) that "we have beheld his glory" (1:14), it is amply clear that he is alluding to the divine aspect of his being and to its revelation as such. When Jesus himself says that the hour has come for the Son of Man to be glorified (12:23), he is pointing ahead to his own death, now viewed as imminent (cf. verses 24–25), and to his death understood as revelatory event: "Father, glorify thy name" (12:28). Glory is the quality of God as God. In the Old Testament the glory of the Lord is his impressive manifestation, even the physical phenomena associated with his presence (Exodus 24:15–18). Particularly in the Exodus tradition the glory of the Lord is associated with his revelation of himself as God, so that Moses can pray "to see thy glory" (Exodus 33:19).

This background and the revelatory connotations of glory are therefore evident in the Fourth Gospel, and particularly in

---

[24] On John's use of Isaiah, see F. W. Young, "A Study of the Relation of Isaiah to the Fourth Gospel," *ZNW* (1955), 215–233. G. Kittel, *doxa*, *TDNT*, II, pp. 2328f., notes the association of the term with revelation in the Old Testament.

the prayer of Jesus in chapter 17. In this so-called Great High
Priestly Prayer Jesus asks God to glorify him even as in his
earthly ministry Jesus has glorified God (17:1, 4). Moreover,
Jesus asks to be glorified in God's own presence "with the glory
which I had with thee before the world came to be" (verse 5).
The glory which Jesus receives from God, and with which he
glorifies God, is ultimately passed on to his disciples (17:22).
Jesus has given the glory to his disciples by manifesting God's
name to them. The name of God, like his glory, is God's reality,
his real presence, as it is manifest to humankind. The crucial
factor in this manifestation is the ministry and death of Jesus
himself.

So Jesus redefines glory, even the glory of God. In his words
and deeds he reveals God's glory (2:11), as his enigmatic
statement to his newly gathered disciples indicates he will
(1:51), and in his death he covers himself with God's glory
even as God gives him glory (12:23; 17:1). In his death as
glorification Jesus revises the meaning of glory and glorification, for God's glory is found precisely in Jesus' death. Thus
when he gives his disciples his God-given glory, he unites them
with himself and with God (cf. 17:22). This is not a union of
being abstractly conceived, but a union of mission: as God has
sent Jesus, so he sends the disciples (20:21). The nature and
content of that mission are defined by Jesus himself in his
amplification of the love commandment (15:12–13), for as
Jesus has loved his followers unto death (cf. 13:1), so they are
to love one another (13:34; cf. 1 John 4:7–12). The icono-
clastic Jesus of the Synoptic tradition overturns the conven-
tions and expectations of his contemporaries, but the revo-
lutionary Jesus of the Fourth Gospel goes even farther by
redefining in a thoroughgoing way what is meant by the glory
of God. Furthermore, John makes the astonishing claim that
Jesus' death reveals the glory of God – the revelatory manifestation of God – and that this glory has existed from the
foundation of the world (17:5,24). John's concept of glory is at
once traditional and radical doctrine, that is, traditional
doctrine placed in a radically new light by the death and
resurrection of Jesus.

f Resurrection

It has been said that in John nothing is added to the revelation of the glory by the resurrection of Jesus, for what Jesus accomplished he accomplished through his death.[25] Indeed, as has been noted, the dying Jesus already transmits the Spirit to his disciples. In fact, the resurrection of Jesus adds nothing theologically to what has already been accomplished through his deeds, words, and death. At the same time, none of it would count as revelation and deliverance apart from Jesus' resurrection from the dead. The resurrection allows Jesus' ministry and message to be seen for what they were, and are. Jesus' resurrection means for John, as for other early Christians and the New Testament writers generally, that God authenticates Jesus as his Son. Already in 2:19–21 the Gospel points us forward to the resurrection, understood as Jesus' assertion of his own authority and mission (10:17f.). It goes without saying that the resurrection is indispensable for the validity or truth of the claims made for Jesus (cf. 1 Corinthians 15:12–14). It is also the case, however, that in the farewell discourses (chaps. 14–16) John allows his thought and teaching about the resurrection to merge with the other traditional motifs of the Holy Spirit and Jesus' coming again.

In the way John handles and presents the resurrection narratives, we see a subtle and not unsophisticated view of the nature of the resurrection and how its truth may be appropriated. While in Luke Jesus shows his wounds, invites his disciples to handle him, and eats fish to show that he is not merely "a spirit" (Luke 24:39–43), in John there is a differently nuanced emphasis in a similar scene. Thomas, when invited to touch Jesus' wounds as proof of the reality of the risen one – or of the identity of the risen one with the crucified Jesus – confesses: "My Lord and my God" (20:28). We are not told whether he actually touched Jesus, although most readers probably assume that he did. Touching *per se* seems to miss

---

[25] For example, by Bultmann, *Theology of the New Testament*, II, p. 56: "If Jesus' death on the cross is already his exaltation and glorification, *his resurrection* cannot be an event of special significance. No resurrection is needed to destroy the triumph which death might be supposed to have gained in the crucifixion."

John's point, however, for Jesus immediately comments (verse 29): "Have you believed because you have seen me? Blessed are those who have not seen and yet believe." Similarly, the risen Jesus tells Mary Magdalene not to hold (or touch) him, for he has not yet ascended to God (20:17). Tangibility may not be the risen Jesus' most important quality.

Jesus breathes the Spirit upon his disciples (20:22), endowing them with his authority (verse 23; cf. Matthew 16:19; 18:18), having just enjoined them to continue his own God-given mission (verse 21). Finally, after Jesus has appeared to his disciples on the Sea of Tiberias (Galilee), in a scene reminiscent of the Synoptics (21:1–14; cf. Luke 5:1–11; Mark 14:28; 16:7), he carries on a pastoral conversation with Peter, who has so recently denied him (21:15–23). Obviously, Peter is reinstated as a leader of Jesus' disciples, literally as pastor (i.e., shepherd) alongside the enigmatic Beloved Disciple. No new theological themes are introduced, but the evangelist uses traditional narratives to show the fulfillment of Jesus' earlier promises to his disciples and to underscore theological points. The reality of Jesus' resurrection is affirmed, through and with tradition, in distinctively Johannine ways.[26]

5   Other christological titles

In our treatment of Johannine christology we have not begun with a study of titles, because the titles accorded Jesus in John, mostly traditional, do not determine the shape and character of Johannine christology.[27] If anything, the opposite is the case. That is, the distinctive Johannine christology lends meaning to the titles. For that reason, we have dealt first with

---

[26] Ashton, *Understanding the Fourth Gospel*, points out the relative lack of sophistication of John's resurrection stories, indeed, their "fairy tale atmosphere" (p. 511): "It is like finding Hans Christian Andersen hand in hand with Søren Kierkegaard." Yet, as I have briefly indicated above, John is using resurrection traditions for his own purposes, and not simply lapsing into fairy tales.

[27] Leander E. Keck has trenchantly and effectively shown the inadequacy of approaching christology through an examination of titles: see his "Toward the Renewal of New Testament Christology," *NTS*, 32 (1986), 362–377, especially 368–370.

the characteristic Johannine motifs of Jesus' origin, the sending of the Son, his descent and ascent, and his relation to the Father. Of course, Christians believed Jesus to be the Messiah or Christ of Jewish expectation, and, as we have seen, John thought it important to establish that point while at the same time radically revising the concept of messiahship itself in light of the career and death of Jesus of Nazareth. In fact, all major New Testament writers both affirm Jesus was the Messiah and revise the concept in light of his unique ministry. The expected Messiah was to be the king of Israel, the heir of the Davidic line; and while John, in contrast to Matthew, Luke, and even Paul, makes nothing of Jesus' Davidic sonship – not even to call him Son of David – he does have him called king of Israel (1:49; 12:13), and his kingship becomes a major theme of the Gospel.

a *Rabbi, prophet, and Elijah*

Among traditional Jewish titles applied to Jesus in John we find also rabbi, prophet, and possibly Elijah. In the case of rabbi (see above, pp. 91–93) and prophet the titles as used in the Gospel often imply an underestimation of who Jesus is (for example, 1:38 for rabbi and 4:19; 6:14–15 for prophet). Yet they are not wrong. Jesus was truly a rabbi or a teacher (1:38), as well as a prophetic figure. Jesus the prophet was not so much a figure like Amos or Hosea, pronouncing God's judgment against a wayward Israel, as he was the prophet like Moses promised in Deuteronomy 18:15–22, that is, a second edition of Moses, Moses redivivus.[28] The figure of Jesus issuing commandments to his followers in the farewell discourses is reminiscent of this prophet of God (Deuteronomy 18:18): "I will put my words in his mouth and he shall speak to them all that I command him."

An important aspect of the Johannine, indeed, all the Gospels', portrayal of Jesus that does not coincide with traditional messianic expectations is his miracle-working activity.

---

[28] On the relationship of Johannine christology to Moses and Mosaic traditions in later Judaism and Samaritanism, see the works cited above in Chapter 2, n. 14, and especially Meeks, *The Prophet-King: Moses Traditions and the Johannine Christology*.

Generally speaking, the Davidic Messiah was not expected to be a miracle worker.[29] Why, then, was Jesus portrayed in this way? One answer that is doubtless correct as far as it goes is that Jesus actually performed mighty works (Greek: *dynameis*) of the sort attributed to him in all the Gospels. His opponents challenge him on the basis of his authority or of the source of his remarkable powers, but do not contest the deeds themselves (Mark 3:23). But such miracle working, particularly the working of signs (Greek: *semeia*), the specifically Johannine term, also belongs to the Mosaic Exodus tradition. Moses, of course, performed miraculous signs before Pharaoh to authenticate his divine commission, which is also what Jesus' signs were intended, in a different historical setting, to do (see Exodus chaps. 4–11 especially). Thus the expected prophet like Moses would also perform signs. Jesus would then be the fulfillment of the expectation of the prophet like Moses as well as of the Davidic Messiah. Not by chance Moses is mentioned a dozen or more times in the Fourth Gospel, more than Abraham, Jacob, or David. Although Jesus' specific role may be related to that of the Mosaic prophet, Jesus is not identified with Moses, but rather placed over against him. This does not mean, however, that Moses, properly understood, is opposed to Jesus. Rather, Moses wrote about Jesus and accuses his opponents (cf. 5:45–47).

Jesus' miracle-working activity seems also to be related to Elijah and Elisha traditions. For example, in the feeding of the five thousand (6:1–15) John alone mentions a small boy with five barley loaves, and in 2 Kings (4:42) Elisha feeds a company of one hundred men with twenty barley loaves. Both Elijah and Elisha are said to have raised the dead to life (1 Kings 17:17–24; 2 Kings 4:32–37), even as Jesus did (John 11:1–44; cf. Mark 5:38–43; Luke 7:11–17). Moreover, at the beginning of John's Gospel John the Baptist is asked whether he is the Christ, Elijah, or the prophet (1:25), and he denies that he is any of these in turn. Since John the evangelist certainly held that Jesus was the Christ, and probably also the

---

[29] See Martyn, *History and Theology in the Fourth Gospel*, pp. 95–100, 110f.

prophet, it is worth asking whether he took him to be Elijah as well.[30] Why else would John the Baptist refuse to accept the title in the Gospel of John, whereas in Matthew (17:10–13) Jesus says quite clearly that John was Elijah? Was the title being reserved for Jesus at an earlier stage of the tradition? In this connection it is worth noting that in the Synoptic tradition Jesus is said by some to be Elijah (cf. Mark 6:14–15), and precisely because of his miracle-working activity. That the fourth evangelist took Jesus to be Elijah redivivus remains uncertain, but some such speculation may underlie the Fourth Gospel. We are, however, now pushing at the boundaries of messianic and related expectation. The christological titles of central importance for John, aside from Messiah (Christ), are Son of Man and Son of God. As we already observed, *kyrios*, Lord, as a christological term is notable for its absence. Interestingly enough, although Jesus is said to be the Messiah or Christ at the very outset of the Gospel of John (1:17,41), he never arrogates this title to himself. When he is asked explicitly whether he is the Christ (10:24), he gives a somewhat evasive answer. In this respect there is a striking agreement with the Synoptic tradition.

b Son of God

"Son of God" is, of course, a traditional christological title, found frequently in Paul's Letters, but also in the Synoptic Gospels and elsewhere. Often it is abbreviated simply to "Son" (for example, Mark 13:32; John 5:19; Galatians 4:4), usually in such a context that it is clear that Son of God (rather than Son of Man) is meant. Already in the Old Testament the anointed king, the Messiah, is said to be God's Son (Psalm 2:7; 89:20–27; 2 Samuel 7:13–14), and the attribution of such sonship to the Messiah was known to the Qumran community.[31] Perhaps it is not necessary to look beyond the Old Testament scripture and

---

[30] As is suggested by J. L. Martyn, *The Gospel of John in Christian History* (New York, 1978), pp. 9–54. But cf. Marinus de Jonge, "John the Baptist and Elijah in the Fourth Gospel," in R. T. Fortna and B. R. Gaventa (eds.), *The Conversation Continues: Studies in Honor of J. Louis Martyn* (Nashville, 1990), pp. 299–308.

[31] See Geza Vermes, *The Dead Sea Scrolls in English*, 3rd ed. (London, 1977), p. 294.

its ancient Jewish interpreters to find the origins of the Son of God title. (In fact, the attribution of divine sonship to kings and rulers was not uncommon in the ancient world, so that the Roman Emperor could be called Son of God, and there were more ancient precedents.[32]) Yet its prominence in the early church can scarcely be explained on this basis, for "Son of God" is not a characteristic title of the Jewish Messiah.

Of course, if the Gospel of John could be viewed as an historical document, presenting the *ipsissima verba* of Jesus, the origin of this Christian usage would be clear enough: Jesus spoke of himself in this way. But precisely such language from Jesus poses the question of the nature of the Johannine account, if for no other reason than that the title is not usually found on Jesus' lips in the Synoptic Gospels and their under-lying traditions. More characteristic, however, is Jesus' use of the term "Father" for God, which is, of course, rooted in biblical and Jewish tradition. A notable example is the Lucan version of the Lord's Prayer (Luke 5:2), in which Jesus addresses God simply as "Father." Not without reason an earlier generation of theological scholarship spoke of Jesus' God-consciousness, and it is not unlikely that the language of later christology has roots in that of Jesus, as well as in the Jewish and biblical tradition. Yet such roots do not explain the development of the concept of divine sonship as a christological category in Paul and John. And while it was once thought that John built upon Pauline usage, this can no longer be easily assumed; both Paul and John relied on earlier, widespread Christian tradition.

That Jesus was named Son of God at the resurrection from the dead (Romans 1:4; Acts 13:33) is probably accurate his-torically, in that it was from, or after, this point that the crucified Jesus' disciples began to refer to him in this way. Psalm 2:7 ("You are my son, today I have begotten you") used of Jesus' resurrection may have paved the way (Acts 13:33; cf. Hebrews 1:5). There is a basis in the Gospels of Matthew and Luke for linking Jesus' divine sonship to the miracle of his

---

[32] See W. von Martitz, *huios*, *TDNT*, VIII, pp. 336f.

conception and birth. Mary is his mother, but God, through the Holy Spirit, begets him without human paternity (Luke 1:35). John, however, if he knew the birth traditions, made nothing of them. (Nor do Paul, Mark, or Hebrews make use of – or appear to know – the birth narratives or traditions.)

Clearly in the Gospel of John, as in Paul, the title "Son of God" expresses Jesus' close unity with God, as it does elsewhere in the New Testament. But John goes further in refining the nature of this unity and restricting it to Jesus, who is said to be the "only" or the "only-begotten" (*monogenēs*) Son of God (1:14,18; 3:16,18). In later christological debates in the ancient church, emphasis fell on the latter half of the Greek word, on Jesus' begottenness, while in contemporaneous Greek usage it fell on the former, "only." In either case, John thereby signals the uniqueness of Jesus' relationship with the Father. Characteristically in John, when this relationship is being presented, "Son of God," or "Son," is the title used.[33] The Father loves the Son (3:35; 5:20), who accomplishes the life-giving work that he sees the Father doing (5:19). To honor the Son is to honor the Father, that is, God (5:23). The unity of the Father and the Son is thus expressed in terms of love and mission. As the Son Jesus addresses the Father in his final prayer and makes this unity quite explicit (17:20–26, especially verse 23). This unity in love and mission is then extended to include Jesus' disciples, that is, the church (cf. 14:21; 15:9; 20:21), and mutual love becomes the ground and basis of the church's existence (13:34–35; 15:12–17).

In the theological, and specifically christological, debates of the fourth and fifth centuries the language of unity between Father and Son, which in the Fourth Gospel had expressed their mutual love and the character of the Son's mission and work, was interpreted ontologically and metaphysically as the question of the nature of that unity was explored.[34] Sub-

---

[33] On "Wisdom," "Word," and "Son" see James D. G. Dunn, *Christology in the Making: A New Testament Inquiry into the Origins of the Doctrine of the Incarnation*, 2nd ed. (Philadelphia, 1989), especially pp. 213–215, 263–265.

[34] For this development see T. E. Pollard, *Johannine Christology and the Early Church* (Cambridge, 1970).

sequently, the character of the coexistence of God and man in Jesus Christ became the focus of discussion, and it too was debated and decided in metaphysical terms. These doctrinal debates and the creeds that emerged from them went beyond anything said in the Fourth Gospel itself, but it would be a mistake to think that they represent the imposition of a completely unrelated set of questions and issues upon that Gospel. Only the Johannine Jesus says, "I and the Father are one" (10:30), and Jesus as Son speaks of his unity with the Father as something grounded in eternity (17:5,24). At the beginning John writes that the word was with God and the word was God (1:1), and at the end Jesus is confessed as Lord (the traditional *kyrios* title) and God (*theos*) by Thomas (20:28). Although John does not engage in metaphysical exploration or ontological construction, the kinds of christological controversies that arose later and drew upon his terminology, and seemingly his conceptuality, were not a misrepresentation of John's own purpose and intent, which cannot be adequately dealt with under functionalist or existentialist categories. The fact that John so consistently centers all talk of God and knowledge of God in the revelation of Jesus as God's Son, and therefore the definitive and exhaustive revelation of God, lends to this fundamental perspective an authoritative role in interpretation. John obviously intends to make far-reaching, extravagant, and extreme claims about who Jesus is, and the interpreter must let him. The fourth- and fifth-century controversies were in their own way an effort to do this also.

That the other christological creeds and controversies concerned with the deity of Jesus Christ or his place in the Godhead did not misrepresent the language and intention of the Fourth Gospel is underscored by the fact that at a couple of crucial points Jesus is, in fact, called God (*theos*). The first is, of course, in the opening line of the prologue (1:1): "and the word was with God and the word was God." Secondly, in the final resurrection scene of chapter 20, Doubting Thomas calls the risen Jesus "my Lord and my God." It is likely significant that the earthly Jesus does not claim the divine title, as often as he asserts his sonship, and that the evangelist reserves it for the preexistent and the risen Christ. Therefore, it does not seem appropriate to treat "God" as a christological title. Nevertheless, it is important to remember that in his role as revealer Jesus Christ is from the standpoint of the believer equivalent to God in that he definitively and finally reveals God and is thus the only true access to God (14:6). Moreover, Jesus emphasizes his unity with God in mission and work. In fact, all the titles point to this reality.

c Son of Man

The Son of Man title differs from "Son of God" in its background in Judaism and early Christianity, but whether it has a different function and meaning within the Gospel of John is a good question. "Son of Man" is the enigmatic title or epithet by which Jesus refers to himself in the Synoptic Gospels, and the problem of the Son of Man sayings in those Gospels has become notorious. They divide themselves into sayings in which Jesus predicts the suffering of the Son of Man, obviously himself; those in which he speaks of the authority of the Son of Man on earth, again obviously himself; and those in which he speaks of the future epiphany of a supernatural figure, traditionally taken to be his own "second coming." In addition there are other scattered references to the Son of Man, sometimes clearly references to Jesus himself (for example, Matthew 16:13), sometimes not necessarily so (Luke 9:58).

As to their assessment of these sayings, scholars can be grouped in several camps. Some think Jesus used the term only for the future, coming Son of Man, who was someone other than himself. Others take only the authoritative Son of Man sayings to be authentic. Still others think Jesus simply used the term as a common periphrasis for "I myself." Finally, some doubt that Jesus used the term or title at all. This last position seems doubtful if only because the turn of phrase is so pervasive in the Gospels, and occurs almost always on the lips of Jesus himself rather than on those of his disciples or interlocutors.

Most scholars assume that the Johannine Son of Man is derivative from the Synoptic, although this may not be the case.[35] The common point between Johannine and Synoptic usage is the fact that the term is used by Jesus of himself, not by others. The so-called apocalyptic Son of Man sayings are represented only once in John (5:27), where the function of holding judgment is said to have been assigned by God to the Son of Man. Otherwise, the title Son of Man does not seem to coincide with a particular function of Jesus' ministry or with a role or status not otherwise dealt with in the Gospel of John. A number of the Johannine Son of Man sayings have to do with Jesus' crucifixion/glorification (3:14; 8:28; 12:23,34; 13:31) and with the related theme of his descent and ascent (1:51; 3:13; 6:62). Therefore, they present Jesus as the revealer of God, so that Jesus can ask the man whose sight he has restored whether he believes in the Son of Man (9:35). The Son of Man gives the bread from heaven (6:27); indeed, his flesh *is* this bread from heaven (6:51).

Apparently, the meaning and function of the Son of Man title in John stands closer to Johannine christology generally than to the several uses of the term in the Synoptic Gospels. Thus it would be difficult to speak of a Son of Man christology in the Gospel of John that stands out distinctly from a Son of God christology. Although "Son of Man" frequently occurs where Jesus' historical, revelatory role, especially his death, is set forth, those aspects of his ministry are also associated with the title "Son of God," or with no title at all. Nevertheless, it is probably not inaccurate to say that "Son of Man" is associated more with Jesus' historic, revelatory work, and "Son of God" with his relationship to the Father. On the other hand, it would certainly be misleading to suggest that in the Gospel of John "Son of Man" is associated with Jesus' human nature, while "Son of God" refers to his divine nature. As the one who reveals God to people, Jesus is *theos* (1:1,18; 20:29). At precisely

---

[35] R. Bultmann, *The Gospel of John: A Commentary* (Oxford and Philadelphia, 1971), derives the Johannine Son of Man from the Gospel's gnostic source (cf. especially p. 105, n. 3; p. 149, n. 4). Delbert Burkett, *The Son of Man in the Gospel of John*, JSNTSS 56 (Sheffield, 1991), argues that it is rooted in scripture, particularly Proverbs 30:1–4. Burkett also presents a valuable discussion of "Son of Man" in Johannine scholarship (pp. 16–37) and of the crucial questions pertaining to it (pp. 38–50).

the points at which Jesus is portrayed as the historic revealer, whether through word, deed, or death, he is transparent to God. Truly to see him is to see who God is.

6 *Jesus' relationship to God*

At the same time, Jesus is careful to define his relationship to God in such a way as to exclude the charge that he has usurped divine prerogatives. "I and the Father are one" (10:30) means that Jesus is completely subject to the will and purpose of God, to carry out the mission that God has given him. "As the Father has sent me, so also I send you," says the risen Jesus to his disciples (20:21). There is an important sense in which Jesus' commission is no different from his disciples'. He too is subject to God's command.

At the point at which he is accused of making himself equal to God (5:18), Jesus does not deny the charge, but says that he only acts at the Father's behest. He only does what he sees the Father doing (verse 19). Then he goes on to describe his work of raising the dead, giving life, and holding judgment (verses 21–29). Prerogatives that scriptural and Jewish tradition have reserved for God Jesus claims for himself. But he denies that they are his independent prerogatives, and insists rather that they have been given him by the Father (verse 30): "I can do nothing on my own authority; as I hear, I judge; and my judgment is just, for I do not seek my own will but the will of him who sent me."

This dispute (John 5) doubtless reflects the fear and accusation that the role ascribed to Jesus in the Johannine community is a threat to monotheism. From the perspective of anyone who does not believe that God in Jesus has acted or revealed himself in a new and definitive way it doubtless seems such a threat. Understandably "the Jews" accuse him of blasphemy for making himself, a mere mortal, equal to God (10:33). How could they think otherwise? Thus questions that are quite reasonable are posed to Jesus. "You are not greater than our Father Jacob, are you?" asks the Samaritan woman (4:12), or, "You are not greater than our Father Abraham, are

you?" the Jews ask (8:53). Both questions in Greek expect
a negative answer, as my translation shows, but both press
Jesus to define the nature and source of his authority. The
highest human authority within scripture or Judaism, Moses, is
invoked on the side of Jesus (5:45–47; cf. 1:45), and the question is how shall Moses be understood. Clearly the Jews or
Pharisees are unwilling to grant Jesus the witness of Moses.
Rather, one must choose between them (9:28).

To the end Jesus views his work and mission as acceptance of
the authority and commission of God. As he dies he says, "It is
finished" (19:30), meaning that he has completed the work
that God gave him to do. Moreover, as Jesus delivers his final
prayer to God, and to the reader of the Gospel (chap. 17), he
characterizes his entire mission and work as obedience to the
mandate that was given him (verse 4): "I glorified thee on
earth, having completed the work that thou gavest me to do."
Jesus does nothing of his own accord. But obviously God speaks
to him in a direct or unmediated way. Who else is privy to such
divine revelation? The answer, in John's view, is no one. So
how, if at all, can the claim be verified – or falsified? It cannot
to everyone's satisfaction. That is, it is impossible to prove the
merit or truth of Jesus' claims, or the claims made for Jesus,
although his signs or works are introduced to bear powerful
testimony (5:36). Of course, John the Baptist has borne testimony (5:33), along with scripture (5:39ff.). But John's authority was debatable (cf. Mark 11:29–33), and the right interpretation of scripture was the crux of the disagreement. The
Father himself has borne testimony, but his work must be
mediated through persons and events on the human scene.
Even if God speaks directly, his word can be mistaken for
thunder (12:29), so fallible are human ears.

On the other hand, how can Jesus' claims, or the claims of
Jesus' followers, be disproved? One may maintain that they
represent a strong misreading of the Hebrew Bible. From any
point within the Bible that would seem to be the case, but the
very point of the claim is that a new vantage point has been
given, outside scripture, so to speak, from which scripture and
tradition must now be interpreted. That claim is supported by

the witnesses mentioned above (5:30–47), as well as by the testimony of the Spirit speaking to and within the community of Jesus' disciples (14:12–14,26; 16:12–15). Moreover, the love of the disciples for one another (13:34) attests the validity of Jesus' mission and message, and the solidarity of the community in love will persuade the world of the validity of the claims made for Jesus (17:21–23).

Of course, the claim that Jesus was the Messiah in any traditional or conventional sense would seem to be refuted by his execution as a criminal or blasphemer. But such a refutation is met by the interpretation of that very death as the expression of God's love (3:16), which underlies all human love. In the eyes of early Christians that expression of love speaks powerfully on the side of the truth and validity of their claims. These Christians, and especially the members of the Johannine community, saw in Jesus' perfect fulfillment of the commission and love of God in his ministry and death the model for their own lives and relationships (John 15:12f.; cf. 1 John 4:7–12). The seemingly exalted christology of the Fourth Gospel presents a Jesus who is God's perfect, in the sense of final or complete, revelation. Yet he does not base that claim on his own authority, but on God's, and his validation of the claim takes the form of obedient self-giving, love, toward his fellows and followers. It is the kind of validation that they can experience and share. Indeed, if they really believe the claim they will manifest this love, and in the only way possible will prove the claim to be true.

C THE REVELATION OF THE GLORY TO THE COMMUNITY

Beginning in chapter 13, at the Last Supper, and continuing through chapter 17, Jesus' prayer, the disciples are constantly in view. In chapters 18 and 19, as Jesus goes to his arrest, trial, condemnation, and death, there is once again a public scenario and Jesus is, as he had predicted (16:42), abandoned by all his disciples except the Beloved Disciple, who is the model of discipleship. But the concluding, resurrection scenes find Jesus and his disciples once again alone together. Thus the latter half of the Gospel consists of Jesus' ministry to his disciples, and it is truly the revelation of the glory to the community.[36]

As we have seen, however, the words Jesus speaks publicly (chaps. 2–12) are also revelatory words, or they become such for the community. For Jesus' disciples now view his entire ministry from the standpoint of his glorification and under the guidance of the Holy Spirit. They have attained not only faith, but a knowledge that was earlier inaccessible to them as well as to Jesus' opponents. Thus the two additional presuppositions (above, pp. 79–80), which have actually been present all along, now come into the foreground, namely, the *church* as the community of Jesus' disciples in the period after his departure, and the *Holy Spirit*.

The church remains, however, a presupposition of Johannine theology, for one can at most *infer* a doctrine of the church. Yet it is hazardous to infer too quickly from what is said, or omitted, the conception of the church underlying the Gospel or its concrete nature and organizational structure. For example, do the absence of a list of the twelve disciples or Apostles and the omission of the term and concept of apostleship imply that their authority was somehow diminished for the fourth evangelist? Does the fact that the individual disciple must relate directly to Jesus (15:1–8) mean that church officers or hierarchy were of no importance theologically? Does the absence of any command to baptize or celebrate the eucharist mean that John's church was without sacraments? Quite possibly John's concept of the church is that of a community with no hierarchy, formal organization, or sacraments and inspired by the Spirit. But it can also be argued that John omits to mention what is assumed and that his sacramental language and his emphasis on the importance of an authoritative witness to Jesus (1:14; 21:24, cf. 19:35) point in an entirely different direction. Clearly the Gospel of John is

---

[36] See Bultmann, *The Gospel of John: A Commentary*, p. 457, for this title. Bultmann used the German *Gemeinde*, rightly translated "community" rather than "church."

focused not upon ecclesiology, but upon christology, about which the evangelist has a great deal to say, much of it fresh and distinctive. That the church as the community of Jesus' followers is not so much discussed but presumed and allowed to emerge by indirection is an important characteristic of the Fourth Gospel. The church is, in a real sense, the *sine qua non* of Johannine theology, the indispensable ground or background. What John writes about the Holy Spirit or Paraclete and what Jesus says to, and commands for, the disciples will allow its character to emerge – perhaps not so much what the Johannine community was as what it should be. This is what happens in the Gospel and presumably what should be allowed to happen in any treatment of the theology of the Gospel.[37]

One thing that can be quite confidently said about the church in John's conception is that it is grounded upon faith in Jesus. In no other Gospel is the disciples' believing in Jesus given quite the prominence it has in the Fourth Gospel. The fact that having faith, believing in Jesus, receives such strong emphasis in John's Gospel is of a piece with its explicit christology, expressed in Jesus' words as well as his signs. Oddly, the noun "faith" (Greek: *pistis*) occurs not at all in the Fourth Gospel, but the verb (*pisteuein*) occurs many times, as often as it does in any of the Synoptic Gospels, and more often even than in Paul. (Perhaps not coincidentally, the noun *gnōsis*, knowledge, is also absent, although the verbs *ginōskein* and *eidenai* occur fairly frequently.) It is as if John wishes to emphasize the act of believing. The characteristic Johannine expression is "to believe in Jesus" (Greek: *pisteuein eis*). (Paul is more likely to use *pisteuein* without an object to mean faith in Jesus Christ.) Apart from belief in Jesus, there can be no valid talk about God or believing in God. To believe in Jesus is to believe in God as Jesus revealed and defined him. But John can also speak of

---

[37] On the ecclesiology of John, Eduard Schweizer, *Church Order in the New Testament*, SBT 32 (London, 1961), pp. 117–136, still represents the predominant position, namely, that John reflects a relatively undeveloped ecclesiology, especially with regard to church organization and office. Cf. Käsemann, *The Testament of Jesus*, pp. 27–32 especially, who essentially agrees with Schweizer.

being born again, and Jesus can tell his disciples that they did not choose him: rather, he chose them (15:16).

While the Gospel of John presupposes the church and presents it indirectly, the disciples as representative of the church are the subject of direct attention and discussion. Not only are their election and faith important themes, but so too is their obedience (see below, pp. 146–149). The true disciples of Jesus obey his commands, particularly the command to love one another (13:34f.). Such love is, of course, a reflection, indeed an extension, of Jesus' love for them and ultimately of God's love. Discipleship, and therefore the church, are impossible concepts apart from obedience to Jesus' love command. Again, if one focuses upon the theme of election, discipleship and church seem to be an inevitable result of God's decision. On the other hand, if one focuses on faith and obedience, everything seems to depend upon the individual's decision and behavior. The paradox is typical, not only of John, but of biblical thought generally.[38]

There is no question that for John the formation of disciples is a matter of fundamental importance. It is one way of bringing the church into the center of attention. Believing obedience is the essence of discipleship and the church. John will talk about the mutual indwelling of the disciples and Jesus (for example, 15:1–11), but such union with Jesus and with one another (17:20–25; cf. 1 John 1:3) is on the human side dependent upon the disciples' obedience to Jesus' love command.

Thus even the intimacy of the model Beloved Disciple with Jesus (for example, 13:23) must not be isolated from the dynamic of faith and obedience. Such intimacy is more than a mystical quality. Moreover, the Beloved Disciple's relationship with Jesus also grounds the community in an historic, as well as theological, relationship with its founder (21:24; cf. 19:35; 1:14; also 1 John 1:1–4). Apart from such an historic relation-

---

[38] See the illuminating remarks of Ed P. Sanders, *Judaism: Practice & Belief 63 BCE–66 CE* (Philadelphia, 1992), pp. 249–251; also his *Paul and Palestinian Judaism*, pp. 257–270, in which he deals with election (and free will) in Qumran, where the parallels with John are significant and obvious.

ship with Jesus of Nazareth, discipleship and the church are quite inconceivable.

1 Spirit-Paraclete

As we have just observed, John has two ways of describing how one becomes a disciple of Jesus Christ: by faith as an act of human allegiance and will; or by God's own action, whereby he chooses one and grants birth from above. From the one side it is a human act of faith in what God has done, but the explanation of how such faith can occur exhausts human possibilities and requires the invocation of God's initiative through the work of the Spirit (3:5–8). That becoming a disciple of Jesus, entering his community, entails baptism is altogether probable (3:5). Not only the Baptist but Jesus himself is said to baptize (3:22; 4:1; but cf. 4:2). As in the case of the eucharist, however, John assumes the sacrament without reporting Jesus' institution of it.

The postresurrection perspective assumed by the evangelist allows him to direct his Gospel to the setting of the early church in a way that is unique. This perspective is not merely given by distance in time. The Gospel of John is retrospective in outlook, but in more than an ordinary sense. The view or interpretation of Jesus given in this Gospel is the work of the Holy Spirit. For John, as well as for Paul and for other early Christians, the work of the Spirit was an important and fundamental aspect in church life, but John articulates a perception of the Spirit's work that is unique to him.

John makes clear that full knowledge and understanding of who Jesus is can only come with his resurrection (2:22) or glorification and the advent of the Spirit (7:39). The work of the Spirit or Paraclete is then laid out in advance and in some detail in the farewell discourses (14:15–17,26; 15:26; 16:7–11,12–15), but one has the impression that the community is already familiar with the Spirit's work, indeed, that the activity of the Spirit among Jesus' disciples is a given for the author of the community. But the Spirit is not simply a presupposition of the Gospel's theology, for the Johannine Jesus says quite explicitly what the Spirit of truth, the Paraclete, will do. Thus one can speak of a concept or doctrine of the Spirit in the Gospel of John.[39]

The greatest problem in understanding the concept of the Spirit in the Fourth Gospel has been the term Paraclete itself, which is used consistently in the farewell discourses whenever the Spirit is mentioned, and only in this Gospel and 1 John. The Greek *parakletos* is derived from the verb *parakalein*, which has several meanings ranging from "summon" (to the side of) to "comfort" or "console." The abstract noun *paraklesis* can mean "encourage" or "comfort" among other things; thus the KJV renders *parakletos* "comforter." The RSV's "Counselor" is probably closer to the intended meaning, however, for outside the Johannine literature *parakletos* frequently meant "advocate" (one called to the side of). Indeed, such a meaning is appropriate for 1 John 2:1 ("We have an advocate with the Father"), and NRSV renders *parakletos* in the Gospel also as "advocate." In one way this rendering seems appropriate, since the Spirit of truth when first introduced is called "another *parakletos*," implying that Jesus was the first (14:16). Yet the actual function of the Spirit-Paraclete as set forth in chapters 14–16 is not so much to represent the disciples before the divine tribunal (as in John 2:1) as to represent Jesus to his disciples left behind on earth. The Spirit-Paraclete speaks to the question of how Jesus will continue with his disciples or church during his physical absence from them. In effect the Spirit-Paraclete continues and interprets the ministry of Jesus himself, and thus is appropriately called "another Paraclete." This Paraclete is given to the community of disciples and to them alone as a permanent Counselor (14:16–17) to teach the disciples "all things," and recall for them what the earthly Jesus had earlier said (14:26). The surest guide to understanding the Paraclete is the description of its functions in the Gospel itself.

A tension is apparently set up between the function of

---

[39] On the concept and work of the Spirit in John the most comprehensive recent treatment is Gary M. Burge, *The Anointed Community: The Holy Spirit in the Johannine Tradition* (Grand Rapids, 1987).

bringing to mind or bearing witness to Jesus (15:26) and delivering a further teaching, for Jesus also promises that the Paraclete will tell the disciples things they cannot yet bear (16:12) and thus will guide them into all truth (verse 13). But the Paraclete is not, like the risen Jesus of gnostic revelation discourses, a purveyor of hidden revelations that could never be imagined on the basis of Jesus' teaching during his ministry. Rather, what this Spirit expounds to Jesus' followers is the truth he already represented, as it is appropriate for their own time, which from the standpoint of Jesus' ministry is future (16:13–15). The coming of the Spirit is anticipated at a number of points in Jesus' public ministry, where the narrator of the Gospel looks forward to the time when the disciples will remember and, presumably, understand what Jesus has said or done (for example, 2:22; 12:16) or when Peter will know or understand what Jesus has done for him in washing his feet (13:7). This fundamental function of the Spirit-Paraclete, to call to remembrance, is set out against the background of Jesus' assurance, "I will not leave you desolate: I will come again to you" (14:18), and Judas' question, "Lord, how is it that you will manifest yourself to us, and not to the world?" (verse 22). When Jesus has been crucified and is risen from the dead, he does what he has promised and bestows the Spirit upon his disciples (20:22; cf. 19:30).

It would be inaccurate to represent the Fourth Gospel as merging the resurrection of Jesus, the coming of the Spirit, and the return of Jesus into one event, for the evangelist can obviously distinguish among them. Yet the fundamental theological reality to which they point is the same, namely, Jesus' continued presence with his disciples after the death that terminates his physically mediated relationship with them. Another, new, relationship is created with his resurrection and ascension (cf. 20:17; 20:27–29). Crucial to this relationship is the manifestation of the Spirit as a living presence. How this spiritual presence was mediated to the community is a question that goes beyond the scope of New Testament theology *per se.* Certainly, the effect of the Spirit was felt in the preaching of the church and in its community life, probably also through the work of specially endowed or spiritually inspired leaders.[40]

Significantly, the risen Jesus' gift of the Spirit to his followers (20:22) stands between his statement that as the Father has sent him (in mission), so he sends the disciples (verse 21) and his words about forgiving and retaining sins (verse 23). The Spirit is taken for granted as inspiring and guiding both mission to the world and inner-church life. The Matthean counterpart to John 20:23, the saying about binding and loosing (Matthew 18:18; cf. 16:19), is followed quickly by Jesus' promise to be present with his disciples "where two or three are gathered in my name" (Matthew 18:20), a promise that clearly applies to the postresurrection period and, in Johannine terms, implies the presence of the Holy Spirit. John articulates what is implied or assumed elsewhere in the New Testament, that is, the working of the Spirit as the continued presence of Christ himself to his church for mission and for community.

The Spirit is Jesus' presence to strengthen and encourage the disciples, or the church, and is not to be thought of as if it were some additive to a redemption and revelation already given. The Spirit is the renewed action and presence of God by which what happened with Jesus and his disciples in the first place is made known as revelation. Only the advent of the Spirit interprets what has happened as God's revelatory, and therefore saving, work. Thus the unity of the revelation, indeed the revelation itself, is incomplete and lacking, awaiting the advent of the Spirit. Only within the ambit of the Spirit's life and work does Christ live for the believer, and correspondingly, only there does the Christian or the church live and know who she is. The revelation of God in the historic, public ministry of Jesus before the world is paralleled by the revelation of God in the Spirit-Paraclete's ministry among the community of his disciples, whereby he makes known to them, as the post-resurrection church, who this Jesus truly was. Undoubtedly

---

[40] See above, n. 4, and note especially Woll, *Johannine Christianity in Conflict*, pp. 109–128. The role of charismatic leaders is also stressed by Paul S. Minear, *John: The Martyr's Gospel* (New York, 1984), pp. 12ff. and passim.

Jesus' disciples did believe in him during his earthly, historic ministry in some real, if inchoate, way – as the Gospel of John indicates. Yet the disciples' knowledge and understanding of which the Gospel speaks (see especially 14:4–7; 15:15) comes only with Jesus' glorification and gift of the Spirit. Then they know who he is because they know that he has come from God; they know Jesus' true origin. (Even when the disciples claim such knowledge during Jesus' earthly ministry, as in 16:30, Jesus makes clear that they do not yet know whereof they speak.) The sending of the Son is paralleled by the sending of the Spirit. Even as the Son's ministry is judgment to those who do not believe, and causes their previous innocence before God to become sin (9:39–41; 15:22–24), so the Spirit's coming convicts the world of sin, righteousness, and judgment (16:8–11), not by direct inspiration or communication, but through the witness of believers on behalf of Jesus Christ. Clearly, therefore, John presents the Spirit-Paraclete as the successor of Jesus who carries on his revelatory work, sustaining the disciples after the rupture represented by Jesus' death.

The unique role assigned the Spirit in the Gospel of John is to a considerable extent paralleled by the role of the Spirit in the Pauline Letters. But John's teaching about the Spirit as Paraclete is scarcely paralleled in the other Gospels. All the Gospels, however, connect John's baptism of Jesus (or, as in the Fourth Gospel, his encounter with him) with the descent of the Spirit upon Jesus himself (John 1:32–33 parr.). In all the Gospels Jesus is designated as the one who will baptize in the Holy Spirit, in contrast with John who baptizes in water, but only in the Fourth Gospel is Jesus' Spirit baptism directly connected (by John the Baptist) with the descent of the Spirit upon him as a dove. Of course, in some contrast to the Synoptics, in the Gospel of John the Baptist himself relates all this. It is Luke's Gospel, however, that portrays Jesus himself as the bearer of the Holy Spirit (4:18), although in John Jesus once speaks of his own endowment with the Spirit (3:34), seeming thereby to take up and confirm the Baptist's word about the Spirit abiding upon him. In any event, the endowment of Jesus with the Spirit at his own baptism is pretty clearly a motif John takes from tradition he shares with the Synoptic Gospels, although with the talk of the Spirit's abiding on Jesus, he gives to his narrative a distinct and characteristic turn. John's principal teaching about the Spirit, however, concerns his role as Paraclete and successor to Jesus.

2   *Unity and community*

As the Spirit effects the continuance of Jesus' ministry among his disciples, so it is only with the Spirit's presence that the disciples as a community become one with Christ. The theme of Jesus' final great prayer of chapter 17 is the disciples as the object of Jesus' ministry. After the proem of the prayer (verses 1–5), in which Jesus declares the completion of his earthly work and prays for glorification, he intercedes for his disciples (verses 6–19), as well as those who will come after (verses 20–26). During the first part of the prayer, Jesus sums up his ministry of the word to his disciples, who have been given him by God (verses 6–8). That Jesus is glorified in them (verse 10) means that he is revealed in and through them, even as Jesus is himself glorified by revealing God in his death (verses 1,5). Those who belong to Jesus believe initially through his word, even as their successors will believe through the word about Jesus that they will speak (verse 20). They differ from Jesus in that they remain in the world as he goes to the Father (verses 11,15). Otherwise, however, there is a remarkable parallel between their destiny and Jesus' (verses 11,14,16–19).

When Jesus turns to pray for the future church as well as his disciples, he asks that they may be one with him even as he is one with the Father (verse 21). This is, as we might have expected, a unity in glory (verse 22), inasmuch as God reveals himself in the Son, so both Father and Son make themselves known in the believers. The end or purpose of this unity is mission, that the world may know and believe (verses 23,21) – here knowledge and belief amount to the same thing. It goes without saying that this prayer for unity includes his contemporary, as well as future, disciples. The key to the unity for which Jesus prays is love (verse 26). Jesus first commands the disciples to love one another (13:34), goes on to say that people will recognize them as disciples by their love, and then prays that the divine love may be in them (17:26). The goal is the unity that also binds together Father, Son, and believers, and such unity or community (1 John 1:3) belongs to the essence of the church. One might even say that it is the church.

When Jesus speaks of the mutual indwelling of Father, Son, and disciples (17:21), the substance of that unity is love (17:26; cf. 14:21,23). When Jesus speaks of the disciples' abiding in him and uses the parable of the vine to portray that relationship (15:1–8), the key to that unity is again love (15:9–10), and Jesus immediately defines love as the kind of self-sacrifice that he himself will display (verses 12–13). There is a wonderful coherence between unity and love, as well as in the way in which the Gospel portrays and, indeed, relates them to other aspects of what we may call – invoking the Apostle Paul's terminology – the new being in Christ (2 Corinthians 5:17).

Whether it is correct to characterize the Gospel's themes of unity, oneness, and love as mysticism is a question that has sometimes troubled the interpretation of the Fourth Gospel. (Certainly Christian mystics have often based themselves in these passages.) Paul, of course, speaks frequently of being in Christ (Greek: *en christō*). The exegesis of an earlier era spoke of the Christ-mysticism shared by Paul and John, and the question of mysticism in John has recently been revived.[41] A theologically informed exegesis unwilling to obscure the distinction between God and the world or God and man once regarded talk of mysticism as misguided and misleading. Certainly the Fourth Gospel knows and respects the difference between the Father and the Son, on the one hand, and human beings, whether believers or unbelievers, on the other. Moreover, faith itself is the essential ingredient of discipleship, whether in coming to Jesus or abiding in him, although the instances of the verb "to believe" (*pisteuein*) do decrease after chapter 12, as

---

[41] See Albert Schweitzer, *The Mysticism of Paul the Apostle* (New York, 1931), especially pp. 334–375. Cf. quite recently L. William Countryman, *The Mystical Way in the Fourth Gospel: Crossing over into God* (Philadelphia, 1987).

more is said about the disciples' abiding in and with Jesus. A believing relation to the Son, and through him to the Father, involves more than simply acknowledgment or even obedience. Believers enter into a new being, a new existence; they are reborn from above, and such imagery implies the reality of a new state and new relationship. Thus talk of mysticism in the Fourth Gospel is not misplaced or misleading. The status of the believer is, of course, dependent on continuing faith and obedience to Jesus.

3 *Love as the commandment of Jesus*

Unity with Jesus, and with the Father, is living one's life in, and on the basis of, love. The believer is loved by the Father and the Son, loves them in return and as an expression of this love keeps Jesus' commandments, which can be summarized as the one new commandment, to love one another (13:34). That not all disciples obey Jesus perfectly is clear enough: Peter denied Jesus, Judas betrayed him, and other unnamed disciples drew back from him (6:66). These episodes all occurred within Jesus' historic ministry, but doubtless reflect what can happen among his disciples at any time. Yet the expectation that Jesus' disciples will obey his commandment to love one another will not be disappointed, for in keeping this commandment they will demonstrate who they are.

It is important that what Jesus commands of his disciples is what he himself has done. Jesus, having loved his own in the world, loved them to the end (13:1). As the good shepherd he lays down his life for his sheep (10:11,15). In enjoining his disciples to lay down their lives for one another, he asks them to do no more than he will do, or has done, for them (15:12–15). Jesus himself lays down his life for his disciples, who are his friends. They show that they are his friends by keeping his commandments, and Jesus treats them as friends rather than servants by taking them into his confidence: "All that I have heard from my Father I have made known to you" (15:15). Thus Jesus' relationship with his disciples is characterized by a certain mutuality in which Jesus nevertheless maintains the priority or primacy.

This relationship is aptly symbolized in the figure (*paroimia*) of the vine (15:1–8), in which Jesus as the vine obviously provides the essential support and sustenance for the disciples, who are the branches. As branches, they are not simply passive, but must bear fruit of love or suffer the pain of excommunication. That the abiding of the disciples in the vine (verse 4) means abiding in love is immediately made explicit in the monologue of Jesus (verses 9–11) that follows the figure itself. The fruit of the branches is, of course, love; the command to love (verse 17) is the command to bear fruit. Jesus' love commandment may be compared to his teaching in the Synoptic Gospels.

In each Gospel Jesus issues a commandment of love. In response to the questioning scribe (Mark 12:28–34 parr.), Jesus gives the "second" commandment: "You shall love your neighbor as yourself," taking up the words of Leviticus 19:18. (The first commandment is, of course, the Shema: Deuteronomy 6:4.) In the Sermon on the Mount, Jesus commands love of enemies, as well as neighbor (Matthew 5:44; cf. Luke 6:35). Paul twice takes up the command to love the neighbor from Leviticus 19:18 (Romans 13:9–10; Galatians 5:14) and says that it is the fulfillment of the law. Perhaps strangely, he does not derive it from Jesus, although it is often argued that Jesus or the Jesus tradition was his source.[42] In any event, the command to love the neighbor is prominent, and one might think central, in the New Testament, so that it is not surprising that we find it in John, where it also appears to sum up Jesus' teaching aptly.

John is then similar to other New Testament writings, but

---

[42] For the view that Paul was extensively dependent upon the Jesus tradition see, for example, W. D. Davies, *Paul and Rabbinic Judaism: Some Rabbinic Elements in Pauline Theology*, 4th ed. (Philadelphia, 1980), pp. 136–145. Victor P. Furnish, *The Love Command in the New Testament* (Nashville, 1972), p. 61, is much more cautious, but allows that "the earliest New Testament formulation of Jesus' teaching on loving enemies is probably to be found in Paul, Rom. 12:14: 'Bless those who persecute you; bless and do not curse them' (RSV)."

with distinct and significant differences. In the first place, the
love command in the Synoptics, and even in Paul, stands in the
midst of a host of traditional sayings, parables, or concrete and
specific injunctions among which it finds a congenial place. In
other words, it summarizes a point of view which is otherwise
expressed more concretely and specifically. In the Gospel of
John, however, it stands more or less alone, as Jesus' one
command, and this is true of 1 John as well. Although the
Johannine command to love can be viewed as a summation of
Jesus' (or the New Testament's) teaching, it is as such the
summation of a teaching found elsewhere in the New Testament, but otherwise not in the Fourth Gospel except as love,
especially the love of God, may be said to characterize Jesus'
entire ministry.

In the second place, while in the Synoptics the focus of
the love command is outward, toward neighbors and even
enemies, in John it is inward, toward and within the community: Love one another. The command of mutual love within
the community does not necessarily exclude or negate the
broader scope of love envisioned by the Jesus of the Synoptic
tradition and by Paul, but there is a difference of focus and
emphasis. This difference coincides with a central theme of the
Fourth Gospel, where, as we have already observed, love serves
the interests of unity between Jesus (and God) and his disciples
and among the disciples. Love of the fellow disciple or fellow
Christian builds the unity of the community or church, which,
of course, is a major goal of the Fourth Gospel (cf. 17:20–26).
The achievement of unity among the disciples is essential to
their unity with God and Jesus Christ (17:21) as well as to their
successful witness to the world (17:21,23). It belongs to the
very character and essence of the revelation of God in Jesus
Christ (cf. 14:21–24; 1 John 1:3): that is, it is not just a
desirable but dispensable by-product of that revelation. The
love of God and Jesus Christ for one another may be real
enough in itself, but it has no tangible or perceptible reality in
this world, and therefore no witness, apart from the love of the
disciples for one another. While the nature of that love is not
spelled out through specific injunctions in the Gospel, in 1 John

it is defined not only as a willingness to lay down one's life (3:16; cf. John 15:12–13), but as supplying the fellow Christian's need for the essentials of this life (3:17).[43]

4　*Life as eschatological gift and goal*

The eschatological goal, the essence of salvation, according to the Fourth Gospel is life (Greek: *zōē*), or eternal life (*zōē aiōnios*). While the eschatological life which God imparts through Jesus Christ occupies an important place in other New Testament books (cf. Matthew 19:29; Romans 6:23), it is particularly prominent in the Gospel of John and 1 John (John 1:4; 3:14–16; 20:30; 1 John 1:1–2).

Exegetes have often observed that according to John eternal life is not only the object of future hope, but already a present possession (5:24; 11:24–25).[44] This is certainly true, but one should also remember that the overcoming of death applies first of all to physical death (5:28–29; 11:1–44) and that the possession or gift of eternal life in the believer's present existence is integrally related to the assurance of its permanence (14:1–4; 17:24). The Johannine community exists under the felt presence of dire or mortal threat (16:2), and the believer knows that his or her life is already safe with God. This assurance is an implication of the concept of unity or oneness that has already been discussed, for such unity implies a sharing of the life of Christ in God. John does not with 2 Peter (1:4) speak of believers' being sharers (Greek: *koinōnoi*) of the divine nature, for "divine nature" is a concept he does not employ, either of Jesus Christ or the believer. Both are fully human. Yet both through union with God come to share in the life of God, which is the only real life there is, and that life is

---

[43] On the seeming limitation of the love command in John see Bultmann, *The Gospel of John: A Commentary*, pp. 524–527. He maintains that limitation has to do with Jesus' unique relationship to the circle of believers who are the recipients of revelation, but "the world always has the possibility of being included with the circle of the *agapan*" (p. 528). Cf. Furnish, *The Love Command in the New Testament*, pp. 139f., 143–148.

[44] Bultmann, *The Gospel of John: A Commentary*, passim, but esp. pp. 257ff., 402–404; Barrett, *The Gospel According to St. John*, pp. 261f., 395f.; Brown, *The Gospel According to John* (i–xii), pp. 218f., 434.

present and permanent. Moreover, the believer is born from above (3:3ff.); born of God (1:13). Interestingly enough, the Gospel of John does not use the hope language that is fairly common elsewhere in the New Testament (*elpis, elpizein*), but disuse of it does not imply that salvation is a present reality only. It is present, but by virtue of its presence the future is already a matter of assurance rather than hope.

What is missing from John's eschatology, however, is the apocalyptic language and conceptuality used in a more-or-less unqualified sense. Assumptions about the resurrection of the dead or a cataclysmic upheaval or end of world history are in the process of being rethought. So it is that when Jesus tells Martha that Lazarus will rise again and she responds by affirming the then traditional and Jewish hope for a resurrection at the last day (cf. John 5:28–29; Daniel 12:2), he informs her that he (already) is the resurrection and the life (11:23–25). In a similar vein, Judas (not Iscariot) in some puzzlement asks Jesus how he will manifest himself to the disciples and not to the world (14:22). So also some members of the Johannine community believed at one point that the Beloved Disciple would not die, but would remain alive awaiting Jesus' return (21:23; cf. 1 Thessalonians 4:15; 1 Corinthians 11:30). Such conventional Christian apocalyptic hopes are apparently still alive in 1 John (2:28). Clearly the Gospel's farewell discourses represent a conscious and deliberate reinterpretation of conventional categories, not so much in view of the necessity of giving them up as because of the realities of revelation and theology already present in the lives of individuals and the community.

Because of the presence of life, the believing community also participates in other aspects of the eschatological age, such as joy (Greek: *chara*) and peace (*eirēnē*). When Jesus says that he has come in order that people may have life and have it more abundantly (10:16) he means life characterized by joy and peace, eschatological life. Jesus speaks of the disciples' joy only in the farewell discourses, and of their peace only there and when he appears to them risen from the dead (20:21,26). Joy and peace, unlike life or eternal life, are not the subject of theological reflection, but are simply spoken of as if the hearer, or reader, would immediately understand. Although abstractions, they nevertheless give color and concreteness to the character of Christian and church life, and are related to the gift or possession of the Spirit, as the chief harbinger of this life. Already for Paul the Spirit's presence betokens the inbreaking of a new age; it is the *arrabōn* or guarantee, the down payment of the new age coming (2 Corinthians 1:22), the first fruits (*aparchē*, Romans 8:23). Characteristically, John sees the eschatological drama as already farther along than does Paul, or one might say that what Paul suggests finds fulfillment in John.

5   *Prayer*

Jesus' ministry is characterized by prayer (12:27–30; 17:1–26), but none of the Synoptic scenes in which Jesus prays is paralleled in the Fourth Gospel. (John 12:27–30 is a reminiscence of the Gethsemane scene, but a quite remote one.) In the Synoptics Jesus prays (Mark 1:35), prays urgently (Mark 14:32–42), and teaches his disciples to pray as well (Matthew 6:7–15). The Johannine Jesus is always in close communion with God, however, and therefore does not need to petition God for anything. In John Jesus does not so much teach his disciples to pray as he tells them what their prayers and the results of their prayers will be like. If they ask anything in Jesus' name, he will do it (14:13–14; 15:16; 16:23–24). Jesus' departure evidently opens up the possibility for prayer *in his name* for the first time (16:24), even as Jesus leaves them his peace (14:27; 16:33).

Understandably, Jesus' seemingly extravagant promise to the disciples about their prayers' fulfillment has raised troubling questions among Christians. Jesus seems to be promising the disciples that whatever they ask for they will receive, and such an expectation is contradicted by harsh experience. But what John writes is scarcely offered as a theology of prayer, and one might suggest that Jesus should not be taken too literally. More to the point is the consideration that Jesus' prayers, as well as the promises to the disciples, reflect the underlying theme of unity so prominent in this Gospel. The disciples come to participate in the same love that the Father has for the Son (3:35) and the Son for the Father (14:31) as they love Jesus (14:21) and one another (15:12–14). Thus they are one with each other, as well as with God. Jesus will scarcely pray in any ordinary sense, because of his unity with God: he is himself *theos*. The prayer of the disciples then also expresses this close unity: they pray for what the Son will give them. Probably it is inapposite to ask whether John presents an unrealistic view of answered prayer. Better to ask whether John reflects an unrealistic, or at least an idealized, view of the community of Jesus' disciples.

Quite possibly this is the case, and if so, we may see already in the Johannine Epistles a return to harsher reality, for there it is clear that the empirical unity is imperfect (1 John 2:18–19; 3 John). Yet quite possibly in the Epistles the ideal of such unity as the obligation of the true community of Jesus' disciples as distinguished from the false is reflected even in its absence, for now each segment of the fragmented community seems to look upon itself as the one true church. Given such an outlook, the prospects of an empirical, tangible unity of the church in this world would seem very slim indeed. One might say that the Johannine literature does not solve the problem of church unity so much as it poses it in an acute and fundamental way. The indispensability of unity is not negated by its absence, and John insists upon its indispensability. The perfection of that unity, with Jesus and among themselves, makes sense of Jesus' seemingly extravagant promises about the fulfillment of his disciples' prayers.

6 *Ecclesiology*

We have seen that John's ecclesiology is based squarely on the concept of unity among believers and with Christ. In fact, it demands that such unity become real. The image of the vine (15:1–11), which expresses that unity, also reveals how it is to be understood. According to the image, each member branch is directly and organically related to Christ, but not otherwise related to other members. The Johannine parable of the vine may then be compared with the Pauline image of the body of Christ (1 Corinthians 12), which is clearly also a metaphor of the church. The image itself, as well as Paul's own exposition of it in 1 Corinthians, underscores not only the unity of believers, but their mutual interdependence. "If one member suffers, all suffer together; if one member is honored, all rejoice together" (1 Corinthians 12:26). John's choice of imagery is more individualistic, as the Fourth Gospel itself seems to be, but nevertheless underscores the unity of believers in and through Christ.[45]

While too much should not be inferred about ecclesiastical organization from the Gospel's imagery of the vine, whether deliberately or not, it is significant and revealing. The ecclesiology implied in the Fourth Gospel emphasizes the importance of the believers' unity and direct relationship with Jesus. While underscoring the importance of individuals' relationships to one another (i.e., love), John does not describe them in structural or functional terms (as Paul does using the image of the body). Moreover, with the possible exception of "elder" as a title (2 John 1; 3 John 1), the Epistles do not mention church office or organization explicitly, and this omission stands in some contrast to the Pauline Letters. This absence, or at least lack of prominence, of church office and organization correlates well with the high view of the function and authority of the Spirit, although we cannot be sure how they were actually related. At least we may say that the view that John mirrors a primitive view of the church, even in comparison to what we see developing in Paul, has a certain plausibility. Perhaps John resists the development toward "early Catholicism."[46] The contours of a conception of the church can be seen beneath the

---

[45] On the imagery of the vine, see Dan O. Via, "Darkness, Christ, and the Church in the Fourth Gospel," *SJT*, 14 (1961), 172–193, esp. 181–185.

[46] Käsemann, *The Testament of Jesus*, p. 32: "The community may take up and use the oldest self-designations and traditions of primitive Christianity, traditions which at the end of the first century appear outdated and obsolete, and thus come into conflict with developing early Catholicism." Similarly, James D. G. Dunn, *Unity and Diversity in the New Testament: An Inquiry into the Character of Earliest Christianity* (Philadelphia, 1977), characterizes the Johannine literature as a reaction against early Catholicism (p. 363).

surface of the Fourth Gospel, but as important as the church and discipleship may be to the author, no doctrine of the church emerges into full view.

In any event, the church of the Gospel of John is the community of Jesus' friends, who know him because he has revealed to them everything he has heard from the Father (15:15). Such knowledge actually came only with the sending of the Spirit-Paraclete to the postresurrection church. Believers who have received this knowledge and live together in mutual love no longer misunderstand Jesus, as those who opposed him did. (Indeed, his disciples during his ministry misunderstood him.) Their unity with Jesus has its positive and negative sides, so to speak. On the one hand, they will continue the mission and work of Jesus (14:12; 20:22; cf. 21:15–19); indeed, they will do "greater works" (14:12). This should not surprise us, given the continuing revelation of Jesus through the Spirit-Paraclete. On the other hand, the church of Jesus' followers will experience in and from the world the same hostility that Jesus himself faced (15:18–21; 16:1–4). The world's hostility will be a kind of demonstration to Jesus' disciples that they truly belong to him and not to the world, for as evil as the world's persecution may be, its love would signify something far worse (15:19; cf. 1 John 4:5).

Probably in all the Gospels the disciples represent or symbolize the church in that they become a means of conveying to the reader a message for or about the church. The church in any age is made up of the followers or disciples of Jesus. John's emphasis on the importance of the individual's faith and relationship to Jesus is, in an important sense, a teaching about discipleship. We have seen how being a disciple means not only believing in Jesus Christ, but belonging to him, being united with him, and obeying his commands. The Johannine Jesus encourages the reader to abide with Jesus, even to seek intimacy with him through believing obedience.

In this regard, the Beloved Disciple plays an important role. He reclines close to Jesus' breast at the Last Supper (13:23); Jesus entrusts his own mother to him at the foot of the cross (19:25–27); he is the first to believe upon seeing the tomb empty (20:8). This disciple seems to understand Jesus and the meaning of his ministry before the others do, perhaps already before the crucifixion and resurrection. Generally speaking, he appears alongside Peter, seemingly in order to surpass him. In his closeness to Jesus he is the paradigmatic disciple, a model not so much for the disciples contemporary with Jesus as for future disciples (cf. 17:20; 20:29). Perhaps for this reason he remains unnamed, for any and all disciples of Jesus may become beloved disciples. Such disciples, whom Jesus loves, are the church.

7   Sacraments

The problem of discerning a doctrine of the church in the Gospel of John is typified by the question of the sacraments, which has been much debated in modern exegesis, with some interpreters claiming that the Gospel is through and through sacramental, while others believe the evangelist's attitude was at best ambiguous.[47] It should be noted at the outset that sacrament, or sacramental, is not a New Testament category, for there is no Greek word in the New Testament that must be, or should be, translated "sacrament." Then there is, of course, the more recent Protestant – Catholic disagreement over the number and nature of sacraments, which we may leave out of account while focusing our attention on the two liturgical acts that are generally accepted and find the broadest support in the New Testament, namely, baptism and the Lord's Supper.

Certainly baptism was widely, if not universally, practiced among the earliest generation of Christians who produced the

---

[47] A classical sacramental view of the Gospel is found in Oscar Cullmann, *Early Christian Worship*, SBT 10 (London, 1953). Cullmann's avowed purpose was "to show how the Gospel of John regards it as one of its chief concerns to set forth the connexion between the contemporary Christian worship and the historical life of Jesus" (p. 37). By worship Cullmann means chiefly baptism and the Lord's Supper. Alternatively, Bultmann, *Theology of the New Testament*, II, pp. 58f., maintains that although the fourth evangelist does not polemicize against the sacraments, they play no role in his Gospel. In his commentary Bultmann had rejected as later editorial additions explicitly sacramental passages such as 6:51b–58 (*The Gospel of John: A Commentary*, pp. 234–237). Most commentators fall somewhere between the extremes represented by Cullmann and Bultmann.

writings of the New Testament. Only in the Gospel of Matthew (28:19) does Jesus himself command baptism, although in the Gospel of John, and only there, Jesus is said to practice it (3:22; 4:1; but cf. verse 2). References to Jesus' baptizing occur alongside John's baptizing, suggesting that the two are related, and indeed it is probable that the Christian practice was originally derived from or related to John's baptism, which was apparently continued among his disciples also (cf. Acts 19:13). The Gospel of John would in any event seem to presuppose the practice among Christians, for Jesus speaks of being born of water as well as Spirit (3:5), and water imagery recurs as symbolic of the salvation that Jesus brings (4:7–42; 7:37–39; 13:1–11). It is characteristic of the Fourth Gospel that this water imagery is never explicitly limited to, or explained as, baptism. At the same time, it is hard to imagine that baptism is not somehow in view. Yet even if it is, the imagery of water seems to connote more than a ritual practice. It is the satisfaction of a fundamental human need as well as a symbol for the cleansing that is also a human necessity. Probably it would be correct to say that the water imagery of the Fourth Gospel alludes to baptism without referring to it. It evokes the liturgical act without being exhausted in it.

Something similar is going on with regard to the Lord's Supper in the use of bread and wine imagery. Wine appears, of course, at the culmination of the very first episode of the Gospel (2:1–11), as it becomes evident to the reader that Jesus has changed the water set aside for the Jewish purification ritual into wine. That this wine symbolizes the purification and life that Jesus brings is altogether probable, but is it also an intentional allusion to the wine of the sacrament that is said in the Synoptics (Mark 14:24 parr.) and Paul (1 Corinthians 11:25) to be Jesus' blood? The vine (15:1–8) is, of course, the source of wine, and although this fact is not specifically noted in Jesus' parable, can it be overlooked? Obviously the point of the image of the vine is to demonstrate the necessity of the disciples' abiding in Jesus, but of course for countless Christians down through the centuries the sacrament of the Lord's Supper has been a principal means of partaking of and abiding in Christ.

In fact, for many Christian readers of the Gospel of John the necessity of this sacrament as a means of participation in Christ is nowhere more forcefully or eloquently expressed than in John 6:52–58, especially verses 53–56.

> So Jesus said to them, "Truly, truly, I say to you, unless you eat the flesh of the Son of man and drink his blood, you have no life in you; he who eats my flesh and drinks my blood has eternal life, and I will raise him up at the last day. For my flesh is food indeed, and my blood is drink indeed. He who eats my flesh and drinks my blood abides in me, and I in him.

The apparently explicit sacramentalism of this passage has led some exegetes to assign it to a later redaction on the grounds that it is out of accord with the thrust or burden of Johannine theology.[48] At the same time, whether even this passage was intended to refer to the sacrament specifically was a matter of discussion among the sixteenth-century reformers, and that question has continued to be debated.[49] Arguably, the intention of the author, whether in this case the evangelist or a later redactor, was to insist upon the earthly reality of Jesus' flesh and blood against the kind of incipient docetism that is found already in 1 John (4:1–6). Needless to say, the two interpretations, the sacramental and the antidocetic, are not mutually exclusive, for both are suggested by the episode of the issue of water and blood (baptism and the Lord's Supper) from Jesus' side (John 19:31–37).[50]

Perhaps the most severe question for any sacramental interpretation of the Fourth Gospel is posed by the absence of the institution of the Lord's Supper from John's account of the Last Supper. The two alternatives, diametrically opposed, are that John assumes, and assumes his readers will know, that Jesus

---

[48] See references to Bultmann in n. 47 above.

[49] Note Robert Kysar, *The Fourth Evangelist and his Gospel: An Examination of Contemporary Scholarship* (Minneapolis, 1975), pp. 252–255; also James D. G. Dunn, "John vi – A Eucharist Discourse?," *NTS*, 17 (1971), 328–338. Both argue that the primary thrust of 6:51c–58 is to combat docetism rather than promote sacramentalism.

[50] Moreover, Ignatius in the early second century combined a strong sacramentalism (*Ephesians* 20:2: "medicine of immortality") with an insistence upon the real humanity of Jesus (*Trallians* chaps. 9–10).

instituted this sacrament on the night he was betrayed, as is the case in the Synoptic Gospels and Paul (1 Corinthians 15:23); or, alternatively, that John is either ignorant of or suppresses the Synoptic and Pauline account of the institution. Even if John did not know the Synoptics and Paul, however, it is difficult to believe that he did not know this sacrament. Conceivably, he knew a tradition that linked it with Jesus' messianic meal by the Sea of Galilee rather than with the Last Supper.[51] The entire problem of John's relation to the Synoptic Gospels and tradition, as well as to early Christianity generally, is here epitomized in a critical way.

That an author (whether the evangelist or a redactor) could write 6:52–58 with no thought of the Lord's Supper is difficult to believe, given the pervasiveness of the sacrament at an early date. At the same time, the allusive character of even this passage suggests that the author does not wish simply to say that partaking of the sacrament is the *sine qua non* of salvation. In the sacrament one partakes of the life that is in Jesus, and therefore one must partake. But to think that such ritual participation alone would guarantee salvation defies everything that is said about the necessity of the believer's faith and obedience in the farewell discourses and elsewhere (cf. 6:63). Moreover, the Johannine Christian could only partake of the sacrament within a community of Jesus' disciples loyal to him. Perhaps participation in, and identification with, that community is the key to understanding 6:52–58. That is, one must depart from the synagogue and its worship and join the congregation of Christ-confessors that worships and partakes of the sacrament in the name of Christ and participates in the life he brings through eating and drinking him together. Participation in the sacraments of baptism and the Lord's Supper has for many centuries set the boundaries of the Christian community, and perhaps this was already the case in John's day, as Chris-

---

[51] Such a linkage occurs, of course, in John 6. The instructions for the eucharist in the *Didachē* (chaps. 9–10), contain no reference to the passion setting. Like the letters of Ignatius, the anonymous *Didachē* dates from the first decades of the second century, but in parts it may be even earlier.

tians excluded from the synagogue establish an alternative community of worship.[52]

To oppose a ministry of the word to that of sacrament would be to impose categories of later theology upon the Fourth Gospel. Nevertheless, the word (*logos*) is important in this Gospel, and not just Jesus as the word or the words of Jesus. Also Jesus prays for those who will believe because of the word of the disciples (17:20), presumably the word they proclaim. Thus John can use "word" of preaching even though he never employs the verb "to preach" (Greek: *kērussein*) or any of its derivatives. Moreover, Jesus says that the disciples have been made clean by the word which he himself has spoken to them (15:3). That the word of the disciples is first of all the announcement of the Gospel about Jesus is suggested by the use of "word of life" in 1 John 1:1, where the life, who is Jesus, seems to be the subject of the word and the object of the proclamation (verse 3). We begin to catch glimpses of a church in which the sacraments are administered and the word proclaimed, to use the terminology that developed later. But such references or allusions to word and sacrament as we may find do not become the center of attention in the Gospel itself.

The concepts and liturgical practices associated with the church enter the picture in John primarily as ways of setting forth or illuminating the theology of the Gospel, rather than as objects of theologizing themselves. They, so to speak, hover in the background. This does not mean that John's concept of what the church should be has no bearing upon his theology. The congregation of Jesus' followers is the indispensable presupposition and background against which the Gospel's theological thoughts are set forth. Presuppositions in this sense may be as important as explicit propositions or proposals. Moreover, the church, made up of Jesus' disciples and those

---

52 See David Rensberger, *Johannine Faith and Liberating Community* (Philadelphia, 1988), pp. 70–81. Rensberger sees the so-called eucharistic passage of John 6:51c–58 as underlining an important social function of the rite, which "separates the Johannine community from the world and unites its members with one another" (p. 80). The background of this need for separation and internal solidarity is the recent conflict with, and separation from, the synagogue.

whom they have gathered, is in a real sense not only the presupposition but the purpose of the Fourth Gospel. The church is the community of those the Father has called together by sending his Son Jesus into the world. For the present, it is God's human dwelling place.

CHAPTER 4

The theology of John and the issues it raises

As we have considered the setting and themes of Johannine theology, there has been ample opportunity to observe the ways in which it relates to, and brings to expression, characteristic doctrines of early Christianity that are stated or suggested elsewhere in the New Testament. Thus the Gospel of John has often been viewed as the culmination of the theology or theological development of the New Testament period, and while the direct dependence that such a developmental concept implies is hard to demonstrate, the basic perspective seems somehow correct. The Gospel of John represents quite well what is distinctive about the New Testament and early Christianity generally. It identifies the central, christological issue and presses it unremittingly. We shall now turn to three important and related issues that the Gospel of John raises and ask about their role and function in the Gospel and in the development of Christian thought as it is mirrored in our own situation. These are the questions of mythology, raised by the heavily supernatural aspect of the christology of the Fourth Gospel; of anti-Semitism, raised by the Gospel's negative view of the Jews who reject christology; and of the nature or character of Christianity, raised by John's relationship to the rest of the New Testament and to the later creeds of the church.

A MYTHOLOGY

The question of the New Testament and mythology was raised in an acute way by Rudolf Bultmann in a famous essay of that title published at the middle of the twentieth century.[1] The point of the essay was that the New Testament writings, and early Christianity generally, took for granted a non-scientific and supernatural world-view that modern people, Christians included, no longer hold. For example, the New Testament writers took for granted a three-storied universe in which the middle tier, inhabited by humans, was subject to incursion from divine emissaries from above and demonic ones from below. Moreover, there was no scientifically understood system of cause and effect, whereby every natural phenomenon has its appropriate natural cause, and nothing happens by divine intervention or fiat. By contrast, modern life is predicated on the assumption of non-intervention by divine or demonic forces. When we become ill we call a doctor rather than – or in addition to – praying, and we do not seek relief through demon exorcism. When we need light, we turn a switch and the forces of nature, scientifically understood and harnessed, produce incandescence in a bulb or tube. (It is important to note, however, that Bultmann's purpose was not so much to absolutize a modern world-view, but to free the New Testament from any world-view, including its own.)

No New Testament book seems to fly in the face of such a modern view of ourselves and the world more than the Gospel of John. In it Jesus is described as a preexistent divine being who descended from heaven and has now returned there. Furthermore, during his stay on earth he performed stupendous miraculous acts, confuted and overcame his enemies, and although seemingly done to death by them actually went to the cross quite of his own intention and volition (10:18). As he returned to the Father he promised his disciples he would come again in order to take them with him (14:4–7). What could be more farfetched or incredible to people living at the close of the twentieth century?

Of course, there are hundreds of millions of people – probably the majority of the human race – who still live and die by

---

[1] Rudolf Bultmann, "The New Testament and Mythology," in Hans Werner Bartsch (ed.), *Kerygma and Myth: A Theological Debate* (London, 1953). Bultmann's essay was written during the Second World War.

myths, whether of Christian or other origin. Moreover, the character and function of such myths, what they contain, express, or accomplish, is a large and important issue, and significant, historic myths may not simply be dismissed on the basis of their most literalistic construal.

1 Spatial imagery

One needs also to ask whether a myth has a meaning or significance that transcends its most literal construal, and how one attains it or determines what that significance might be. To take two examples from the Fourth Gospel, we read there not only about Jesus' descent from and ascent to heaven, but about the necessity of rebirth or birth from above for anyone who would truly accept Jesus and become his follower. We have, so to speak, both a major christological myth, and a myth of human redemption. How shall we understand them if we pass beyond the crudest possible terms?

In fact, the evangelist obviously expects the reader to be able to pass beyond such terms to attain the true meaning. Thus in John's chapter 3, Nicodemus' initial understanding of what Jesus could possibly mean when he speaks of being born *anōthen* ("again" or "from above") is quickly transcended and corrected by Jesus himself, who clearly thinks that Nicodemus should know better than to think birth from above would entail once more passing through the womb. Whatever is meant by birth from above, it can only come about through the work of the Spirit; it cannot be self-generated. It is in fact a miracle, but a miracle that is spiritual in the strictest sense of the word. As we have also observed, God's role in such rebirth is a correlate of human decision, so that it does not make faith superfluous. Rather, God's action through the Spirit explains how faith is possible. Behind the mythological language one finds a sophisticated understanding of the redemption of human life. To use a much overworked technical term, the concept of rebirth is already being *demythologized* by the evangelist within the Gospel itself. For Bultmann this fact was the basis and justification of his own program.

As to the descent and ascent of Jesus as the revealer, it is a good question whether such talk is to be taken literally, or in terms of the three-storied universe. It is worth observing that although John speaks of Jesus' ascent and of his being lifted up, there is no account of the physical ascension of Jesus such as is found in the Book of Acts. What is more, it is quite clear from the Gospel that Jesus' own statement in 1:51 about the heavens' opening and the angels of God ascending and descending upon the Son of Man is to be understood symbolically or metaphorically of the coming revelation of God in Jesus' words and deeds. And while those seem to be presented in such a way as to be unambiguously clear, they do not come across as such to Jesus' first hearers and observers. One could see the signs Jesus performed, recognize that they testified to his commission from Goa, and yet fail to appreciate their full and proper significance (2:23–25). Even when the voice of God was heard from heaven, many people thought only that it thundered (12:29). Jesus' own disciples did not really understand him during his earthly ministry (16:31–32). In a variety of ways, the evangelist's sophistication and subtlety become clear. If his world-view is not our own, and it evidently is not, it would nevertheless be unfair and misleading to characterize it as crude or primitive. John in fact rejects crude and primitive interpretations within the Gospel itself.

2   *Miracles*

What, then, of the miracles in John and the Jesus who performs them? Although John did view Jesus as a healer and miracle worker, the interpreter must nevertheless observe carefully the way in which the miracles are presented and the hints about their proper or deeper meaning that are occasionally dropped. Clearly the final two signs, the gift of sight to the man born blind (chap. 9) and the gift of life to the thoroughly dead Lazarus (chap. 11), are the most awesome miracles, not only in the Gospel of John, but in the New Testament, and, in fact, they seem to be intended as such (cf. 9:32; 11:14,37,39; 12:9–11).

Their amazing character is doubtless related to their intended effect. They demonstrate that Jesus comes from God and does the work of God. Thus, at the conclusion of chapter 9, the gift of sight to the blind man is taken to be symbolic of the total, saving work of Jesus, as he says that he has come into the world, "that those who do not see may see, and that those who see may become blind" (verse 39). The language is not, however, to be understood literally; obviously, Jesus blinds no one physically. So the interpreter must ask whether or in what sense the gift of physical sight is really the point. Earlier on in the Gospel, in discussing his life-giving work, Jesus says that the hour is coming when the dead (5:25) or those in the tombs (5:28) will hear the voice of the Son of God, clearly referring to the life-giving work that God has given him to accomplish for all who believe, and at the same time pointing forward to the concrete manifestation of this work that will come with the raising of Lazarus. When one reads the words about the Son's life-giving work for the first time, he has no reason to think of Lazarus, but when the Lazarus episode is read it is then understood in light of those statements about Jesus' work.

In the Gospel tradition there are other instances in which Jesus brings back to life a person seemingly dead (Mark 5:35–43; Luke 7:11–17; the Secret Gospel of Mark). Perhaps John has taken such a traditional story and stretched it, even exaggerated it, in every dimension with the quite conscious purpose of setting forth the incredible and unprecedented nature of the life-giving work that Jesus performs. The same thing may have happened in the case of the man born blind (cf. Mark 8:22–26; 10:46–52). Although John believed Jesus accomplished such things, he used those stories to elaborate upon, and make concrete, the saving and life-giving work of Jesus so that their principal point becomes that work itself. It is somewhat anomalous therefore that the chief priests then seek to kill Lazarus, who has been brought back from the dead (12:10), and precisely because he has now become such a powerful witness to Jesus (12:11). Anomalous though it may be, just the fact that Lazarus is still subject to death implies that the whole episode is a sign. It betokens what Jesus can and will do, but it is not itself that eschatological life-giving work, which is something greater yet. The miracles or signs of Jesus are transparent or symbolic of that work, as Jesus himself represents or symbolizes God in the precise sense that a true symbol participates in the reality it symbolizes but is not identical with it.

3   The humanity of Jesus

When we turn to the figure of Jesus in the Fourth Gospel, there is always the question of whether he is a real human being or a docetic Christ, only seemingly human, God striding across the face of the earth.[2] Such a question would hardly arise on the basis of the Synoptic accounts or Paul. The amazing character of the Johannine Jesus' miracles scarcely speaks on the side of his humanity, however, although John, like the other evangelists (for example, Mark 3:22), is aware that Jesus' signs could be rejected by some and misinterpreted by others. Moreover, as we have just observed, those miracles as signs are intended to play a distinct and definite role in interpreting Jesus' life-giving work, which was the effect of his entire ministry and glorification. Therefore, one should not too quickly conclude from them that in the Fourth Gospel we are dealing with some sort of naive, superhuman christology.

That the Gospel of John reckons with Jesus' humanity becomes clear at points where Jesus himself manifests normal human characteristics (for example, 4:6; 7:1; 11:35), but also in the repeated references to Jesus' origins. His opponents (7:52) but also his disciples-to-be repeatedly stumble over the matter of his origin, that is, his natural or geographic origin. In fact, the Gospel takes full account of Jesus' natural, human origins and does not deny them, despite the negative connotations they may have for many people. Jesus' origins bespeak his humanity. Thus we find here (4:44), as in the other Gospels,

---

[2] See E. Käsemann, *The Testament of Jesus: A Study of the Gospel of John in the Light of Chapter 17* (Philadelphia and London, 1968), pp. 9 (where Käsemann cites F. C. Baur) and 66.

the famous saying about a prophet not having honor in his own country.[3]

There is, indeed, a kind of paradox of the incarnation in the Gospel of John, despite the seemingly obvious manifestations of God in Jesus' words and deeds. To say that the Johannine Jesus is a mere human being scarcely does justice to the evangelist's portrayal. Yet whatever else Jesus is, he is also that. This paradoxical character of the incarnation is underlined by the fact that in the evangelist's own view the true perception of Jesus only became possible, even for his disciples, with his glorification, his crucifixion and resurrection. There were indications, signs (*semeia*) of it, during Jesus' historic ministry, but the truth about who Jesus was, and is, was not known and could not have been known until his death and resurrection. Thus the revelation of God in Jesus was truly historical, and even contingent, in that it was accomplished through the very human event of Jesus' own death, brought about by people who did not see in him the revelation of God's glory. It could not, however, have been simply read off the observation of the earthly Jesus, although the signs were already present. That the figure of Jesus in the Fourth Gospel has mythological aspects is then clear enough, even apart from his preexistence, descent, and ascent. Nevertheless, when one looks closely at the presentation of this figure, it becomes clear that this Jesus is anything but simply and naively conceived.

The evangelist and his faithful readers, inspired by the Spirit, know whence Jesus has come and whither he has gone. Jesus' contemporaries, however, had less clarity about him. His opponents reject him as an impostor and deny the truth of his words and the actuality or legitimacy of his deeds. Even his disciples, who believe in Jesus, do not fully understand him. Not only faith, but also insight, will be required to apprehend the truth about Jesus. During his earthly ministry it could not be fully known. The evangelist paints a picture of Jesus as God

---

[3] For a full discussion of the humanity of Jesus and how it figures in the theology of the Gospel, see Marianne Meye Thompson, *The Humanity of Jesus in the Fourth Gospel* (Philadelphia, 1988). Thompson shows, among other things, that Jesus' humanity is not the subject, but the premise, of John's christology.

knew him and as Christians would know him, but he is aware that Jesus' earthly ministry evoked more than one perception and interpretation.

4   *"Demythologizing"*

In his interpretation of the Gospel of John, which provided the justification of his program of demythologizing, Bultmann envisioned an evangelist who dealt with mythological sources, a sign source and a revelation discourse source. The one was drawn from primitive Christian circles in contact with the John the Baptist sect, the other from perhaps more sophisticated gnosticism that had developed in a similar milieu. The evangelist then employed, and deployed, these sources in his Gospel, interpreting their miracles and mythological concepts in such a way that the point was no longer the crassly miraculous or the mythological (for example, Jesus' preexistence and descent), but rather the revelatory, saving work of Jesus as it impinged upon human existence and consciousness. This is demythologizing, and, in Bultmann's view, the evangelist demythologized his sources. Bultmann's position involved complex and largely hypothetical theories of these sources and their history-of-religions background, both of which he painstakingly reconstructed out of the Gospel itself.[4] Not surprisingly, these theoretical aspects of his work have not stood the test of time very well. On the other hand, the insight into the theological profundity and sophistication enshrined in this ancient Gospel is not misplaced.

Whether it is any longer helpful to think of John as demythologizing sources may be questionable, but he certainly works with the traditions and conceptuality available to him to construct a narrative of Jesus' ministry and a portrait of Jesus that is at once simple and rich. It has complex dimensions but raises issues that are finally rather simple. Whether they are too

---

[4] Bultmann's source-critical work is carried out in *The Gospel of John: A Commentary* (Oxford and Philadelphia, 1971). See D. Moody Smith, *The Composition and Order of the Fourth Gospel: Bultmann's Literary Theory* (New Haven, 1965), for an explanation and critique of Bultmann's work.

simple, or simply cast, is a question the thoughtful reader must in due course entertain. But it is undeniable that John has written a Gospel that puts the christological question before the reader in a way that is powerful and compelling. He evokes an answer that will be either decidedly positive or sharply negative. If positive, it will not be so primarily because of the elements dubbed mythological but because the word and work of Jesus find a powerful resonance in the hearer. To use John's terms, he rejects the claims of the world, finds life, and manifests that the Spirit is already at work. If negative, it will probably not be so because of the Gospel's incredible dimensions, but because of its offense against ordinary human sensibilities and against established cultural and religious traditions. Thus, no one who is Jewish is likely to find the Fourth Gospel congenial reading. (In fact, when read aright, it will scarcely comfort most nominal Christians.) The mythology of the Gospel is not conceived out of thin air, but is a correlative and expression of the conflict between Jesus and people identified as "the Jews," those who reject him. And so we must turn now to the question of whether this Gospel is anti-Jewish or even anti-Semitic.

B ANTI-SEMITISM

The Gospel of John has proved to be a dangerous document, for although it may not itself be anti-Semitic, it has given aid and comfort to anti-Semites. If a text is nothing more than what its community of interpretation makes of it,[5] then the Gospel of John is, or at many points in the history of its interpretation has been, anti-Semitic. It seems to portray the Jews as the mortal enemies of Jesus, who by their forethought and intention do him in. Thus on John's terms Matthew's infamous cry of the Jerusalem crowd, "His blood be upon us and upon our children" (27:25), would seem a proper invocation of doom upon the Jewish people, whether or not the

---

[5] See Stanley E. Fish, *Is There a Text in this Class? The Authority of Interpretive Communities* (Cambridge, MA, 1980), especially the opening essay, which gives the book its title.

fourth evangelist knew the First Gospel. At the very least, the Gospel of John has lent itself to such a reading.[6]

As we have seen, John's pressing of the christological issue did not take place in a vacuum. The Gospel reflects the point in the history of at least a segment of the community of Jesus' followers when they had begun to define themselves over against Judaism. Jesus' opponents, the Jews or Pharisees, say to the man born blind, "You are disciples of that man, but we are disciples of Moses" (9:28). Such a statement, while scarcely conceivable at the time, or in the setting of Jesus himself, accurately depicts a state of affairs toward the end of the first century. One had to choose between Jesus and Moses or, as it seems, between Judaism and Christianity. The Apostle Paul already saw that most of his fellow Jews were not accepting the preaching of Jesus as the Messiah (Romans 1–5), but he still resisted the divisive implications of this fact. In this regard, what seemed a threat on the horizon to Paul now appears to be an accomplished fact in the Gospel of John. Christianity and Judaism have now separated, and the hostility appears to reflect the anger engendered on both sides.

One of the amazing aspects of the New Testament is the way so many of its premises, or promises, have been fulfilled in subsequent history (a fact that has little or nothing to do with the espousal of literal fulfillment of biblical prophecy). If one looks, for example, at the portrayal of the triumphal spread of Christianity through the Mediterranean world in the Book of Acts, there is little reason for surprise, given the success of the church during subsequent centuries and the dawn of the Constantinian era. Yet when Luke wrote, toward the end of the first century, the prospect of the success of Christianity on this scale would not have been obvious to the unprejudiced eye. Indeed, there is little or no reason to think that Luke himself

---

[6] The alleged anti-Semitism of the Fourth Gospel has been a major subject of discussion among Christian theologians and exegetes, and the literature is now considerable. For an introduction to the issue and citation of relevant literature, see D. Moody Smith, "Judaism and the Gospel of John," in James H. Charlesworth (ed.), *Jews and Christians: Exploring the Past, Present, and Future* (New York, 1990), pp. 176–199.

would have imagined such worldly success before the return of Jesus or the culmination of the age.

By the same token, the division of Christianity from Judaism, so that the two become distinct, although closely related and often mutually hostile, religions, seems to be anticipated, if not an already established fact, in the Gospel of John. Probably most Christians since the end of the first century have read the Gospel in this way, or at least have taken for granted that this is the proper reading of it. Certainly there is ample justification in such a reading, given the conflict and division that obviously underlie, and find expression in, the Fourth Gospel. That "the Jews" appear as the representation of the world, over against Jesus and his disciples, is a fair reading of the Gospel.

Of course, "the Jews" are, historically, the heirs of the Pharisees, with whom Jesus had considerable conflict according to the Synoptic tradition. Thus they were, in a real sense, a historical given in the time of Jesus as well as in that of the evangelist, although their role had sharpened and changed in the intervening years. But, as we have seen, a close reading of the text reveals that "the Jews" are not all Jewish people, or even all Jewish people contemporary with Jesus or with the Johannine community. Rather, "the Jews" represent the emerging authoritative group, those who are seeking to establish a canonical interpretation of what Judaism is, and, moreover, one that excludes Christians (9:22; 12:42; 16:2). It is therefore not coincidental that they are identified with the Pharisees. In John there are plenty of Jewish people who are open to Jesus (3:1; 11:37) and even accept him (chap. 9), but they too may be in danger of being excluded from an emerging Jewish community that is identifying itself in part over against something that will be called Christianity (12:42; cf. Acts 11:26).

It is sometimes said that the Gospel of John is anti-Jewish without being anti-Semitic, and there is reason to make such a distinction. Modern anti-Semitism is racist in that it falsely views Jewishness as a racial rather than an historic religious or cultural identity. Thus the Nazis drew a distinction between Aryan and Jewish racial types and did not regard conversion to

Christianity as a way of divesting one's self of Jewishness. Certainly the Gospel of John is not anti-Semitic in this sense, for this sort of racial anti-Semitism emerged only in modern times. Yet one must face the question of whether or not the Gospel of John is anti-Jewish, and, if so, what does its anti-Jewishness mean for Judaism and Christianity? Does the Gospel, rightly understood, promote anti-Semitism?

As we have observed, it is all too easy to read later religious developments and hostility back into the Gospel of John, for enough mutual hostility and rejection are reflected there already. To take a prime example, the Gospel of John seems to be thoroughly supersessionist, as is the Epistle to the Hebrews, for it anticipates the displacement of Jews as God's people by Christians and appropriates the Jewish scripture as its own (5:39,45–47). Moreover, "the Jews" themselves disavow the lordship of God by avowing that they have no king but Caesar (19:15) just before Pilate hands Jesus over to them for crucifixion. Interestingly enough, however, it is clear from the Gospel of John itself that Jesus was put to death by a detail of Roman soldiers (19:23–25; cf. 18:3), not by the Jews (who in 19:21–22 seem to be distinguished from the soldiers who appear in the next paragraph). Yet John leaves the impression that "the Jews" did Jesus in.

Although "Jews" (*Ioudaioi*) is characteristically, though not always, a term of opprobrium in the Fourth Gospel, "Israel" and "Israelite" uniformly appear in a positive sense. Nathanael, Jesus' disciple to be, is "truly an Israelite" (1:47), and John the Baptist's mission is to reveal Jesus as the Christ to Israel (1:31). Jesus himself is the king of Israel (1:49; 12:13). Moreover, the evangelist knows quite well that Jesus is a Jew, for the Samaritan woman identifies him as such (4:9), while Jesus himself will say to her, "Salvation is of the Jews" (4:22). Although Nicodemus proves woefully ignorant, the fact that he was a teacher of Israel means that he should have been prepared to understand Jesus (3:10). "Israel" and "Israelite," the designations preferred by the Jews themselves, remain entirely positive terms. Perhaps John sees the church as the true Israel and the replacement of fallen Israel, but, as we have already observed, he does not express himself in these terms.

It is all too easy for Christians to supply what seems to be implied by the Fourth Gospel, and thus to extend and fortify the gulf between Christianity and Judaism, but those who do so should remain aware of what they are doing, namely, coming to conclusions that are not as explicitly drawn in the Gospel of John as may at first appear. John can be said to point in that direction, but such a view of the Fourth Gospel also has much to do with the fact that most Christians can agree that whatever Christianity may be, it is not Judaism – and vice versa. John tends to confirm that perception, which also has some basis elsewhere in the New Testament, particularly in Paul's attitude toward the law. But what is Christianity in John's view, or what would it be if he undertook to define it? What is its distinguishing feature or characteristic? If the most that can be said is that it is not Judaism, that is little enough, too little, to say about it. John has much more to say than that.

C THE NATURE OF CHRISTIANITY[7]

Christianity is not Judaism because of its belief that Jesus was the Messiah of Israel and no one as great as he may any longer be expected. Judaism is, or became, what it is by virtue of the rejection of this claim, and we see this self-definition in the process of taking place on both sides in the Gospel of John. It is too bad that we have no Jewish, or pro-Jewish, document saying what Judaism is and is not as a kind of counterpoise to the Gospel of John. Yet it might be possible on the basis of the Fourth Gospel to write a description of Judaism under the heading "Whatever else Judaism is, it is not Christianity." The

---

[7] See Adolf von Harnack's famous book *What is Christianity?* (New York, 1957; ET 1901), translated from the German *Das Wesen des Christentums*, "The Nature (or Essence) of Christianity." This book, based on Harnack's orally delivered lectures in Berlin, became a classic statement of nineteenth-century, liberal Protestant theology. Harnack states the essence of Christianity on the basis of Jesus' own message of the kingdom of God. There is a sense in which John's emphasis on christology, especially the person of Christ, stands at the opposite end of the theological spectrum from Harnack's liberalism.

Johannine Jews in rejecting Jesus, while obviously not set in a positive light, nevertheless in their defense of monotheism (5:18; 19:7) and their insistence on their own freedom as children of Abraham (8:33), assert their heritage clearly.[8]

Yet it is necessary to press beyond Jewish-Christian issues to ask what is the essence of Christianity according to the Gospel of John, for it is not simply the negation or rejection of Judaism. To answer this question we may once again invoke the Gospel's christological and soteriological mythology: the descent of Jesus as Son of God and supernatural birth from above. Christianity is the religion of salvation through Jesus Christ. Jesus, who comes down from above, saves his own, who are themselves born again in the sense of being born from above (1:13; 3:3–8). These myths correspond to the widespread Christian sensibility, through the centuries, that being Christian has to do with believing dogma about Jesus Christ and experiencing life (i.e., salvation) through him. Moreover, to experience life through Christ means belonging to him and, in a very tangible sense, to others who belong to him. Thus the Johannine, like the Pauline doctrine of salvation, is a communal one: *extra ecclesia nulla salus* (outside the church there is no salvation). For both John and Paul, christology, soteriology, and ecclesiology are bound together, and the development of theology in the ancient church follows their lead.

The ancient church's christological controversies look something like an exercise in the development of Johannine thought. The Nicene-Constantinopolitan Creed, which in the fourth century emerged from these controversies, obviously centers upon the doctrine of Christ, christology, and uses terminology that is largely Johannine to set forth this doctrine. In this so-called Nicene Creed Jesus is called the only, or

---

[8] On the historical relationship between Judaism and Christianity a most helpful perspective has been provided by Alan F. Segal, *Rebecca's Children: Judaism and Christianity in the Modern World* (Cambridge, MA, 1986), who regards both Judaism and Christianity as equally the offspring of ancient biblical religion. Obviously, Judaism's roots antedate the rise of Christianity, but, as Segal argues, Judaism's "greatest transformation, contemporary with Christianity, was rabbinic Judaism, which generally became the basis of the future Jewish religion" (p. 1).

more literally, the only begotten Son of God.[9] The same term, *monogenēs*, is found in John 1:14 and 18. The Creed goes on to elaborate upon the *monogenēs* to say that Jesus Christ was begotten by the Father eternally or before all the ages. John does not say this directly, but the idea that Jesus was begotten before the ages can be, and evidently was, seen as an implication of the word's coexisting with God in the beginning (1:1–2). By saying the word was God (verse 1), John makes a fundamental assertion which the Creed explains, or elaborates upon: "light from light, true God from true God." The Creed thus seems to take up the theme of light from 1:5 and Jesus Christ's origin in God from 1:18 (as well as 1:1): "No one has ever seen God, the only-begotten God who is in the bosom of the Father, that one has made him known." The Creed's "begotten, not made" can then be seen as making clear how John is to be understood: Jesus Christ the *logos* is not a creature. Rather, as the Creed now elaborates, he is of one and the same being (*homoousios*) with the Father. With the choice of *homoousios* rather than *homoiousios* (like being), the Creed reflects Athanasius' triumph over the Arians. The Creed's "through whom all things were made" simply takes up John 1:3, which asserts, and perhaps reiterates (depending upon the punctuation) the creation of "all things" through the *logos*. The Creed's "for us human beings and for our salvation he came down from heaven" reflects not so much a specific statement of the prologue as the entire Johannine christology, in which the descent (and ascent) of the Son are fundamental. For example, John 6:38–39: "I have come down from heaven not to do my own will, but the will of him who sent me. This is the will of him who sent me, that all that he gave me I should lose none of it, but I shall raise it up at the last day." The descending and ascending Christ is the hallmark of the Fourth Gospel. He appears also in the Pauline Letters (Philippians 2:5–11), but one would scarcely picture Jesus' saving work in these terms on the basis of the Synoptic Gospels.

---

[9] See Philip Schaff, *The Creeds of Christendom* (New York, 1877), II, pp. 57f., for the Eastern version of the Nicene Creed (AD 381). The translations in the text are mine.

Finally, the doctrine of the virgin birth, known only from Matthew and Luke, is in the Creed made to serve the doctrine of the incarnation, which is distinctively Johannine.[10] Jesus is said to have been "incarnate (*sarkōthenta*) of the Holy Spirit and the Virgin Mary." Thus a verb not found in John, except in nominal form (*sarx*), is used at the crucial point to express the theological truth of the incarnation, and another non-Johannine word says unequivocally what is meant: "having become truly human" (*enanthrōpēsanta anthrōpos*). This is apparently an exegesis of the Fourth Gospel, particularly the assertion that the word became flesh (1:14), combined with the virgin birth, derived from Matthew or Luke.

John has, so to speak, authorized the great ecumenical, christological creed of Christendom. Thus John, more than any other New Testament writing, authorizes the preaching of the Christ of Christian dogma, as distinguished from the historical Jesus. Indeed, in John's view there is no historical Jesus who is not the cosmic creator and savior. It would be inaccurate to say that John's own christological line was simply developed further by the Nicene Creed, as if John shared the same metaphysical and philosophical interests. Yet John and Nicaea evidently have in common the conviction that God was fully present in Jesus Christ, or the word, in creation as well as redemption. As is apparently the case with the Nicene Creed, for John christology and soteriology, as well as ecclesiology, are closely woven together.

Moreover, the christology of John is not a given apart from, or prior to, the transformation Jesus Christ has effected and effects, and that transformation is not simply an individual experience but involves unity with one's fellow believers as well as with Christ. That is, the expression of that unity – indeed, its very nature – is love, and love in turn is nothing other than

---

10 See James D. G. Dunn, *Christology in the Making: A New Testament Inquiry into the Origins of the Incarnation*, 2nd ed. (Philadelphia, 1989), p. 258: "In short as the first century of the Christian era drew to a close we find a concept of Christ's real preexistence begin to emerge, but only with the Fourth Gospel can we speak of a full blown conception of Christ's personal preexistence and a clear doctrine of incarnation."

obedience to Jesus' command. The unity and interpenetration
of the elements of Johannine theology are impressive, but so, it
seems, is its inwardness.

That is, love in John would seem to be a closed circle in
which Father, Son, and believers participate mutually, the
Holy Spirit being nothing other than the continued presence of
Jesus among his own. Nevertheless, the initial impression that
the world is left to go its own way, to its destruction, is finally
misleading. For the love of the disciples, of all followers of Jesus
for one another, will be their effective witness to the world of
the truth of the Christian claims about Jesus (13:35; 17:21,23).
He is the One whom God has sent, the savior of the world
(4:42). There is in John, as in the New Testament and early
Christianity generally, a strong missionary impulse.

Nevertheless, John differs from some other New Testament
witnesses, particularly from other Gospel traditions and also
from Jesus himself, in the emphasis the Gospel places on the
primacy or priority of christological confession. (As we have
observed, the sense of priority has something to do with the
polemical setting in which this Gospel was conceived and
written.) For John, questions of ethics, indeed all questions
including theological questions, can only be dealt with on the
basis of belief in, and confession of, Jesus as Christ and Son of
God (20:31). This means that the Gospel of John seems to
support those Christians for whom conversion is always the first
order of business.

In his emphasis upon christology, John seems within the
New Testament to stand closest to Paul. One can easily understand how modern criticism viewed John as standing on the
shoulders of Pauline theology and, so to speak, representing
and interpreting Paul for a new day, for the theological agreements between them are, on a broad scale, remarkable. God
sends the Son, Jesus Christ, into a world hopelessly locked in
sin and darkness to provide a means of redemption for all
people, particularly those who believe. Both Paul and John
find the meaning of Christ's coming in his crucifixion and
resurrection, albeit in different ways. This is an act of God's
grace, but it requires the response of faith for men and women

to avail themselves of it. Those who believe are not, however, transported from this world, but are challenged to live in faith and obedience in it. Nevertheless, their lives are no longer under the dominion of this world. Inspired and guided by the Spirit, believers participate in the new age that God has brought into being, which already impinges on this world, rendering the lives of those who will live in it blessed. A harbinger of this new age is the existence of the church as the eschatological people of God, united with Christ and with each other through mutual, reciprocal love. The church stands over against the world, but becomes, as an extension of Christ's ministry, God's means of redeeming the world, which is, after all, his creation. Already Paul hints at Christ's role in creation (1 Corinthians 8:6), a major theme of the prologue of the Gospel of John, and in the deutero-Pauline Letter to the Colossians there is the closest parallel to the prologue (Colossians 1:15–20).

John, along with Paul, thus appears to stand in some contrast to the Sermon on the Mount or the Matthean Jesus generally, for that Jesus warns his disciples against the vain illusion that right confession has any validity apart from obedience:

Not every one who says to me, "Lord, Lord" will enter the kingdom of heaven, but the one who does the will of my Father in heaven. On that day many will say to me, "Lord, Lord, did we not prophesy in your name and cast out demons in your name, and do many mighty works in your name?" Then I will declare to them, "I never knew you; depart from me, you evildoers." (Matthew 7:21–23)

At the very end of his ministry, in what is in fact the conclusion of his teaching, the Matthean Jesus poses for his disciples a sharp alternative (Matthew 25:31–46). Those who have ministered to the needs of "the least of these my brethren" have done it for Jesus himself. On the other hand, those who have ignored their needs face a dire but appropriate fate:

Then he will say to those at his left hand, "Depart from me, you cursed, into the eternal fire that has been prepared for the devil and his angels; for I was hungry and you gave me nothing to eat, I was thirsty and you gave me nothing to drink, I was a stranger and you did not receive me, naked and you did not clothe me, sick and in prison and you did not visit me." Then they also will answer, "Lord, when did we see you hungry or thirsty or a stranger or naked or sick or in prison, and did not take care of you?" Then he will answer them, "Truly, I say to you, inasmuch as you did not do it for one of the least of these, you did not do it for me." And they will go away into eternal punishment, but the righteous into eternal life. (Matthew 25:41–46)

At first glance, the fideistic theology of John (or Paul) seems to be at odds with the works righteousness of Matthew. In other ways also Matthew's Gospel seems to be the antithesis of John's. Matthew delights in exactly the kind of scriptural, traditional, midrashic argument that John abjures because of his concept of revelation. Just at the beginning of his Gospel, Matthew presents Jesus' birth and infancy as the precise fulfillment of scriptural prophecy and traditional expectation, while John alludes to such expectations (7:41–42), but pointedly fails to embrace them. Yet Matthew, like John, ultimately portrays Jesus in sharp conflict with contemporary Jewish authorities, particularly the Pharisees. Thus it can easily be imagined that John and Matthew represent different ways of responding to the question of the relationship of Jesus to Judaism, for both reflect the same kinds of tension and hostility.[11]

Matthew, along with Luke, gathers and presents the tradition of Jesus' teaching in all its concreteness, richness, and variety, and in this respect seems to stand in contrast with John's rigorous and austere concentration on christology. Yet Matthew's own christology can scarcely be characterized as low, for only Matthew describes Jesus as Emmanuel, God with us (1:23), and it is at the end of Matthew's Gospel that Jesus

[11] See J. L. Martyn, *History and Theology in the Fourth Gospel*, rev. ed. (Nashville, 1979), and W. D. Davies, *The Setting of the Sermon on the Mount* (Cambridge, 1963), esp. pp. 256–315. Davies' understanding of the setting in Judaism of Matthew's Gospel has some striking parallels to Martyn's view of the setting of the Fourth Gospel. See also D. Moody Smith, "The Contribution of J. Louis Martyn to the Understanding of the Gospel of John," in R. T. Fortna and B. R. Gaventa (eds.), *The Conversation Continues: Studies in Paul and John in Honor of J. Louis Martyn* (Nashville, 1990), especially pp. 383–385.

says to his disciples that all authority has been given him in heaven and earth (28:18) and promises them that he will be with them until the close of the age (28:20). Both these high christological notes are also characteristically Johannine, if expressed in other terms. So to oppose John and Matthew in that way is simplistic and misleading, not because there cannot be disagreement within the New Testament, but because in many ways Matthew and John stand on common ground.

Moreover, both Gospels have as their primary audience, or implied readers, the community of Christian believers, or would-be believers, and are addressing the question of how disciples of Jesus should show themselves to be such and be recognized. Both assume that followers of Jesus must obey his commands, and that simply pledging allegiance is not enough. In other words, faith is the beginning of a journey and not the end. Both John and Matthew can describe Christian life as the way (*hodos*). By the same token, Paul can describe his life in Christ as a race (1 Corinthians 9:24–27; Philippians 3:13f.).

Matthew's Jesus speaks of the narrow way that leads to life (Matthew 7:14); John has Jesus claim that he himself is the way (John 14:6). Matthew typically describes the way that leads to life in very specific, concrete terms, whether by parable or injunction, while in John Jesus gives a blanket, general commandment: Love one another. Doubtless Matthew is more accurate historically in depicting a Jesus who spoke as a Jewish teacher to a Jewish audience, from which he would draw followers as disciples. At the same time, Matthew, like John, presupposes a community of disciples, followers of Jesus, to whom Jesus' teaching is addressed and for whom it is primarily meant.

This fact does not mean, however, that Jesus' word, whether in Matthean or Johannine form, does not have universal relevance and applicability. In Matthew, and only in Matthew, Jesus says, "Come to me, all you who labor and are heavy laden, and I will give you rest" (Matthew 11:28), while in John he says, "I, if I am lifted up from the earth, will draw all people to myself" (John 12:32). The assertion that few will choose, or be chosen (Matthew 22:14; cf. John 15:19), reflects the empirical realities with which the Johannine and Matthean churches are faced, not the horizon of the Gospel message.

Perhaps Matthew's points of contact with those realities are indicated more graphically and directly than John's. But, as we have seen, John arises out of a set of historical circumstances that very much affects, if not the content of the message, certainly the way it is shaped and focused. The hostility faced by the Johannine church, the oppression and threat of persecution from without, caused the disciples of Jesus to look intensely inward to their own relationship with Jesus and with one another.[12] Thus in the Fourth Gospel we find a severe concentration upon the themes of christology, faith, abiding in Jesus, and mutual love. Yet, as we have seen, the nurturing and securing of the church is not an end in itself but serves the church's mission to the world.

God out of his love sends his Son not to judge the world, but to save it (3:16–17). As God has sent Jesus, so he sends his followers (20:21), who are to remain in the world, although they are not of it (17:15–16). They will bear witness to the world, through their unity in love (17:21,23; cf. 13:35), to the end that the world will know the truth about Jesus, namely, that he has been sent by God to manifest God's love. As one moves from 3:16–17 to chapter 17, it seems that God's love narrows down from the world to his disciples. There is an obvious sense in which that is true, but it is a tactical or even a strategic narrowing, a narrowing in present, historic appearance but not in principle. God's love is universal, and precisely through this narrowing will be shown to have as its object all people.

Standing where it does in the New Testament, at the conclusion of the Gospel canon and before Acts and the Epistles, John sums up the mission and message of Jesus in terms of what is to

---

[12] Paul S. Minear, *John: The Martyr's Gospel* (New York, 1984), p. 43: "Because the charismatic leaders of the [Johannine] church would bear the brunt of the world's brutality, it would be their falling away that would be most disastrous to their cause. Only a continued victory over fear of social ostracism and death could give them the necessary stamina to carry out their assignments." Cf. D. Rensberger, *Johannine Faith and Liberating Community* (Philadelphia, 1988), pp. 120f.

be proclaimed as the message about Jesus, and he has Jesus proclaim it. Thus the Fourth Gospel provides the key to the other three while laying out in some detail the substance of the gospel about Jesus Christ. That gospel is then preached, according to the Book of Acts (for example, by Peter in 2:14–36 and by Paul in 13:16–41), and is presumed, frequently alluded to, and occasionally expounded in the Epistles, most extensively, of course, by Paul in Romans. From its pivotal position, John guides and deeply influences the reading of the New Testament.

The obverse is also the case: there is a real and important sense in which John begs to be read in light of the rest of the New Testament, particularly the Synoptic Gospels. The claims of the Johannine Jesus are given a certain shape, intelligibility, and justification if they are read in conjunction with the other New Testament witnesses. When this is done, the Jesus who says, "I am the way, the truth, and the life" is also the Jesus who proclaims the will of God in the Sermon on the Mount and the parables of the kingdom, as well as the Jesus who befriends harlots, tax collectors, and the outcasts of society. Despite the tensions already observed, the Jesus of the Fourth Gospel shows himself to be this same Jesus as he assumes the role of a servant to wash his disciples' feet and sits down tired and thirsty at Jacob's well to strike up a conversation with a Samaritan woman, astonishing his own disciples. The portrayal of Jesus in the Fourth Gospel resonates with that of the Jesus of the broader gospel tradition and the New Testament generally.

Further reading

COMMENTARIES ON THE GOSPEL OF JOHN

There are many good commentaries on the Gospel of John. Barrett remains the standard English-language commentary on the Greek text, although Beasley-Murray may now also be consulted. Brown's commentary serves a wider readership, since it is not based on the Greek text, although there are references to it. Lindars' commentary is more compact than Brown's but also serves the English reader well. Kysar's commentary, intended for the general reader, is a balanced, up-to-date treatment. Bultmann's commentary is an important theological document as well as a watershed in Johannine exegesis. Hoskyns' commentary, which first appeared the same year as Bultmann's, is likewise a significant piece of theological exegesis. Haenchen's commentary, left incomplete at the author's death and published posthumously, is of uneven quality, but the bibliographies are uniformly valuable. Among more conservative commentaries, Carson's recent work stands out. Schnackenburg's massive commentary remains a valuable resource. Only works in English or English translation are listed in this bibliography.

Barrett, C. K. *The Gospel According to St. John: An Introduction with Commentary and Notes on the Greek Text*, 2nd ed., London and Philadelphia, 1978.

Beasley-Murray, G. R. *John*, Word Biblical Commentary, Waco, TX, 1987.

Brown, R. E. *The Gospel According to John: Introduction, Translation and Notes*, 2 vols., Anchor Bible 29, 29A, Garden City, NY, 1966, 1970.

Bultmann, R. *Das Evangelium des Johannes*, Kritisch-exegetischer Kommentar über das Neue Testament, Göttingen, 1941; ET *The Gospel of John: A Commentary*, Oxford and Philadelphia, 1971.

Carson, D. A. *The Gospel According to John*, Grand Rapids, 1991.
Haenchen, E. *Das Johannesevangelium: Ein Kommentar aus den nachgelassen Manuskripten herausgegeben*, Tübingen, 1980; ET *John 1/2: A Commentary on the Gospel of John*, 2 vols., Hermeneia, Philadelphia, 1984.
Hoskyns, E. C. *The Fourth Gospel*, ed. F. N. Davey, 2nd ed., London, 1947.
Kysar, R. *John*, Augsburg Commentary on the New Testament, Minneapolis, 1986.
Lindars, B. *The Gospel of John*, New Century Bible, London and Grand Rapids, 1972.
Schnackenburg, R. *Das Johannesevangelium*, 4 vols., Herders theologischer Kommentar zum Neuen Testament, Freiburg, Basle and Vienna, 1965–1984; ET *The Gospel According to St. John*, 3 vols., Herder's Theological Commentary on the New Testament, New York and London, 1968–1982.

JOHANNINE THEOLOGY

Bultmann's treatment of Johannine theology in his *Theology of the New Testament*, based on the exegesis of his commentary, remains a benchmark. His student, Ernst Käsemann (*The Testament of Jesus*), has developed a perspective on that theology significantly at odds with Bultmann's. J. Louis Martyn (*History and Theology in the Fourth Gospel*) lays out another approach to Johannine theology decidedly different from either. The possible backgrounds of Johannine thought, as well as its interpretation, are dealt with by C. H. Dodd, *The Interpretation of the Fourth Gospel*. Ashton's *Understanding the Fourth Gospel* is in some ways comparable to Dodd, but focuses much more specifically and directly on John's background in Judaism. Also of value is the same author's *The Interpretation of John*, a collection of important essays by various scholars, for example: de la Potterie ("The Truth in Saint John"), Borgen ("God's Agent in the Fourth Gospel"), Dahl ("The Johannine Church and History"), and Meeks ("The Man from Heaven in Johannine Sectarianism").

Ashton, J. *The Interpretation of John*, Issues in Religion and Theology 9, Philadelphia and London, 1986.
Understanding the Fourth Gospel, Oxford, 1991.
Bultmann, R. *Theologie des Neuen Testaments*, Tübingen, 1951; ET *Theology of the New Testament*, 2 vols., New York, 1952, 1955. See Part III (in vol. II) for the theology of the Gospel and Epistles of John.

Burge, G. M. *The Anointed Community: The Holy Spirit in the Johannine Tradition*, Grand Rapids, MI, 1987.

Dodd, C. H. *The Interpretation of the Fourth Gospel*, Cambridge, 1953.

Forestell, J. T. *The Word of the Cross: Salvation as Revelation in the Fourth Gospel*, Analecta Biblica 57, Rome, 1974.

Jonge, M. de *Jesus: Stranger from Heaven: Jesus Christ and the Christians in Johannine Perspective*, Society of Biblical Literature Sources for Bible Study, Missoula, MT, 1977.

Käsemann, E. *Jesu letzter Wille nach Johannes 17*, Tübingen, 1966; ET *The Testament of Jesus: A Study of the Gospel of John in the Light of Chapter 17*, Philadelphia and London, 1968.

Loader, W. R. G. *The Christology of the Fourth Gospel: Structure and Issues*, Beiträge zur biblischen Exegese und Theologie 23, Frankfurt-on-Main, Berne, New York, and Paris, 1989.

Martyn, J. L. *History and Theology in the Fourth Gospel*, rev. ed., Nashville, 1979.

Meeks, W. A. *The Prophet-King: Moses Traditions and the Johannine Christology*, Supplements to Novum Testamentum 14, Leiden, 1967.

O'Day, G. R. *Revelation in the Fourth Gospel: Narrative Mode and Theological Claim*, Philadelphia, 1986.

Painter, J. *The Quest for the Messiah: The History, Literature and Theology of the Johannine Community*, Edinburgh, 1991.

Rensberger, D. *Johannine Faith and Liberating Community*, Philadelphia, 1988.

Scroggs, R. *Christology in Paul and John: The Reality and Revelation of God*, Proclamation Commentaries, Philadelphia, 1988.

Thompson, M. M. *The Humanity of Jesus in the Fourth Gospel*, Philadelphia, 1988.

SPECIAL STUDIES

A number of studies deal with the historical context of the Fourth Gospel or its literary character as they impinge on the understanding of its theology or of specific theological themes. Therefore the classifications "Theology" and "Special studies" are in the nature of the case overlapping and somewhat arbitrary.

Barrett, C. K. *Essays on John*, London, 1982.

Borgen, P. *Bread from Heaven: An Exegetical Study of the Concept of Manna in the Gospel of John and the Writings of Philo*, Supplements to Novum Testamentum 10, Leiden, 1965.

Logos Was the True Light and Other Essays on the Gospel of John, Trondheim, 1983.

Brown, R. E. *The Community of the Beloved Disciple*, New York, 1979.

Charlesworth, J. H. (ed.), *John and the Dead Sea Scrolls*, New York, 1990.

Cullmann, O. *Der johanneischen Kreise, sein Platz im Spätjudentum, in der Jüngerschaft Jesu und im Urchristentum: zum Ursprung des Johannesevangelium*, Tübingen, 1975; ET *The Johannine Circle*, Philadelphia and London, 1976.

Culpepper, R. A. *Anatomy of the Fourth Gospel: A Study in Literary Design*, Louisville, 1983.

Dodd, C. H. *Historical Tradition in the Fourth Gospel*, Cambridge, 1963.

Fortna, R. T. *The Fourth Gospel and its Predecessor: From Narrative Source to Present Gospel*, Philadelphia, 1988.

Hengel, M. *The Johannine Question*, London and Philadelphia, 1989.

Kysar, R. *The Fourth Evangelist and his Gospel: An Examination of Contemporary Scholarship*, Minneapolis, 1975.

Minear, P. S. *John: The Martyr's Gospel*, New York, 1984.

Segovia, F. F. *The Farewell of the Word: The Johannine Call to Abide*, Minneapolis, 1991.

Smith, D. M. *Johannine Christianity: Essays on its Setting, Sources, and Theology*, Columbia, SC, and Edinburgh, 1984, 1987.

John Among the Gospels: The Relationship in Twentieth-Century Research, Minneapolis, 1992.

BIBLIOGRAPHY

Belle, G. van *Johannine Bibliography 1966–1985: A Cumulative Bibliography on the Fourth Gospel*, Bibliotheca Ephemeridum Theologicarum Lovaniensium 82, Louvain, 1988.

Malatesta, E., *St. John's Gospel 1920–1965: A Cumulative and Classified Bibliography of Books and Periodical Literature on the Fourth Gospel*, Analecta Biblica 32, Rome, 1967.

Index of references

Index of modern authors

Index of subjects

Abraham, 31, 49, 58, 76, 82, 112, 126,
    133, 174
Acts, Book of, 52, 66, 92, 164, 170, 181–182
Amos, 125
anti-Semitism in John, 169–173
apocalyptic, 40, 84, 85, 105–106
    categories in Paul, 56
apocryphal gospels, 35, 46, 47, 69–71
Arians, 175
arrest of Jesus, *see* Jesus
Athanasius, 175

baptism, 136, 139, 155–160, *see also*
    sacraments
belief, *see* faith
Beloved Disciple, 45, 46, 47, 93, 124,
    135, 138, 150, 154
birkat ha-minim, see Twelfth Benediction
birth narratives, *see* Jesus
blindness, 109
    man born blind, 20, 32, 48, 165
bread, 112, 156
bread discourse, bread from heaven, 30,
    31, 113, *see also* "I am" sayings
burial of Jesus, *see* Jesus

Calvin, John, 64
Cana, 25
Christianity, 79, 173–182, *see also*
    Judaism
christology, 106, 124–135, 181
    later christological debates, 129–131
church, 9, 79, 129, 135–160 passim, esp.
    152–155, 172, 174, 178
    mission to the world, 181
    organization, 136–137, 152–155
Clement of Alexandria, 4, 62, 63
community, Johannine, 42, 44, 46, 79,
    96, 135–160 passim, 180

in Epistles and Revelation, 61
    relation to synagogue, 62
conversion, *see* rebirth
1 Corinthians, 78
cosmic dimension, 102
creation, 22, 71, 77, 175, 176
creeds, 130–131, 174–176
    Nicene Creed, 100, 174–176
crucifixion, *see* Jesus

darkness, 16–17, 73, 81, 83–84
Daniel, 84
David, 49, 76, 89, 126
    Davidic lineage, 86, 87, 125–126
Dead Sea Scrolls, 16
    Qumran, 50, 67, 70, 71, 127
death, human condition, 81, 83–84,
    149–151
death of Jesus, *see* Jesus
demythologizing, 168–169
descent and ascent motif, 99, 101, 162,
    163–164, 174, 175
devil, or Satan, 31, 96, 105
Diatessaron, 4
didachē (teaching), 78
Dionysius of Alexandria, 60
disciples, 21, 23–24, 26, 39, 40, 41, 42,
    44, 70, 77, 102–103, 103–105, 107,
    111, 113–114, 118, 122, 129,
    135–160 passim, 162, 167
    the twelve, 46, 104, 136
    unity with Jesus and God, 138,
    144–146, 147–149, 151–152,
    152–155, 176–177, 178, 180–181
docetism, 58, 157
dualism, 13, 15, 16, 21, 39, 42, 69, 85

early Christianity, 9
ecclesiology, *see* church

198